A Longman Cultural Edition

William Shakespeare's

THE MERCHANT OF VENICE

Edited by

Lawrence Danson
Princeton University

PEARSON
Longman

New York   San Francisco   Boston
London   Toronto   Sydney   Tokyo   Singapore   Madrid
Mexico City   Munich   Paris   Cape Town   Hong Kong   Montreal

Vice President and Editor-in-Chief: Joseph P. Terry
Development Editor: Barbara Santoro
Executive Marketing Manager: Ann Stypuloski
Production Coordinator: Shafiena Ghani
Project Coordination, Text Design, and Electronic Page Makeup: Dianne Hall
Cover Designer/Manager: John Callahan
Manufacturing Buyer: Mary Fischer
Printer and Binder: R R Donnelley and Sons Company / Harrisonburg
Cover Printer: Coral Graphics Services

Cover Image: Michele Marieschi (1696–1743), "Rialto Bridge and Palazzo Camer-
lenghi," detail (c. 1740). By permission of Scala/Art Resource, NY.

Library of Congress Cataloging-in-Publication Data

CIP data is on file with the Library of Congress.

Please visit our website at http://www.ablongman.com

ISBN 0-321-16419-9

1 2 3 4 5 6 7 8 9 10—DOH—07 06 05 04

Contents

List of Illustrations

About Longman Cultural Editions

Reading always seems to vibrate with the transformation of the day—now, yesterday, and centuries ago, when the presses first put printed language into wide circulation. Correspondingly, literary culture has always been a matter of change: of new practices confronting established traditions; of texts transforming under the pressure of new techniques of reading and new perspectives of understanding; of canons shifting and expanding; of informing traditions getting reviewed and renewed, recast and reformed by emerging cultural interests and concerns; of culture, too, as a variable "text"—a reading. Inspired by the innovative *Longman Anthology of British Literature*, Longman Cultural Editions respond creatively to the changes, past and recent, by presenting key texts in contexts that illuminate the lively intersections of literature, tradition, and culture. A principal work is made more interesting by materials that place it in relation to its past, present, and future, enabling us to see how it may be reworking traditional debates and practices, how it appears amid the conversations and controversies of its own historical moment, how it gains new significances in subsequent eras of reading and reaction. Readers new to the work will discover attractive paths for exploration, while those more experienced will encounter fresh perspectives and provocative juxtapositions.

Longman Cultural Editions serve not only several kinds of readers but also (appropriately) their several contexts, from various courses of study to independent adventure. Handsomely produced and affordably priced, our volumes offer appealing companions to *The Longman Anthology of British Literature*, in some cases enriching and expanding units originally developed for the *Anthology*, and in other cases presenting this wealth for the first time. The logic and composition of the contexts vary across the series. The constants are the complete text of an important literary work, reliably edited, headed by an inviting introduction, and supplemented by helpful annotation; a table of dates to track its composition, publication, and public reception in relation to biographical, cultural, and historical events; and a guide for further inquiry and study. With these common measures and uncommon assets, Longman Cultural Editions encourage your literary pleasures with resources for lively reflection and adventurous inquiry.

Susan J. Wolfson
General Editor
Professor of English
Princeton University

About This Edition

The Merchant of Venice, written in 1596 or 1597, was first published in 1600 in a small single-play volume, called a quarto (Q1). In 1623 it was included in the first collected edition of Shakespeare's plays, edited by his theatrical colleagues and now generally called the First Folio (F1). The two texts, Q1 and F1, agree in most important details. David Bevington, who edited the text used in this Longman Cultural Edition, bases his readings on Q1. The textual situation is relatively simple; nothing else about the play is.

This is the play about the Jew Shylock. But its title refers to the Christian merchant Antonio. Its heroine, Portia, is rich and in the course of the play literally wears the pants, but her dead father controls her choice of husband, and when the choice is made she gives all her wealth to her husband-to-be, the penniless Bassanio. This is a play, then, about religion, money, parents, children, and sex. Not surprisingly it has become one of the most controversial plays Shakespeare ever wrote.

I say is has *become* controversial because no other play's reception is more entangled in history than that of *The Merchant of Venice*. All Shakespeare's plays present challenges to modern audiences. The culture within which they were written is like a foreign country. We hear the people speak but we miss some of the words; their customs seem familiar but turn out to have meanings different from those we would attach to similar actions. Plays that surprised their original audiences with their novelty have become only more surprising as history has made them stranger but no less compelling. We who live after the Holocaust, after the creation of Israel, in the midst of war and insurrection, terrorism and retaliation, must hear the word *Jew* with a difference.

This volume provides material that can help us know important things about the cultural context in which the play was written. I have modernized the spelling of all texts and occasionally altered punctuation for the sake of clarity; and I have provided explanatory notes where necessary. I have selected writings about Jews and about Christian theology; about English ideas of Venice; about the economic and social controversy over money-lending; about the figure of Shylock in the theater, including the Yiddish theater of the early twentieth century; about male friendship and the status of women; and about the music that is both discussed and heard in the play. The selections come from many different kinds of writing. I have included accounts by contemporary travelers and historians, by playwrights, and by essayists, theologians, and polemicists of various stripes. Some are well known, such as the selections from essays by Francis Bacon and Michel de Montaigne. Some are well known but seldom read, such as the selection from Robert Burton's *Anatomy of Melancholy*. Some were once well known, such as Boethius on music and the Elizabethan homily on matrimony. Others are known to few but are colorful and interesting, such as the traveler Thomas Coryate's account of his meeting with Jews in Turkey, Robert Wilson's play *Three Ladies of London* in which a character named Merchant cheats a Jew, and the Puritan Philip Stubbes's diatribe against music. I have also included two selections by Shakespeare himself, who is, after all, very much part of the play's cultural context.

My Introduction points ahead to some of these contexts, but all of them together will not resolve our questions and controversies about the play. A culture is not monolithic. We can't say how all the people in Shakespeare's audience reacted any more than we can say how all the people in a modern audience will react. But there are some broad parameters. It's extremely unlikely that many people in Shakespeare's audience would have concluded, as many modern critics do, that the play's Christian characters are hypocrites, or worse. The idea to which the modern word *anti-Semitism* points was unavailable to them, despite the fact that from our modern standpoint we can find its defining characteristic thoughout the culture. Notice that we have various perspectives to negotiate: Each of us must try to know his or her own mind while also trying to understand our differently minded contemporaries, and we must try to know the minds of Shakespeare's culture, recognizing that they too are diverse and that no single expression of the culture expresses it all.

The relation between Shakespeare's peculiar, brilliant play and other cultural artifacts of the time is at best indirect. We can know what dozens of early modern writers said about Jews, but we still have to come to grips with Shakespeare's unique Shylock. And we have to see him in the dramatic place Shakespeare created for him, which in some ways resembles the historical Venice but in other important ways resembles the generic place of romantic comedy, with its forest of Arden or coast of Illyria. The genre of Elizabethan romantic comedy is one of the play's contexts.

What this volume offers, then, is not a resolution to the differences of opinion about the play but a way of clarifying them, even while perhaps multiplying them. The Contexts section presents documents that are more or less directly—sometimes very indirectly—in conversation with Shakespeare's play; and Shakespeare's play has its own voice or voices, none of which merely ventriloquizes the documents I have assembled.

The explanatory notes to the play are David Bevington's, used with my thanks and admiration. I have occasionally added a note to draw attention to contextual material; such notes are indicated by my initials, LD.

My thanks to the General Editor of the Longman Cultural Editions, Susan Wolfson, a good friend and colleague, and a real sharp editor.

Lawrence Danson
Princeton University

Introduction

Antonio, a merchant in the great trading city of Venice, knows not why he is so sad. His friends make the plausible diagnosis that he is worried about business. All his money is tied up in the ships that carry his merchandise eastward through the Mediterranean to India and westward across the Atlantic to Mexico. The vast world of his trading empire is a dangerous one, where rocks and winds and murderous pirates lie in wait. The merchant's friends try to transform this risky business of international trade into fanciful images. Their language begins with a simple life at home ("My wind cooling my broth / Would blow me to an ague") and moves outward to the destructive ocean ("when I thought / What harm a wind too great might do at sea" [1.1.22–24]). The sight of a stone church would make any merchant think

> of dangerous rocks
> Which, touching but my gentle vessel's side,
> Would scatter all her spices on the stream,
> Enrobe the roaring waters with my silks,
> And, in a word, but even now worth this,
> And now worth nothing[.] (1.1.31–36)

A pretty picture, this, of the scattered spices and floating silks, but one that keeps contact with the actual historical world of an age of exploration, when great fortunes could be made or lost by those who had the money and fortitude to brave the risks. The language evokes a world where a person's fortunes can change swiftly (now this, now nothing), where danger comes from unexpected quarters, where the beauty of life can give way suddenly to the horror of loss and death. It is a dark and disturbing way to open a play called, in its first printed edition (Q1, the quarto of 1600), *The Comical History of the Merchant of Venice.* Antonio rejects the mercantile explanation for his somber mood. His commercial bets are hedged, and he insists that business is not what makes him sad. What then can it be? Love! To which Antonio's answer is a quick dismissal that allows no further discussion. Shakespeare never does provide a simple explanation for the merchant's sadness. Many factors seem to crowd into it and flow out from it as the play progresses. Perhaps it is a premonition of the danger that awaits, not on distant seas, but in Venice. Perhaps it is also an uneasy feeling about the young man he loves. Perhaps it is just a reasonable response that any person might have to living in a sinful world, unsure of the future, incapable of taking joy in wealth that buys no security, no peace.

To Antonio comes his friend Bassanio, bursting with the high spirits that have gotten him into trouble before. He has borrowed money without repaying it, and now he wants more money to pursue the woman of his dreams, a rich, beautiful, and, above all, virtuous woman who lives in a place of mystery, like a princess enchanted by her dead father's will. That *will*—the word suggests both a legal document and a paternal desire exerting itself from beyond the grave—ties her to Belmont, her home, until one man, the only right man, can answer the riddles locked in three containers, or caskets, and thereby free her into love. (When we meet Portia, her very first words, "By my troth, Nerissa, my little body is aweary of this great world" [1.2.1–2], remind us of Antonio's first words about his sadness.)

Antonio does not have the money to give to Bassanio but he has good credit, so he proposes that they go to a money-lender, a Jew named Shylock. (The 1600 quarto edition gives the play a subtitle: "Otherwise Called *The Jew of Venice*"). With only a few strokes Shakespeare has set in motion one of his greatest plays. And with the introduction of Shylock he has embroiled that play in history—what came before as well as what still lay ahead in the darkness that would become our history—in ways that challenge our methods for engaging the works that most profoundly disturb our beliefs and emotions.

The Merchant of Venice is a play, a fantasy, a comic world creating and obeying its own dramatic rules. But it is also part of the actual historical world from which it emerged, reflecting the culture of a world in many ways very different from our own, and different also from the fictional world of the play. To enter into either world, of fiction or of history, requires many acts of imagination. To find the relation between them requires more.

Why, for instance, a merchant and a Jew of *Venice*? All but one of Shakespeare's comedies are set outside England, in locations more or less identifiable with places in the real world. Those written up to the time of *The Merchant of Venice* belong to sunnier climates than England's: *The Comedy of Errors* and *A Midsummer Night's Dream* are set in Greece, *Love's Labor's Lost* in Spain, *The Two Gentleman of Verona* and *The Taming of the Shrew* in Italy. These exotic locales mark out the comedies as the world of not-history, a dramatic place of possibilities different from those Shakespeare was simultaneously exploring in his English history plays. But even the most extravagant fantasy bears a relation to the culture it transforms: we are our dreams as much as we are the actors of our waking lives. Without diminishing the fantastic aspect of *The Merchant of Venice* we can ask what that island city of winding canals and grand palaces meant to Shakespeare and his audience.

Venice was one of the great trading and commercial centers of the world. Set at a crossroad between Christian Europe and the Islamic east, it was a cosmopolitan place where, as Antonio says, "the trade and profit of the city / Consisteth of all nations" (3.3.30–31). Its central square, St. Mark's, was, according to a visiting Englishman, Thomas Coryate, not the marketplace of the city (*urbis*) but of the world (*orbis*). In addition to the gowned Venetians themselves, this Englishman encountered "Polonians, Slavonians, Persians, Grecians, Turks, Jews, Christians of all the [most famous] regions of Christendom, and each nation distinguished from another by their proper and peculiar habits." It was, Coryate remarks, "A singular show, and by many degrees the worthiest of all the European countries." In Shakespeare's play, the "show" of otherness is more limited. To Portia's Belmont, a place Bassanio likens to the land where the mythical Jason sought the golden fleece, "the four winds blow in from every coast / Renownèd suitors" (1.1.168–169). We hear about a Neapolitan, an Englishman, and a German, and we meet the impressive princes of Aragon and of Morocco. But in Venice itself, foreignness is represented only by the Jews. All that energy of otherness of which the English traveler admiringly writes is concentrated in the deeply troubling figure of Shylock.

Pieter Paul Rubens (1577–1640), "Portrait of Mulay Ahmad," (c. 1610), copyright 2004 The Museum of Fine Arts, Boston, M. Theresa B. Hopkins Fund.

Ruben's painting is supposedly of a Tunisian, not a Moroccan, prince, but it can give a general idea of what an English audience might have expected Portia's suitor to look and dress like. (In fact, Rubens's may never have seen the real Mulay Ahmad, since he uses the same model in another painting on an entirely different subject.) The ruined walls of the ancient city of Carthage, which supposedly stood on the site of modern Tunis, serve as background for the noble-looking prince. The real Mulay Ahmad was not as genial as the Prince of Morocco in *The Merchant of Venice*, who immediately accepts the terms of his dismissal: the Prince of Tunis blinded and deposed his own father.

The Venice of the early modern English imagination was an ambiguous place, idealized by some, vilified by others: a wonderful place to set a play. To one English enthusiast, Venice was simply the best place in the whole world. Lewis Lewkenor claims that visitors who have been to Africa and Asia think that Venice is the "most infinitely remarkable city they had seen in the whole course of their travels." In Venice, they say, foreigners find a humane welcome, the women are beautiful, "all pleasure and delight" flow abundantly, and the government is grave and majestic, the laws inviolable, the people zealous in religion but also moderate and just. But another English writer at almost the same time paints a very different, dark and lurid, picture: "[T]he Italians, above all other nations, most practice revenge by treasons, and especially are skillful in making and giving poisons." He says they are a sexually voracious people, worse than the worst an Englishman could conceive: "For fleshly lusts, the very Turks . . . are not so much transported therewith as the Italians are. . . . [C]hastity is laughed at among them and hissed out of all good company. . . ." Both of these supposedly factual descriptions are bundles of prejudice that tell us as much about the writers as about Venice or Italians. For this very reason they show the range of ideas that Shakespeare could draw on and manipulate. In *The Merchant of Venice* the imputation of sexual licentiousness is at once acknowledged and made harmless by the joke about "Nerissa's ring" in Act 5. The claim that Venice's legal system is inviolable becomes riddlingly complex. And the whole business about revenge and devious ways of killing is, again, concentrated in a single source, not the merchant but the Jew of Venice: two sides, perhaps, of the same idea, the same remarkable place?

For the visiting Englishman, nothing about Venice was more exotic than its Jewish residents. Jews had been officially banished from England by King Edward I in 1290. In the diaspora that followed, many settled in Spain, where they were relatively unmolested until the Catholic reconquest drove out Spain's former Muslim rulers and then, in 1492, drove out all Jews who refused to convert. Many made their way eastward to relatively more hospitable Islamic countries; others joined the communities of Jews who were gathered in the ghettos of Europe. (According to the *Oxford English Dictionary*, the first English use of the Italian word *ghetto* was in 1611, in a portion of Thomas Coryate's *Crudities* included in the Contexts materials.) Even there Jews remained in peril. In Germany the great theologian and religious leader Martin Luther proposed burning down their synagogues, confiscating their books, outlawing them from worshiping or even mentioning the name of God; and (in case all that didn't work), he advised, "They must be driven from our country."

It is a curiosity of anti-Semitism that it can thrive even in the absence of Jews. The fact that there had been no openly practicing Jews in England for three hundred years did not mean that England had no "Jewish problem": *The Merchant of Venice* is a symptom of it. The prejudice drew on ancient myths, of the sort that Shakespeare's contemporary, Christopher Marlowe, satirized in *The Jew of Malta*. The cartoonishly wicked Jew of this play boasts that he poisons wells and walks abroad at night to kill sick people groaning under walls; by the end of his gleeful confession of ingenious villainies he has made himself into the monster of international intrigue and treachery that the popular imagination wants him to be. Such grotesqueries derived in part from misreadings of biblical history. Supposedly, the Jews as a group had killed Christ, and their descendants just went right on ritually slaughtering Christians, especially innocent little ones. Prejudicial myths about people who belong to minority groups at home or to enemy groups abroad do not require evidence in order to survive; they are their own proof, their telling alone sustains them. Traces of such long-standing myths find their way into *The Merchant of Venice*, where Shylock's intention to cut a pound of Antonio's flesh seems to have leapt out of a collective European nightmare. Such traces of a vicious mythology, however, are mixed with material of a different sort. Shakespeare creates in Shylock not a monster but an all-too-human being, with strengths and weaknesses, a family, a history, a capacity for pain that bogey-men do not feel. The play's mingling of popular superstition and sympathetic understanding makes it especially challenging to modern audiences.

One of the most durable anti-Semitic myths virtually equates Jews and usury—the practice, that is, of taking interest for the loan of money. There is some historical reason for the connection: before their banishment in 1290, the Jewish community in England had in fact been kept as a source of royal revenue and forced by a succession of kings into the occupation of money-lenders. That was in the distant past. Elizabethan England had an expanding economy and plenty of certifiably non-Jewish entrepreneurs to service it. In his *Description of England* (1587), William Harrison described usury as "a trade brought in by the Jews, now perfectly practiced almost by every Christian and so commonly that he is accounted but for a fool that doth lend his money for nothing." In the absence of organized banks, almost anyone with money could do it, often well beyond the legal limit of 10 percent. The main business, however, was carried on by Antonio's real-life counterparts, the great London merchants who first accumulated money in trade and then put that money to use supplying, at a price, the needs of other merchants or of aristocrats who were rich in land but poor in cash. When Portia enters the courtroom in Venice disguised as a young legal scholar, her first question is, "Which is the merchant here, and which the Jew?" (4.1.171). Presumably the answer is obvious because Shylock would be wearing a distinctively Jewish costume and would likely be made up with distinctively "Jewish" nose and hair. Shakespeare seems to make the distinction between merchant and Jew absolute in terms of their attitude toward the use of money. Antonio says he neither borrows nor lends "by taking nor by giving of excess" (1.3.56), while Shylock defends taking interest as blessed "thrift" (1.3.85). It can look like a simple case of opposites: Antonio as victim, the "tainted wether of the flock" (4.1.114), patiently awaiting the fury of Shylock, the victimizer whetting his knife upon the sole of his shoe. Portia's little question about the identity of the merchant and the Jew points to the complexity of the European cultural and economic situation, where the merchant often played the social role supposedly reserved for the Jew. One of the ways in which *The Merchant of Venice* remains always fresh and controversial is that it, too, puts those identities under pressure.

The "merry sport" Shylock devises—not to take interest but to engage Antonio in an all-or-nothing bond for the repayment of the loan—makes a stunningly simple statement: usury cuts the heart out of a person. Money-lending is like taking blood. The equation of money with flesh and blood is a guiding metaphor in the play, not only in the flesh-bond. It figures in Shylock's defense of his profession, his retelling of the biblical story of Jacob and his uncle Laban. That story as it appears in Genesis is already suffused with a kind of magic of equivalency. The two men agreed that all multi-colored lambs would be Jacob's and all solid-colored lambs would be Laban's. When, as Shylock wonderfully puts it, "the work of generation was / Between these woolly breeders in the act" (1.3.77–78), Jacob made sure that the copulating sheep saw multi-colored sticks, or wands, and therefore gave birth to an unusually high proportion of multicolored lambs. This is genetically absurd, but for Shylock it is a cunning way to justify human intervention in supposedly natural acts. Jacob's trick brought about the birth of multicolored sheep; by an analogous trick, Shylock makes gold and silver "breed as fast" (1.3.91) as if they were alive and procreative. Art is above nature in that respect.

Antonio stands firmly on the other side of this argument. Like many conservative economic and social critics of Shakespeare's time, he claims it is wrong, because supposedly unnatural, to make "barren metal" beget more metal (1.3.129). Taking interest for the loan of money seems to evade God's judgment that human beings will live by the productive sweat of their brows: usury is a no-sweat occupation. Usury blurs the line between the animate and the inanimate, between life and death. The almost superstitious horror many Elizabethans express toward usury may be incomprehensible to the modern reader bombarded by blandishments for new and more expensive credit cards. Capitalist society cannot exist without money-lending; paying interest, if only on the national debt, is an inescapable experience for citizens of a developed modern economy. An economy like that of Elizabethan England, still largely agrarian and only beginning to adjust to the realities of a modern economic system, finds the processes of finance mysterious and threatening. Making money out of money seems not just to substitute an impersonal market for a living connection between trading partners but also to threaten the very foundation of civil society. So threatening is it, indeed, that only devils would engage in it. Since, against the evidence of eyes and ears, Christians supposedly don't do it, the blame tends to fall on the usual suspects for social distress, the Jews.

We cannot expect from Shakespeare the same respect for social diversity that has become a moral virtue of modern liberal democracy. Nonetheless, he makes Shylock's defense of himself and his trade as money-lender a virtuoso performance, even if he does not have it all his own way. His great series of rhetorical questions, beginning "Hath not a Jew eyes?" (3.1.49), is his bitter response to a previous question: Salerio says incredulously, "Why, I am sure, if he forfeit, thou wilt not take his flesh. What's that good for?" Shylock's implacable answer is: "To bait fish withal. If it will feed nothing else, it will feed my revenge" (3.1.42–45). Shylock's plea about our common humanity—"If you prick us, do we not bleed? . . . If you poison us, do we not die?" (3.1.53–55)—cannot help but move an audience. But it leads by steps to a justification for acting according to the lowest common denominator: "And if you wrong us, shall we not revenge? If we are like you in the rest, we will resemble you in that" (3.2.55–57). The speech is moving as the response of a man who has been repeatedly humiliated and literally spat upon by the unrepentant Antonio; and it brilliantly turns the tables on his accusers. But it is also an attempt to justify murder: "The villainy you teach me I will execute, and it shall go hard but I will better the instruction" (3.1.59–61).

Shylock's defense is equally compelling in the trial scene, when he reminds the Christians, "You have among you many a purchased slave" (4.1.90). (He refers to the Mediterranean slave trade, carried on by Ottoman Turks, North Africans, and Europeans.) Even there, however, his point is not exactly to condemn the practice of slavery; rather, Shylock claims he has as much right to the pound of Antonio's flesh as a slave-holder has to the body of the slave—that is, an apparently unquestionable right. We notice again how Shakespeare subtly suggests a structural similarity between the merchant and the Jew. Both are men of property; both depend on the law to defend their property.

The play, however, treats the issue of property—of money, of gold, silver, and lead, even of people when they are treated as property—in two radically different ways. Shylock stands on the proverb, "Fast bind, fast find" (2.5.53); he is all for thrift, for keeping things tied down and locked away behind the doors of his house, behind casement windows shut against the sound of frivolity. He is faithful to his precise principle, and he expects the laws of Venice to support him. A contract is a contract; a thing purchased belongs to its owner: "I'll have my bond. . . . I'll have my bond. . . . I will have my bond" (3.3.12, 13, 17). Another way is Antonio's, who is ready to give everything he has to Bassanio. And even more spectacularly it is Portia's way: "Pay him six thousand and deface the bond; / Double six thousand, and then treble that" (3.2.297–298). Portia's way is to let riches loose, to make her overflowing abundance a principle as absolute in its way as Shylock's principle of holding property tight.

Portia is a treasure: that, at least, is the statement the play makes by equating her with the golden fleece, making her the object of suitors from every coast, giving her an apparently endless supply of money. Her dramatic figure is as complexly enmeshed in the play's enactment of economic fantasies as are the figures of the merchant and the Jew. The elements of Portia's configuration may seem contradictory. She is a golden girl (even her hair, Bassanio says, is "A golden mesh t'entrap the hearts of men" [3.2.122]), yet only the man who chooses "meager lead" can have her. She is active, independent, and apparently the only character in the play with the brains to save Antonio's life. Yet her immediate response to Bassanio's choosing is to commit her "gentle spirit" to be directed by him, "her lord, her governor, her king" (3.2.165). She wishes (in the expansive arithmetic that is so different from Shylock's measured way) that she could be "trebled twenty times [her]self, / A thousand times more fair, ten thousand times more rich" (3.2.153–154), all on Bassanio's account.

Shakespeare did not invent the clever and sexually desirable cross-dressing heroine (she was a staple of folk tale and comedy when women had to assume a conventionally male role in order to exercise power), but he brought it to comic perfection in characters such as Rosalind in *As You Like It*, Viola in *Twelfth Night*, Imogen in *Cymbeline*, and of course Portia. Such characters do double dramatic duty. They arouse men's anxieties about women's social and sexual roles, but their participation in the marriage quest also allays those anxieties. Elizabethan law followed the principle laid down by the apostle Paul, that the husband is the head of the wife and that wives should be in subjection to their husbands (Ephesians 5.22–23). Upon marriage, a woman's property became her husband's property; her rights of self-ownership were severely limited. In *The Taming of the Shrew*, Petruchio's comic boast about his new wife Katharina, "She is my goods, my chattels; she is my house, / My horse, my ox, my ass, my anything" (3.2.231–232), is absurd—Kate is a person, not an animal or thing—but it is an almost literal statement of the legal reality. The smart young women of Shakespeare's romantic comedies potentially threaten the masculine arrangement. How could any mere husband tame a Kate or put into subjection a Beatrice (*Much Ado about Nothing*) or a Rosalind? The masculine fear that women would refuse to be treated as manageable property contributed to the ubiquitous jokes about cuckolds (men with adulterous wives). Cuckoldry was the stuff of comedy. All an actor had to do was make the sign of the horns, the cuckold's sign, to get a laugh; but in certain instances, of which *Othello* is the outstanding example, it could be tragic as well.

It is clear that between the ways in which men and women were supposed to behave under the ideology of masculine possessiveness and the real conditions of living men and women, there was sometimes a bewildering distance. The Shakespearean comic heroine (played by a boy) turns her energetic inventiveness to shortening it. Portia's independent spirit, like that of Nerissa and Jessica, enables the play's ending in marriage. It is the privilege of comedy simultaneously to acknowledge historical conditions and to make them a source of pleasure. In all three of *The Merchant*'s interconnected episodes (the casket plot, the trial, and the episode of the rings), harsh cultural facts are converted into the elements of comic release. (Significantly, Shylock is locked outside the charmed circle where these adjustments happen; his conversion and the terms of his release bring pleasure only to those within.) For instance, Portia is subject to her father's will, a situation, however fantastic, that has a basis in the practice of arranged marriages. But when Portia submits to the letter of her dead father's law, she gets the man of her own desires. In this comic world, it turns out, the father's decree anticipates the woman's wish. Portia brings to the marriage not only her wealth but her wit, a quality potentially threatening to a supposedly superior man; but she uses both wit and wealth to save the male world from the disaster its own laws and economic arrangements have brought upon it. In the final action of the rings, the threat of cuckoldry, of wives who cannot be controlled by their husbands, is raised only to become the comedy's punch line.

There are cultural contexts for Portia's principle of giving rather than keeping. It carries echoes of ancient ideas. The first-century writer Seneca, whose work was widely influential in Shakespeare's time, had described an ideal economy based not on payments but on gifts or "benefits." According to Seneca, social life should be like a circular dance in which each participant must give willingly, receive willingly, and return willingly, in order that the cycle can begin again. In this ideal economy, benefits are constantly in motion, never hoarded; and giving, not lending, creates the links between human beings.

Another context is Christian theology. In the trial scene, Shylock demands the letter of the law and Portia pleads for (but acknowledges that she cannot constrain) "the quality of mercy" (4.1.181). In Christian thought, the relation of these two commendable principles, justice and mercy, was similar to the relation of the Old Testament to the New Testament, or, as it was sometimes put, of the Synagogue to the Church. According to this Christian interpretation, under God's law all human beings have already been judged and found guilty by contagion from Adam's original sin. The law of the Old Testament, in this theological understanding, leads only to mankind's condemnation. Christ, however, took humanity's sin upon himself; he paid the penalty, fulfilling the law's requirements and saving mankind, or at least some portion of it.

This admittedly sketchy summary of complex issues can suggest a theological context for the debate between Shylock, who claims that he "stand[s] for judgment" (4.1.103) and "crave[s] the law" (4.1.203), and Portia, who argues "That in the course of justice none of us / Should see salvation" (4.1.196–197). Portia links human law to God's law. According to principles of Venetian justice, Antonio is apparently bound to death. Her recourse is to mercy, which in this context means much more than niceness or leniency. It is "an attribute to God himself" (4.1.192), since God sent Christ to pay the penalty for his guilty creatures. We pray for God's mercy, says Portia, and the best we can do as human beings is to imitate God by rendering "the deeds of mercy" to others (4.1.199). The languages of theology and economics ("render" suggests payment, "deeds" are both actions and documents of ownership) are inextricable in Portia's courtroom speech, as they have been throughout the play.

The Merchant of Venice does not simply pit justice and mercy against one another; rather, it recognizes the necessity of both principles. Shylock's demand that he get what is lawfully his is not ruled out of court. How could it be when "the trade and profit of

"Ecclesia et Synagoga" (Church and Synagogue), by the "Master of the Ursula Legend." The Legend of St. Ursula, the Church, and The Synagogue. Stedeljka Musea Brugge, Groeningemuseum. By permission.

The contrast between the dispensation of the Hebrew Bible and the new dispensation of the Christian revelation was a common theme for artists from the early Medieval period through the Renaissance. The relationship is represented from the Christian point of view by allegorical figures of Synagogue and Church. In this painting from the late 15th century, Eccelesia, on the left, is an upright queenly figure bearing the cross, communion cup, and wafer. On the right, Synagoga, blind-folded to represent Judaism's supposed refusal to see the truth, wears an Oriental turban; her staff is broken; the upside-down tablets of the Mosaic Law seem about to fall from her hand. The courtroom scene in *The Merchant of Venice*, in which Shylock demands "justice" (an attribute of Old Testament law) and Portia extols "mercy" (an attribute of Christ as redeemer), suggests the kind of opposition embodied in the painting.

the city" (3.3.30) requires the inviolability of contracts? It is seldom easy, in or out of courtrooms, to balance the demands of justice and mercy: How to be merciful without violating the law, how to be just without forsaking the claim of mercy? Is mercy to one party an injustice to the other? These are the intractable kinds of issues Shakespeare plays out in the trial. His solution is itself controversial. For some readers and audiences, Portia plays a cruel trick when she goes to the law's small print, which allows the flesh but not the blood and condemns any "alien" who conspires against a Venetian's life. According to this view, she has set up Shylock, giving him assurances, allowing him to pursue his claim, then suddenly springing the trap on him. Others see Portia's method as a way of finding mercy for Antonio without disregarding the claims of the law. As if in imitation of the Christian understanding (in Matthew 5.17–18, Christ says he comes not to destroy but to fulfill the law), Portia reads the letter of the law and finds that its ultimate meaning is the mercy that spares life. According to a reading of this sort, the play reconciles the claims of justice and mercy.

Shylock says, "I stand for judgment. . . . I stand here for law" (4.1.103, 142). Holding the balancing scales, the symbol of justice, to weigh an exact pound of flesh, Shylock seems almost to be declaring himself what the characters so frequently call him: "the Jew," the allegorical figure (from a certain Christian point of view) of the Old Testament dispensation of law, the embodied principle of justice untempered by mercy. But Shakespeare has a way of unraveling our neat interpretations. Throughout the play Shylock refuses to be a mere symbol and demands to be recognized as an individual. He is too distinctive, too strange merely to "stand for" an idea. He has a daughter whose betrayal pains him. He had a wife, Leah, who gave him a turquoise ring when he was a bachelor. Touches such as these create a dramatic figure that approximates our idea of a person like ourselves, not the allegorical figure of an abstract principle. Modern audiences are unlikely to take pleasure from Shylock's humiliation. We have had to learn repeatedly the difference between symbols and people and to recognize that the reduction of individuals to types is a precondition for their oppression.

Perhaps Shylock's resistance to being dismissed accounts for the play's odd structure. The trial that might seem its grand conclusion occurs when there is still a full act to come. Seen from a distance,

Shylock plays a dramatic role similar to Malvolio's in *Twelfth Night*: Both characters are keepers-in rather than givers-out, both are impediments to the other characters' happy endings, both are expelled from the comic conclusion in which (in both plays) three couples are destined for marriage. But no one worries very much about the false-Puritan Malvolio; he makes his exit only ten lines before the song that concludes the play, leaving hardly a wet eye in the house. Shylock's expulsion is different. The power of it— whether we emphasize the death averted or the pain inflicted—requires an entire fifth act to manage.

Lorenzo and Jessica begin that act exchanging teasing references to the most disastrous of legendary love affairs. Once again, the play glances at danger at the same time that it tries to charm it away, this time by the lovers' banter. Music plays throughout much of the act and becomes the subject of Lorenzo's and Jessica's conversation. According to Lorenzo, the music we hear is only an intimation of the music made by the heavenly spheres in their perfect circulation. Earthly music is a fainter version of heavenly music. The play draws into itself these powerful ideas about an ultimate harmony as if in an attempt to balance Shylock's powerful dissonance. And finally Portia and Nerrisa play the joke of the rings. It is an interesting variation on the idea of giving, receiving, and giving again. In giving away the ring to "Balthazar," Bassanio breaks the letter of his vow to Portia; now "Balthazar" gives the ring back to Bassanio, only so that he can restore it to Portia. Some readers find in this action another instance of the Christian characters' profligate ways; others see it as a last instance of the principle that giving is the condition for getting. In the fantastic world of *The Merchant of Venice*, even the conflict between male friendship and heterosexual marriage can, apparently, be reconciled.

It is appropriate that even this ending is controversial. Since the nineteenth century, *The Merchant of Venice* has been one of the most frequently performed of Shakespeare's plays but also the one that has aroused the most controversy, even including calls for its censorship. In 1974, for instance, *The New York Times* ran a column by a member of its editorial board arguing, as the headline put it, "Why Shylock Should Not Be Censored." The article was inspired by protests against the television presentation of the National Theatre Company production, directed by Jonathan Miller and starring Sir Laurence Olivier. The case against censorship was made easier because the writer found in Olivier's performance a Shylock who forced one to "question and reject the stereotypes . . . who, though vengeful, had much to be vengeful about."[1] Olivier's sympathetic Shylock was at a vast distance from one of the earliest and most famous Shylocks, Charles Macklin's 1741 performance of him as a terrifying villain. Cultural conditions had radically changed by 1817 when the critic William Hazlitt, referring to the performance by Edmund Kean, wrote that "In proportion as Shylock has ceased to be a popular bugbear . . . he becomes a half-favorite with the philosophical part of the audience, who are disposed to think that Jewish revenge is at least as good as Christian injuries."

It may seem unnecessary to ask why a play in which Christian characters call a Jew "dog," "cur," "inhuman wretch," and so on, and which then requires the Jew, against his will, to convert to Christianity, is controversial. (And that's to say nothing about Portia's comment about the Prince of Morocco's complexion.) In fact, however, these matters have not always or in all places seemed as self-evidently troubling as they do to most readers today. Some of our most fundamental ideas about human rights and freedom of religion are of recent invention, and they are by no means universally shared. To experience *The Merchant of Venice* we must be sensitive to the ideas of other times and other places while also scrutinizing our own most intimate beliefs about, among other things, the relation of imaginative literature to our personal histories and to world history. The materials in this volume are intended to help meet that challenge.

[1]Fred M. Hechinger, March 31, 1974.

Note on Sources

Shakespeare read widely: the evidence is all over the plays. Some of that reading provided traceable hints for the plots and characters of his plays. Scholars refer to this kind of writing as a *source*. The word can be misleading if it implies a direct act of taking over, as if the so-called source were the original and Shakespeare's play somehow a copy. True, in some cases Shakespeare did draw closely on a source. Enobarbus's description of Cleopatra on her barge (*Antony and Cleopatra*) borrows directly from his source, Thomas North's translation of Plutarch; and Gonzalo's description of his ideal commonwealth (*The Tempest*) borrows directly from John Florio's translation of Montaigne. (But even in such instances, the interesting things to notice are the swerves, the additions or emendations that make these speeches distinctively Shakespearean despite their derivations.) In other cases we find that the source may have suggested a character or situation but that Shakespeare made something radically different from it. In such cases the source belongs among the plays' contexts, but it may be a less interesting cultural context—less revealing of attitudes within Shakespeare's world—than some other writing that Shakespeare may not have read.

For *The Merchant of Venice* the probable sources are very distant from the spirit and feel of the play. Also, the stories these sources tell are themselves versions of widespread motifs with ancient lineages. For instance, Shakespeare may have found inspiration for the bond story and the pound of flesh in the Italian story collection *Il Pecorone* by Ser Giovanni Fiorentino. He also would have there found the name "Belmonte" as the home of a rich woman (but in this case a widow). *Il Pecorone* was published in

Italy in 1558. We do not know how and in what version Shakespeare (who probably did not read Italian) found it.

The story about a pound of flesh appears in other texts, and these versions too may have suggested specific elements that Shakespeare radically revised. Alexander Silvayn's *The Orator* (English translation 1596) has speeches by the Jew and the Christian that may have contributed ideas to the trial scene. Anthony Munday's *Zelauto* (1588), although it does not involve a Jew and the usurer demands an eye rather than a pound of flesh, seems to have some faint echoes in Shakespeare's play.

These and other work that have plausible claim to being sources can be found in Geoffrey Bullough's multivolume collection, *Narrative and Dramatic Sources of Shakespeare* (London; Routledge and Paul; New York, Columbia University Press, 1957–1975).

Table of Dates

1558	Queen Elizabeth I begins her reign upon the death of Mary I.
1564	William Shakespeare is born on April 23 in Statford-upon-Avon, Warwickshire, the son of Mary Shakespeare and John Shakespeare, a glover.
	Christopher Marlowe is born.
1582	Shakespeare marries Anne Hathaway.
1583	Shakespeare's daughter Susanna is born.
1585	The twins, Hamnet and Judith Shakespeare, are born.
1588	The Spanish Armada is defeated by England.
1592	Robert Greene's *A Groatsworth of Wit* contains the first extant reference to Shakespeare ("Shake-scene") as an actor or playwright.
	Christopher Marlowe's *The Jew of Malta* has its first performance.
1593	Christopher Marlowe dies on May 30.
1596–97	*The Merchant of Venice* and *1 Henry IV* are performed for the first time.
1598	Francis Meres publishes *Palladis Tamia* in which he lists some of Shakespeare's work up to that time: under "comedies" he names *The Two Gentlemen of Verona*, *The Comedy of Errors*, *Love's Labor's Lost*, *A Midsummer Night's Dream*, and *The Merchant of Venice*.

1600	The first quarto of *The Merchant of Venice* is published.
1600–01	The first performances of *Hamlet* take place.
1603	Queen Elizabeth dies and is succeeded by King James I.
1616	Shakespeare dies and is buried in Holy Trinity Church, Stratford-upon-Avon.
1623	*Mr. William Shakespeare's Comedies, Histories, and Tragedies* (the First Folio) is published.

The Merchant of Venice

by William Shakespeare

The Merchant of Venice

Dramatis Personae

THE DUKE OF VENICE
ANTONIO, *a merchant of Venice*
BASSANIO, *his friend, suitor to Portia*
GRATIANO, *a follower of Bassanio, in love with Nerissa*
SOLANIO, } *friends to Antonio*
SALERIO, } *and Bassanio*
LORENZO, *in love with Jessica*
LEONARDO, *servant to Bassanio*

PORTIA, *a rich heiress of Belmont*
NERISSA, *her waiting-gentlewoman*
BALTHASAR, *servant to Portia*
STEPHANO, *servant to Portia*
THE PRINCE OF MOROCCO, *suitor to Portia*
THE PRINCE OF ARAGON, *suitor to Portia*
A MESSENGER *to Portia*

SHYLOCK, *a rich Jew*
JESSICA, *his daughter*
TUBAL, *a Jew, Shylock's friend*
LANCELOT GOBBO, *a clown, servant to Shylock and then to Bassanio*
OLD GOBBO, *Lancelot's father*

Magnificoes of Venice, Officers of the Court of Justice, Jailor, Servants to Portia, and other Attendants

SCENE: *Partly at Venice and partly at Belmont, the seat of Portia*

ACT 1
SCENE 1

Location: A street in Venice

Enter Antonio, Salerio, and Solanio

ANTONIO In sooth,° I know not why I am so sad.°
It wearies me, you say it wearies you;
But how I caught it, found it, or came by it,
What stuff 'tis made of, whereof it is born,
I am to learn;°   5
And such a want-wit sadness makes of me°
That I have much ado to know myself.

SALERIO Your mind is tossing on the ocean,
There where your argosies° with portly° sail,
Like signors° and rich burghers on the flood,°   10
Or as it were the pageants° of the sea,
Do overpeer° the petty traffickers
That curtsy° to them, do them reverence,
As they fly by them with their woven wings.°

SOLANIO Believe me, sir, had I such venture forth,°   15
The better part of my affections would
Be with my hopes abroad. I should be still°
Plucking the grass to know where sits the wind,
Peering in maps for ports and piers and roads;°
And every object that might make me fear   20
Misfortune to my ventures, out of doubt
Would make me sad.

SALERIO   My wind cooling my broth
Would blow me to an ague° when I thought
What harm a wind too great might do at sea.

---

1 **In sooth** truly | **sad** morose, dismal-looking 5 **am to learn** have yet to learn
6 **such . . . of me** sadness makes me so distracted, lacking in good sense
9 **argosies** large merchant ships (so named from *Ragusa*, the modern city of
Dubrovnik) | **portly** majestic 10 **signors** gentlemen | **flood** sea 11 **pageants**
mobile stages used in plays or processions 12 **overpeer** look down upon
13 **curtsy** bob up and down, or lower topsails in token of respect (**reverence**)
14 **woven wings** canvas sails 15 **venture forth** investment at risk 17 **still**
continually 19 **roads** anchorages, open harbors 23 **blow . . . ague** start me
shivering

I should not see the sandy hourglass run   25
But I should think of shallows and of flats,°
And see my wealthy *Andrew*° docked in sand,
Vailing° her high-top° lower than her ribs
To kiss her burial.° Should I go to church
And see the holy edifice of stone   30
And not bethink me straight° of dangerous rocks
Which, touching but my gentle vessel's side,
Would scatter all her spices on the stream,
Enrobe the roaring waters with my silks,
And, in a word, but even now° worth this,°   35
And now worth nothing? Shall I have the thought
To think on this, and shall I lack the thought
That such a thing bechanced° would make me sad?
But tell not me. I know Antonio
Is sad to think upon his merchandise.   40
ANTONIO   Believe me, no. I thank my fortune for it,
My ventures are not in one bottom° trusted,
Nor to one place; nor is my whole estate
Upon the fortune of this present year.°
Therefore my merchandise makes me not sad.   45
SOLANIO   Why then, you are in love.
ANTONIO   Fie, fie!
SOLANIO   Not in love neither? Then let us say you are sad
Because you are not merry; and 'twere as easy
For you to laugh and leap, and say you are merry
Because you are not sad. Now, by two-headed Janus,°   50
Nature hath framed° strange fellows in her time:
Some that will evermore peep through their eyes°
And laugh like parrots at a bagpiper,°
And other° of such vinegar aspect°

---

26 **flats** shoals   27 *Andrew* name of a ship (perhaps after the *St. Andrew*, a Spanish galleon captured at Cadiz in 1596)   28 **Vailing** lowering (usually as a sign of submission) | **high-top** topmast   29 **burial** burial place   31 **bethink me straight** be put in mind immediately   35 **even now** a short while ago | **this** the cargo of spices and silks   38 **bechanced** having happened   42 **bottom** ship's hold   44 **Upon . . . year** risked upon the chance of the present year   50 **two-headed Janus** a Roman god of all beginnings, represented by a figure with two faces   51 **framed** fashioned   52 **peep . . . eyes** look with eyes narrowed by laughter   53 **at a bagpiper** even at a bagpiper, whose music was regarded as melancholic   54 **other** others | **vinegar aspect** sour, sullen looks

That they'll not show their teeth in way of smile   55
Though Nestor° swear the jest be laughable.

                    Enter Bassanio, Lorenzo, and Gratiano

Here comes Bassanio, your most noble kinsman,
Gratiano, and Lorenzo. Fare ye well.
We leave you now with better company.
SALERIO   I would have stayed till I had made you merry,   60
If worthier friends had not prevented° me.
ANTONIO   Your worth is very dear in my regard.
I take it your own business calls on you,
And you embrace th'occasion° to depart.
SALERIO   Good morrow, my good lords.   65
BASSANIO   Good signors both, when shall we laugh?° Say, when?
You grow exceeding strange. Must it be so?°
SALERIO   We'll make our leisures to attend on yours.°
                    Exeunt Salerio and Solanio
LORENZO   My lord Bassanio, since you have found Antonio,
We two will leave you, but at dinnertime,   70
I pray you, have in mind where we must meet.
BASSANIO   I will not fail you.
GRATIANO   You look not well, Signor Antonio.
You have too much respect upon the world.°
They lose it that do buy it with much care.   75
Believe me, you are marvelously changed.
ANTONIO   I hold the world but as the world, Gratiano—
A stage where every man must play a part,
And mine a sad one.
GRATIANO   Let me play the fool.
With mirth and laughter let old wrinkles come,   80
And let my liver rather heat with wine°
Than my heart cool with mortifying° groans.

---

56 Nestor venerable senior officer in the *Iliad*, noted for gravity   **61 prevented** forestalled   **64 th'occasion** the opportunity   **66 laugh** be merry together   **67 strange** distant | **must it be so?** must you go? or, must you show reserve?   **68 We'll . . . yours** we'll adjust our spare time to accommodate your schedule   **74 respect . . . world** concern for worldly affairs of business   **81 heat with wine** (the liver was regarded as the seat of the passions and wine as an agency for inflaming them)   **82 mortifying** penitential and deadly (sighs were thought to cost the heart a drop of blood)

Why should a man whose blood is warm within
Sit like his grandsire cut in alabaster?°
Sleep when he wakes, and creep into the jaundice°   85
By being peevish? I tell thee what, Antonio—
I love thee, and 'tis my love that speaks—
There are a sort of men whose visages
Do cream and mantle° like a standing° pond,
And do a willful stillness entertain   90
With purpose to be dressed in an opinion
Of wisdom, gravity, profound conceit,°
As who should say,° "I am Sir Oracle,
And when I ope my lips let no dog bark!"°
Oh, my Antonio, I do know of these   95
That therefore only are reputed wise
For saying nothing, when, I am very sure,
If they should speak, would almost damn those ears
Which, hearing them, would call their brothers fools.°
I'll tell thee more of this another time.   100
But fish not with this melancholy bait
For this fool gudgeon, this opinion.—°
Come, good Lorenzo.—Fare ye well awhile.
I'll end my exhortation after dinner.
LORENZO [*to Antonio and Bassanio*]
Well, we will leave you then till dinnertime.   105
I must be one of these same dumb° wise men,
For Gratiano never lets me speak.
GRATIANO Well, keep° me company but two years more,
Thou shalt not know the sound of thine own tongue.
ANTONIO Fare you well. I'll grow a talker for this gear.° 110

---

84 in alabaster in a stone effigy upon a tomb **85 jaundice** (regarded as arising from the effects of too much choler or yellow bile, one of the four humors, in the blood) **89 cream and mantle** become covered with scum, i.e., acquire a lifeless, stiff expression | **standing** stagnant **90–2 And . . . conceit** and who maintain a willful silence in order to acquire a reputation for gravity and deep thought **93 As . . . say** as if to say **94 let . . . bark** let no creature dare to interrupt me **98–9 would . . . fools** would virtually condemn their hearers into calling them fools (compare Matthew 5.22, in which anyone calling another a fool is threatened with damnation) **101–2 fish . . . opinion** don't go fishing for a reputation of being wise, using your melancholy silence as the bait to fool people (*gudgeon*, a small fish, was thought of as a type of gullibility) **106 dumb** mute, speechless **108 keep** if you keep **110 for this gear** in view of what you say

GRATIANO Thanks, i'faith, for silence is only commendable
In a neat's° tongue dried and a maid not vendible.°

Exeunt [Gratiano and Lorenzo]

ANTONIO Is that anything now?°
BASSANIO Gratiano speaks an infinite deal of nothing, more
than any man in all Venice. His reasons° are as two grains of   115
wheat hid in two bushels of chaff; you shall seek all day ere
you find them, and when you have them they are not worth
the search.
ANTONIO Well, tell me now what lady is the same°
To whom you swore a secret pilgrimage,   120
That you today promised to tell me of.
BASSANIO 'Tis not unknown to you, Antonio,
How much I have disabled mine estate
By something showing a more swelling port°
Than my faint means would grant continuance.°   125
Nor do I now make moan to be abridged
From such a noble rate;° but my chief care
Is to come fairly off° from the great debts
Wherein my time,° something too prodigal,
Hath left me gaged.° To you, Antonio,   130
I owe the most, in money and in love,
And from your love I have a warranty°
To unburden° all my plots and purposes
How to get clear of all the debts I owe.
ANTONIO I pray you, good Bassanio, let me know it;   135
And if it stand, as you yourself still do,
Within the eye of honor,° be assured
My purse, my person, my extremest means
Lie all unlocked to your occasions.
BASSANIO In my schooldays, when I had lost one shaft,°   140
I shot his° fellow of the selfsame flight°

112 neat's ox's | not vendible not yet salable in the marriage market   113 Is . . .
now? was all that talk about anything?   115 reasons reasonable ideas   119 the
same the one   124 By . . . port by showing a somewhat more lavish style of living
125 grant continuance allow to continue   126–27 make . . . rate complain at being
cut back from such a high style of living   128 to . . . off honorably to extricate
myself   129 time youthful lifetime   130 gaged pledged, in pawn   132 warranty
authorization   133 unburden disclose   136–37 if . . . honor if it looks honorable,
as your conduct has always done   140 shaft arrow   141 his its | selfsame flight
same kind and range

The selfsame way with more advisèd° watch
To find the other forth,° and by adventuring° both
I oft found both. I urge this childhood proof
Because what follows is pure innocence.°   145
I owe you much, and, like a willful youth,
That which I owe is lost; but if you please
To shoot another arrow that self° way
Which you did shoot the first, I do not doubt,
As I will watch the aim, or° to find both   150
Or bring your latter hazard° back again
And thankfully rest° debtor for the first.
ANTONIO   You know me well, and herein spend but time°
To wind about my love with circumstance;°
And out of doubt you do me now more wrong   155
In making question of my uttermost°
Than if you had made waste of all I have.
Then do but say to me what I should do
That in your knowledge may by me be done,
And I am prest° unto it. Therefore speak.   160
BASSANIO   In Belmont is a lady richly left;°
And she is fair and, fairer than that word,
Of wondrous virtues. Sometimes° from her eyes
I did receive fair speechless messages.
Her name is Portia, nothing undervalued   165
To° Cato's daughter, Brutus' Portia.°
Nor is the wide world ignorant of her worth,
For the four winds blow in from every coast
Renownèd suitors, and her sunny locks
Hang on her temples like a golden fleece,   170
Which makes her seat of Belmont Colchis'° strand,°

---

142 **advisèd** careful   143 **forth** out | **adventuring** risking   145 **innocence**
ingenuousness, sincerity   148 **self** same   150 **or** either   151 **hazard** that which
was risked   152 **rest** remain   153 **spend but time** only waste time   154 **To . . .**
circumstance in not asking plainly what you want (**circumstance** here means
"circumlocution")   156 **In . . . uttermost** in showing any doubt of my intention to
do all I can   160 **prest** ready   161 **richly left** left a large fortune (by her father's
will)   163 **Sometimes** once   165–66 **nothing undervalued to** of no less worth than
166 **Portia** (known for bravery and loyalty to her husband; a character in
Shakespeare's *Julius Caesar*) [LD]   171 **Colchis'** (Jason adventured for the golden
fleece in the land of Colchis, on the Black Sea) | **strand** shore

And many Jasons come in quest of her.
Oh, my Antonio, had I but the means
To hold a rival place with one of them,
I have a mind presages° me such thrift°   175
That I should questionless be fortunate.
ANTONIO   Thou know'st that all my fortunes are at sea;
Neither have I money nor commodity°
To raise a present sum.° Therefore go forth.
Try what my credit can in Venice do;   180
That shall be racked° even to the uttermost
To furnish thee to Belmont, to fair Portia.
Go presently° inquire, and so will I,
Where money is, and I no question make°
To have it of my trust° or for my sake.°   185

Exeunt

❖

ACT 1
SCENE 2

Location: Belmont. Portia's house

Enter Portia with her waiting woman, Nerissa

PORTIA   By my troth,° Nerissa, my little body is aweary of this
great world.
NERISSA   You would be,° sweet madam, if your miseries were in
the same abundance as your good fortunes are; and yet, for
aught I see, they are as sick that surfeit° with too much as   5
they that starve with nothing. It is no mean° happiness, therefore, to be seated in the mean.° Superfluity comes sooner by°
white hairs, but competency° lives longer.
PORTIA   Good sentences,° and well pronounced.°

175 **presages** that presages | **thrift** profit and good fortune   178 **commodity**
merchandise   179 **a present sum** ready money   181 **racked** stretched   183 **presently**
immediately   184 **no question make** have no doubt   185 **of my trust** on the basis
of my credit as a merchant | **sake** personal sake

1 **troth** faith   3 **would be** would have reason to be (weary)   5 **surfeit** overindulge
6 **mean** small (with a pun; see next note)   7 **in the mean** having neither too much
nor too little | **comes sooner by** acquires sooner   8 **competency** modest means
9 **sentences** maxims | **pronounced** delivered

NERISSA They would be better if well followed.   10

PORTIA If to do were as easy as to know what were good to do,
chapels had been churches and poor men's cottages princes'
palaces. It is a good divine° that follows his own instructions.
I can easier teach twenty what were good to be done than to
be one of the twenty to follow mine own teaching. The   15
brain may devise laws for the blood,° but a hot temper leaps
o'er a cold decree; such a hare is madness, the youth, to skip
o'er the meshes° of good counsel, the cripple.° But this reasoning is not in the fashion to choose me a husband.° Oh,
me, the word "choose"! I may neither choose who I would   20
nor refuse who I dislike; so is the will of a living daughter
curbed by the will° of a dead father. Is it not hard, Nerissa,
that I cannot choose one nor refuse none?

NERISSA Your father was ever virtuous, and holy men at their
death have good inspirations; therefore the lottery that he   25
hath devised in these three chests of gold, silver, and lead,
whereof who° chooses his° meaning chooses you, will no
doubt never be chosen by any rightly but one who you shall
rightly° love. But what warmth is there in your affection towards any of these princely suitors that are already come?   30

PORTIA I pray thee, overname them,° and as thou namest them
I will describe them; and according to my description level°
at my affection.

NERISSA First, there is the Neapolitan prince.

PORTIA Ay, that's a colt° indeed, for he doth nothing but talk   35
of his horse, and he makes it a great appropriation° to his
own good parts° that he can shoe him himself. I am much
afeard my lady his mother played false with a smith.

NERISSA Then is there the County Palatine.°

---

13 **divine** clergyman 16 **blood** (thought of as a chief agent of the passions, which
in turn were regarded as the enemies of reason) 18 **meshes** nets (used here for
hunting hares) | **good counsel, the cripple** (wisdom is portrayed as old and no
longer agile) 18–19 **But . . . husband** but this talk is not the way to help me choose
a husband 21–2 **will . . . will** volition . . . testament 27 **who** whoever | **his** the
father's 28–9 **rightly . . . rightly** correctly . . . truly 31 **overname them** name
them over 32 **level** aim, guess 35 **colt** wanton and foolish young man (with a
punning appropriateness to his interest in horses) 36 **appropriation** addition
37 **good parts** accomplishments 39 **County Palatine** a count entitled to supreme
jurisdiction in his province

PORTIA He doth nothing but frown, as who should say,° "An° 40
you will not have me, choose."° He hears merry tales and
smiles not. I fear he will prove the weeping philosopher°
when he grows old, being so full of unmannerly sadness° in
his youth. I had rather be married to a death's-head with a
bone in his mouth than to either of these. God defend me 45
from these two!

NERISSA How say you by° the French lord, Monsieur Le Bon?

PORTIA God made him, and therefore let him pass for a man.
In truth, I know it is a sin to be a mocker, but he! Why, he
hath a horse better than the Neapolitan's, a better bad habit 50
of frowning than the Count Palatine; he is every man in no
man.° If a throstle° sing, he falls straight° a-capering. He will
fence with his own shadow. If° I should marry him, I should
marry twenty husbands. If he would despise me, I would
forgive him, for if he love me to madness, I shall never re- 55
quite him.

NERISSA What say you, then, to° Falconbridge, the young
baron of England?

PORTIA You know I say nothing to him, for he understands not
me, nor I him. He hath neither Latin, French, nor Italian, 60
and you will come into the court and swear that I have a
poor pennyworth in the English.° He is a proper man's picture,° but alas, who can converse with a dumb show?° How
oddly he is suited!° I think he bought his doublet° in Italy,
his round hose° in France, his bonnet° in Germany, and his 65
behavior everywhere.

NERISSA What think you of the Scottish lord, his neighbor?

PORTIA That he hath a neighborly charity in him, for he
borrowed° a box of the ear of the Englishman and swore he

40 **as who should say** as one might say | **An** if   41 **choose** do as you please
42 **the weeping philosopher** Heraclitus of Ephesus, a melancholic and retiring
philosopher of about 500 BCE, often contrasted with Democritus, the "laughing
philosopher"   43 **sadness** melancholy   47 **How . . . by** what do you have to say
about   51–2 **he is . . . no man** he borrows aspects from everyone but has no
character of his own   52 **throstle** thrush | **straight** at once   53 **if** even if
57 **say you . . . to** do you say about (but Portia wittily puns, in her reply, on the
literal sense of "speak to")   61–2 **come . . . English** bear witness that I can speak
very little English   62 **He . . . picture** he looks handsome   63 **dumb show**
pantomime   64 **suited** dressed | **doublet** upper garment corresponding to a jacket
65 **round hose** short, puffed-out breeches | **bonnet** hat   69 **borrowed** received
(but with a play on the idea of something that must be repaid)

would pay him again when he was able. I think the 70
Frenchman became his surety and sealed under for another.°

NERISSA How like you the young German, the Duke of
Saxony's nephew?

PORTIA Very vilely in the morning, when he is sober, and most
vilely in the afternoon, when he is drunk. When he is best he 75
is a little worse than a man, and when he is worst he is little
better than a beast. An° the worst fall° that ever fell, I hope I
shall make shift° to go without him.

NERISSA If he should offer° to choose, and choose the right casket, you should refuse to perform your father's will if you 80
should refuse to accept him.

PORTIA Therefore, for fear of the worst, I pray thee, set a deep
glass of Rhenish wine° on the contrary° casket, for if° the
devil be within and that temptation without, I know he will
choose it.° I will do anything, Nerissa, ere I will be married 85
to a sponge.

NERISSA You need not fear, lady, the having any of these lords.
They have acquainted me with their determinations, which
is indeed to return to their home and to trouble you with no
more suit, unless you may be won by some other sort° than 90
your father's imposition° depending on the caskets.

PORTIA If I live to be as old as Sibylla,° I will die as chaste as
Diana,° unless I be obtained by the manner of my father's
will. I am glad this parcel° of wooers are so reasonable, for
there is not one among them but I dote on his very absence, 95
and I pray God grant them a fair departure.

NERISSA Do you not remember, lady, in your father's time, a
Venetian, a scholar and a soldier, that came hither in company of the Marquess of Montferrat?

PORTIA Yes, yes, it was Bassanio—as I think, so was he called. 100

---

71 became . . . another offered to back up the Scottish lord and promised (with as
solemn a vow as if he were signing and sealing a document) to add a blow of his
own (an allusion to the age-old alliance of the French and the Scots against the
English) **77 An** if | **fall** befall **78 make shift** manage **79 offer** undertake
83 Rhenish wine a German white wine from the Rhine Valley | **contrary** wrong | **if**
even if **85 it** the tempting red wine **90 sort** means (with perhaps a suggestion too
of "casting or drawing of lots") **91 imposition** command, charge **92 Sibylla** the
Cumaean Sibyl, to whom Apollo gave as many years as there were grains in her
handful of sand **93 Diana** goddess of chastity and of the hunt **94 parcel**
assembly, group

NERISSA True, madam. He, of all the men that ever my foolish eyes looked upon was the best deserving a fair lady.

PORTIA I remember him well, and I remember him worthy of thy praise.

Enter a Servingman

How now, what news?   105

SERVINGMAN The four° strangers seek for you, madam, to take their leave; and there is a forerunner° come from a fifth, the Prince of Morocco, who brings word the Prince his master will be here tonight.

PORTIA If I could bid the fifth welcome with so good heart as I   110 can bid the other four farewell, I should be glad of his approach. If he have the condition° of a saint and the complexion of a devil,° I had rather he should shrive me° than wive me. Come, Nerissa. [*To Servingman*] Sirrah,° go before. Whiles we shut the gate upon one wooer, another knocks at the   115 door.

Exeunt

❖

ACT 1
SCENE 3

Location: Venice. A public place

Enter Bassanio with Shylock the Jew

SHYLOCK Three thousand ducats,° well.

BASSANIO Ay, sir, for three months.

SHYLOCK For three months, well.

BASSANIO For the which, as I told you, Antonio shall be bound.

SHYLOCK Antonio shall become bound, well.   5

---

106 four (Nerissa actually names six suitors; possibly a sign of revision or the author's early draft)   **107 forerunner** herald   **112 condition** disposition, character   **112–13 complexion of a devil** (devils were thought to be black; but **complexion** can also mean "temperament," "disposition")   **113 shrive me** pardon me, excuse me from having to be wooed (literally, act as my confessor and give absolution)   **114 Sirrah** (form of address to social inferior)

1 ducats gold coins

BASSANIO May you stead° me? Will you pleasure° me? Shall I
know your answer?

SHYLOCK Three thousand ducats for three months and Antonio
bound.

BASSANIO Your answer to that.   10

SHYLOCK Antonio is a good° man.

BASSANIO Have you heard any imputation to the contrary?

SHYLOCK Ho, no, no, no, no! My meaning in saying he is a
good man is to have you understand me that he is sufficient.°
Yet his means are in supposition.° He hath an argosy bound   15
to Tripolis, another to the Indies. I understand, moreover,
upon the Rialto,° he hath a third at Mexico, a fourth for England, and other ventures he hath squandered° abroad. But
ships are but boards, sailors but men. There be land rats and
water rats, water thieves and land thieves—I mean pirates—   20
and then there is the peril of waters, winds, and rocks. The
man is, notwithstanding, sufficient. Three thousand ducats.
I think I may take his bond.

BASSANIO Be assured you may.

SHYLOCK I will be assured I may; and that I may be assured,° I   25
will bethink me. May I speak with Antonio?

BASSANIO If it please you to dine with us.

SHYLOCK Yes, to smell pork, to eat of the habitation which
your prophet the Nazarite° conjured the devil into. I will
buy with you, sell with you, talk with you, walk with you,   30
and so following,° but I will not eat with you, drink with
you, nor pray with you. What news on the Rialto? Who is
he comes here?

Enter Antonio

BASSANIO This is Signor Antonio.

---

6 **stead** supply, assist | **pleasure** oblige   11 **good** (Shylock means "solvent," a
good credit risk; Bassanio interprets it in the moral sense)   14 **sufficient** a good
security   15 **in supposition** doubtful, uncertain   17 **the Rialto** the merchants'
exchange in Venice and the center of commercial activity   18 **squandered** scattered
25 **assured** (Bassanio means that Shylock may trust Antonio, whereas Shylock
means that he will obtain legal assurances)   29 **Nazarite** Nazarene (for the
reference to Christ's casting evil spirits into a herd of swine, see Matthew 8.30–2,
Mark 5.1–13, and Luke 8.32–3)   31 **so following** so forth

SHYLOCK [*aside*] How like a fawning publican° he looks! 35
I hate him for he is a Christian,
But more for° that in low simplicity°
He lends out money gratis° and brings down
The rate of usance° here with us in Venice.
If I can catch him once upon the hip,° 40
I will feed fat° the ancient grudge I bear him.
He hates our sacred nation,° and he rails,
Even there where merchants most do congregate,
On me, my bargains, and my well-won thrift,
Which he calls interest.° Cursèd be my tribe 45
If I forgive him!
BASSANIO   Shylock, do you hear?
SHYLOCK I am debating of my present store,°
And, by the near guess of my memory,
I cannot instantly raise up the gross°
Of full three thousand ducats. What of that? 50
Tubal, a wealthy Hebrew of my tribe,
Will furnish me. But soft,° how many months
Do you desire? [*To Antonio*] Rest you fair, good signor!
Your Worship was the last man in our mouths.°
ANTONIO Shylock, albeit I neither lend nor borrow 55
By taking nor by giving of excess,°
Yet, to supply the ripe wants° of my friend,
I'll break a custom. [*To Bassanio*] Is he yet possessed°
How much ye would?°
SHYLOCK Ay, ay, three thousand ducats. 60
ANTONIO And for three months.
SHYLOCK I had forgot—three months, you told me so.
Well then, your bond. And let me see—but hear you,

---

35 **publican** Roman tax gatherer (a term of opprobrium; see Luke 18.9–14); or, innkeeper **37 for** because | **low simplicity** humble foolishness **38 gratis** without charging interest **39 usance** usury, interest **40 upon the hip** at my mercy (a figure of speech from wrestling; see Genesis 32.24–9) **41 fat** until fatted for the kill **42 our sacred nation** the Hebrew people **44–5 thrift . . . interest** (for these terms and others in this scene, see documents in the "Usury" section of the Contexts materials, including Bacon's essay "Of Usury") [LD] **47 I am . . . store** I am considering my current supply of money **49 gross** total **52 soft** wait a minute **54 Your . . . mouths** we were just speaking of you (but with ominous connotation of devouring; compare line 41) **56 excess** interest **57 ripe wants** pressing needs **58 possessed** informed **59 ye would** you want

Methought you said you neither lend nor borrow
Upon advantage.°
ANTONIO   I do never use it.   65
SHYLOCK When Jacob° grazed his uncle Laban's sheep—
This Jacob from our holy Abram° was,
As his wise mother wrought in his behalf,
The third° possessor;° ay, he was the third—
ANTONIO And what of him? Did he take interest?   70
SHYLOCK No, not take interest, not as you would say
Directly interest. Mark what Jacob did.
When Laban and himself were compromised°
That all the eanlings° which were streaked and pied°
Should fall as Jacob's hire,° the ewes, being rank,°   75
In end of autumn turnèd to the rams,
And when the work of generation° was
Between these woolly breeders in the act,
The skillful shepherd peeled me certain wands,°
And in the doing of the deed of kind°   80
He stuck them up before the fulsome° ewes,
Who then conceiving did in eaning° time
Fall° parti-colored lambs, and those were Jacob's.
This was a way to thrive, and he was blest;
And thrift° is blessing, if men steal it not.   85
ANTONIO This was a venture, sir, that Jacob served for,°
A thing not in his power to bring to pass,
But swayed and fashioned by the hand of heaven.
Was this inserted to make interest good?°
Or is your gold and silver ewes and rams?   90
SHYLOCK I cannot tell.° I make it breed as fast.
But note me, signor—
ANTONIO   Mark you this, Bassanio,

---

65 **advantage** interest 66 **Jacob** (see Genesis 27, 30.25–43) 67 **Abram** Abraham
69 **third** after Abraham and Isaac | **possessor** of the birthright of which, with the
help of Rebecca, he was able to cheat Esau, his elder brother 73 **compromised**
agreed 74 **eanlings** young lambs or kids | **pied** spotted 75 **hire** wages, share |
rank in heat 77 **work of generation** mating 79 **peeled . . . wands** partly stripped
the bark of some sticks (**me** is used colloquially) 80 **deed of kind** copulation
81 **fulsome** lustful, well-fed 82 **eaning** lambing 83 **fall** give birth to 85 **thrift**
thriving, profit 86 **venture . . . for** uncertain commercial venture on which Jacob
risked his wages 89 **inserted . . . good** brought in to justify the practice of usury
91 **I cannot tell** I don't know about that

The devil can cite Scripture° for his purpose.
An evil soul producing holy witness
Is like a villain with a smiling cheek,   95
A goodly apple rotten at the heart.
Oh, what a goodly outside falsehood hath!
SHYLOCK Three thousand ducats. 'Tis a good round sum.
Three months from twelve, then let me see, the rate—
ANTONIO Well, Shylock, shall we be beholding° to you?   100
SHYLOCK Signor Antonio, many a time and oft
In the Rialto you have rated° me
About my moneys and my usances.
Still have I borne it with a patient shrug,
For sufferance° is the badge of all our tribe.   105
You call me misbeliever, cutthroat dog,
And spit upon my Jewish gaberdine,°
And all for use of that which is mine own.
Well then, it now appears you need my help.
Go to,° then. You come to me and you say,   110
"Shylock, we would have moneys"—you say so,
You, that did void your rheum° upon my beard
And foot me as you spurn° a stranger cur
Over your threshold. Moneys is your suit.°
What should I say to you? Should I not say,   115
"Hath a dog money? Is it possible
A cur can lend three thousand ducats?" Or
Shall I bend low, and in a bondman's key,°
With bated° breath and whispering humbleness,
Say this: 120
"Fair sir, you spit on me on Wednesday last,
You spurned me such a day, another time
You called me dog, and for these courtesies
I'll lend you thus much moneys"?
ANTONIO I am as like° to call thee so again,   125
To spit on thee again, to spurn thee too.

---

93 devil . . . Scripture (see Matthew 4.6) 100 beholding beholden, indebted
102 rated berated, rebuked 105 sufferance endurance 107 gaberdine loose outer
garment like a cape or mantle 110 Go to (an exclamation of impatience or
annoyance) 112 rheum spittle 113 spurn kick 114 suit request
118 bondman's key serf's tone of voice 119 bated subdued 125 like likely

If thou wilt lend this money, lend it not
As to thy friends, for when did friendship take
A breed for barren metal° of° his friend?
But lend it rather to° thine enemy,   130
Who,° if he break,° thou mayst with better face
Exact the penalty.

SHYLOCK   Why, look you how you storm!
I would be friends with you and have your love,
Forget the shames that you have stained me with,
Supply your present wants, and take no doit°   135
Of usance for my moneys, and you'll not hear me.
This is kind° I offer.

BASSANIO   This were° kindness.

SHYLOCK   This kindness will I show.
Go with me to a notary, seal me there
Your single bond;° and, in a merry sport,   140
If you repay me not on such a day,
In such a place, such sum or sums as are
Expressed in the condition, let the forfeit
Be nominated for° an equal° pound
Of your fair flesh, to be cut off and taken   145
In what part of your body pleaseth me.

ANTONIO   Content, in faith. I'll seal to such a bond
And say there is much kindness in the Jew.

BASSANIO   You shall not seal to such a bond for me!
I'll rather dwell° in my necessity.   150

ANTONIO   Why, fear not, man, I will not forfeit it.
Within these two months—that's a month before
This bond expires—I do expect return
Of thrice three times the value of this bond.

SHYLOCK   O father Abram, what these Christians are,   155
Whose own hard dealings teaches them suspect
The thoughts of others! Pray you, tell me this:

---

129 **A breed . . . metal** offspring from money, which cannot naturally breed (one of the oldest arguments against usury was that it was thereby "unnatural") | **of** from 130 **to** as if to   131 **Who** from whom | **break** fail to pay on time   135 **doit** a Dutch coin of very small value   137 **kind** kindly | **were** would be (if seriously offered)   140 **single bond** bond signed alone without other security; unconditional (Shylock pretends the **condition**, line 143, is only a joke)   144 **nominated for** named, specified as | **equal** exact   150 **dwell** remain

If he should break his day, what should I gain
By the exaction of the forfeiture?
A pound of man's flesh taken from a man   160
Is not so estimable,° profitable neither,
As flesh of muttons, beefs, or goats. I say
To buy his favor I extend this friendship.
If he will take it, so;° if not, adieu.
And for my love, I pray you, wrong me not.°   165
ANTONIO   Yes, Shylock, I will seal unto this bond.
SHYLOCK   Then meet me forthwith at the notary's.
Give him direction for this merry bond,
And I will go and purse the ducats straight,
See to my house, left in the fearful° guard   170
Of an unthrifty knave, and presently
I'll be with you.   *Exit*
ANTONIO   Hie thee, gentle° Jew.—
The Hebrew will turn Christian; he grows kind.
BASSANIO   I like not fair terms and a villain's mind.
ANTONIO   Come on. In this there can be no dismay;   175
My ships come home a month before the day.
                                              [*Exeunt*]

❖

ACT 2
SCENE 1

Location: Belmont. Portia's house

[*Flourish of cornets.*] *Enter* [*the Prince of*] *Morocco,
a tawny Moor all in white, and three or four followers
accordingly,° with Portia, Nerissa, and their train*

MOROCCO   Mislike me not for my complexion,
The shadowed livery° of the burnished sun,

---

161 **estimable** valuable   164 **so** well and good   165 **wrong me not** do not think
evil of me   170 **fearful** to be mistrusted   172 **gentle** gracious, courteous (with a
play on "gentile")
0.4 **accordingly** similarly (dressed in white and dark-skinned like Morocco)
2 **shadowed livery** dark complexion, worn as though it were a costume of the sun's
servants

To whom I am a neighbor and near bred.°
Bring me the fairest creature northward born,
Where Phoebus'° fire scarce thaws the icicles,   5
And let us make incision for your love
To prove whose blood is reddest,° his or mine.
I tell thee, lady, this aspect° of mine
Hath feared° the valiant. By my love I swear,
The best-regarded virgins of our clime   10
Have loved it too. I would not change this hue,
Except to steal your thoughts, my gentle queen.°
PORTIA   In terms of choice I am not solely led
By nice direction° of a maiden's eyes;
Besides, the lott'ry of my destiny   15
Bars me the right of voluntary choosing.
But if my father had not scanted° me,
And hedged me by his wit° to yield myself
His wife who° wins me by that means I told you,
Yourself, renownèd prince, then stood as fair°   20
As any comer I have looked on yet
For my° affection.
MOROCCO   Even for that I thank you.
Therefore, I pray you, lead me to the caskets
To try my fortune. By this scimitar
That slew the Sophy° and a Persian prince,   25
That won three fields° of Sultan Solyman,°
I would o'erstare° the sternest eyes that look,
Outbrave the heart most daring on the earth,
Pluck the young sucking cubs from the she-bear,
Yea, mock the lion when 'a° roars for prey,   30
To win thee, lady. But alas the while!
If Hercules and Lichas° play at dice
Which is the better man, the greater throw

---

3 near bred closely related   **5 Phoebus'** the sun's   **7 reddest** (red blood was regarded as a sign of courage)   **8 aspect** visage   **9 feared** frightened   **12** (see the portrait by Rubens, page xviii) [LD]   **14 nice direction** careful guidance **17 scanted** limited   **18 wit** wisdom   **18–19 yield . . . who** give myself to be the wife of him who   **20 then . . . fair** would then have looked as attractive and stood as fair a chance (with a play on "fair-skinned")   **22 For my** of gaining my **25 Sophy** Shah of Persia   **26 fields** battles I   **Solyman** a Turkish sultan ruling from 1520 to 1566   **27 o'erstare** outstare   **30 'a** he   **32 Lichas** a page of Hercules (Alcides); see the note for 3.2.55

May turn by fortune from the weaker hand.
So is Alcides beaten by his page,   35
And so may I, blind Fortune leading me,
Miss that which one unworthier may attain,
And die with grieving.
PORTIA   You must take your chance,
And either not attempt to choose at all
Or swear before you choose, if you choose wrong   40
Never to speak to lady afterward
In way of marriage. Therefore be advised.°
MOROCCO   Nor will not.° Come, bring me unto my chance.
PORTIA   First, forward to the temple.° After dinner
Your hazard shall be made.
MOROCCO   Good fortune then!   45
To make me blest or cursed'st among men.

                                        [*Cornets, and*] *exeunt*

                                ❖

                          ACT 2
                          SCENE 2

                Location: Venice. A street

                Enter [*Lancelot*] *the clown,*° *alone*

LANCELOT   Certainly my conscience will serve° me to run from
this Jew my master. The fiend is at mine elbow and tempts
me, saying to me, "Gobbo, Lancelot Gobbo, good
Lancelot," or "Good Gobbo," or "Good Lancelot Gobbo,
use your legs, take the start, run away." My conscience says,   5
"No, take heed, honest Lancelot, take heed, honest
Gobbo," or, as aforesaid, "Honest Lancelot Gobbo, do not
run; scorn running with thy heels."° Well, the most coura-
geous fiend bids me pack.° "Fia!"° says the fiend. "Away!"
says the fiend. "For the heavens,° rouse up a brave mind,"   10

---

42 **be advised** take warning, consider   43 **Nor will not** nor indeed will I violate the
oath   44 **to the temple** in order to take the oaths

0.1 *clown* (1) country bumpkin (2) comic type in an Elizabethan acting company
1 **serve** permit   8 **with thy heels** emphatically (with a pun on the literal sense)
9 **pack** begone | **Fia!** via, away!   10 **For the heavens** in heaven's name

says the fiend, "and run." Well, my conscience, hanging
about the neck of my heart,° says very wisely to me, "My
honest friend Lancelot, being an honest man's son," or
rather an honest woman's son—for indeed my father did
something smack, something grow to, he had a kind of   15
taste°—well, my conscience says, "Lancelot, budge not."
"Budge," says the fiend, "Budge not," says my conscience.
"Conscience," say I, "you counsel well." "Fiend," say I,
"you counsel well." To be ruled by my conscience, I should
stay with the Jew my master, who, God bless the mark,° is a   20
kind of devil; and to run away from the Jew, I should be
ruled by the fiend, who, saving your reverence, is the devil
himself. Certainly the Jew is the very devil incarnation;°
and, in my conscience, my conscience is but a kind of hard
conscience to offer to counsel me to stay with the Jew. The   25
fiend gives the more friendly counsel. I will run, fiend. My
heels are at your commandment. I will run.

Enter Old Gobbo, with a basket

GOBBO Master young man, you,° I pray you, which is the way
to master Jew's?

LANCELOT [*aside*] Oh, heavens, this is my true-begotten father,   30
who, being more than sand-blind,° high-gravel-blind,°
knows me not. I will try confusions° with him.

GOBBO Master young gentleman, I pray you, which is the way
to master Jew's?

LANCELOT Turn up on your right hand at the next turning, but   35
at the next turning of all on your left; marry,° at the very
next turning, turn of no hand,° but turn down indirectly to
the Jew's house.

11–12 hanging . . . heart timidly   **15–16 something smack . . . taste** had a tendency
to lechery   **20 God . . . mark** (an expression by way of apology for introducing
something potentially offensive, as also in *saving your reverence* in line 22)
23 incarnation (Lancelot means "incarnate")   **28 you** (Gobbo uses the formal *you*
but switches to the familiar *thou*, line 83, when he accepts Lancelot as his son)
31 sand-blind dim-sighted | **high-gravel-blind** blinder than sand-blind (a term
seemingly invented by Lancelot)   **32 try confusions** (Lancelot's blunder for "try
conclusions," experiment, though his error is comically apt)   **36 marry** by the
Virgin Mary, indeed (a mild interjection)   **37 of no hand** neither right nor left

GOBBO By God's sonties,° 'twill be a hard way to hit. Can you
tell me whether one Lancelot, that dwells with him, dwell   40
with him or no?

LANCELOT Talk you of young Master Lancelot? [*aside*] Mark
me now; now will I raise the waters.°—Talk you of young
Master Lancelot?

GOBBO No master,° sir, but a poor man's son. His father,   45
though I say't, is an honest exceeding poor man and, God be
thanked, well to live.°

LANCELOT Well, let his father be what 'a° will, we talk of young
Master Lancelot.

GOBBO Your Worship's friend, and Lancelot,° sir.   50

LANCELOT But I pray you, ergo, old man, ergo,° I beseech you,
talk you of young Master Lancelot?

GOBBO Of Lancelot, an't please Your Mastership.

LANCELOT Ergo, Master Lancelot. Talk not of Master Lancelot,
father,° for the young gentleman, according to Fates and Des-   55
tinies and such odd sayings, the Sisters Three° and such
branches of learning, is indeed deceased, or, as you would
say in plain terms, gone to heaven.

GOBBO Marry, God forbid! The boy was the very staff of my
age, my very prop.   60

LANCELOT Do I look like a cudgel or a hovel post,° a staff, or a
prop? Do you know me, father?

GOBBO Alack the day, I know you not, young gentleman. But I
pray you, tell me, is my boy, God rest his soul, alive or dead?

LANCELOT Do you not know me, father?   65

GOBBO Alack, sir, I am sand-blind. I know you not.

LANCELOT Nay, indeed, if you had your eyes you might fail of
the knowing me; it is a wise father that knows his own
child.° Well, old man, I will tell you news of your son. [*He
kneels.*] Give me your blessing. Truth will come to light;   70

39 **sonties** little saints 43 **raise the waters** start tears 45 **master** (the title was
applied to gentlefolk only) 47 **well to live** prospering, in good health 48 **'a** he
50 **Your . . . Lancelot** (again, Old Gobbo denies that Lancelot is entitled to be called
"Master") 51 **ergo** therefore (but Lancelot may use this Latin word with no
particular meaning in mind) 55 **father** (1) old man (2) father 56 **the Sisters Three**
the three Fates 61 **hovel post** post holding up a hovel or open shed 68–9 **it is . . .
child** (reverses the proverb "it is a wise child that knows his own father")

murder cannot be hid long; a man's son may, but in the end truth will out.

GOBBO   Pray you, sir, stand up. I am sure you are not Lancelot, my boy.

LANCELOT   Pray you, let's have no more fooling about it, but   75
give me your blessing. I am Lancelot, your boy that was, your son that is, your child that shall be.°

GOBBO   I cannot think you are my son.

LANCELOT   I know not what I shall think of that; but I am Lancelot, the Jew's man, and I am sure Margery your wife is   80
my mother.

GOBBO   Her name is Margery indeed. I'll be sworn, if thou be Lancelot, thou art mine own flesh and blood. Lord worshiped might he be, what a beard° hast thou got! Thou hast got more hair on thy chin than Dobbin my fill horse° has on   85
his tail.

LANCELOT [*rising*]   It should seem then that Dobbin's tail grows backward.° I am sure he had more hair of his tail than I have of° my face when I last saw him.

GOBBO   Lord, how art thou changed! How dost thou and thy   90
master agree? I have brought him a present. How 'gree you now?

LANCELOT   Well, well; but for mine own part, as I have set up my rest° to run away, so I will not rest° till I have run some ground. My master's a very° Jew.° Give him a present? Give   95
him a halter!° I am famished in his service; you may tell° every finger I have with my ribs.° Father, I am glad you are come. Give me° your present to one Master Bassanio, who indeed gives rare° new liveries.° If I serve not him, I will run as far as God has any ground. Oh, rare fortune! Here comes   100

---

77 your . . . shall be (echoes the *Gloria* from the Book of Common Prayer: "as it was in the beginning, is now, and ever shall be")   **84 beard** (stage tradition has Old Gobbo mistaking Lancelot's long hair for a beard)   **85 fill horse** cart horse   **87–8 grows backward** grows at the wrong end   **89 of** on   **93–4 set up my rest** determined, risked all (a metaphor from the card game *primero*, in which a final wager is made, with a pun also on *rest* as "place of residence")   **94 not rest** not stop running (more punning on *rest*)   **95 very** veritable | **Jew** (1) Hebrew (2) grasping old usurer   **96 halter** hangman's noose | **tell** count   **96–7 tell . . . ribs** (comically reverses the usual saying of counting one's ribs with one's fingers)   **98 Give me** give (*me* suggests "on my behalf")   **99 rare** splendid | **liveries** uniforms or costumes for servants

the man. To him, father, for I am a Jew° if I serve the Jew
any longer.

Enter Bassanio, with [Leonardo and] a follower or two

BASSANIO   You may do so, but let it be so hasted° that supper be
ready at the farthest° by five of the clock. See these letters
delivered, put the liveries to making, and desire Gratiano to   105
come anon to my lodging.

[*Exit a Servant*]

LANCELOT   To him, father.

GOBBO [*advancing*]   God bless Your Worship!

BASSANIO   Gramercy.° Wouldst thou aught° with me?

GOBBO   Here's my son, sir, a poor° boy—   110

LANCELOT   Not a poor boy, sir, but the rich Jew's man, that
would, sir, as my father shall specify—

GOBBO   He hath a great infection,° sir, as one would say, to
serve—

LANCELOT   Indeed, the short and the long is, I serve the Jew,   115
and have a desire, as my father shall specify—

GOBBO   His master and he, saving Your Worship's reverence,
are scarce cater-cousins—°

LANCELOT   To be brief, the very truth is that the Jew, having
done me wrong, doth cause me, as my father, being, I hope,   120
an old man, shall frutify° unto you—

GOBBO   I have here a dish of doves that I would bestow upon
Your Worship, and my suit is—

LANCELOT   In very brief, the suit is impertinent° to myself, as
Your Worship shall know by this honest old man, and,   125
though I say it, though old man, yet poor man, my father.

BASSANIO   One speak for both. What would you?

LANCELOT   Serve you, sir.

GOBBO   That is the very defect° of the matter, sir.

---

101 a Jew a villain (punning on the literal sense in *the Jew;* compare with line 95)
103 hasted hastened, hurried   **104 farthest** latest   **109 Gramercy** many thanks |
aught anything   **110 poor** (1) unfortunate (2) penniless (contrasted with *rich* in the
next line)   **113 infection** (blunder for "affection" or "inclination")   **118 cater-
cousins** good friends   **121 frutify** (Lancelot may be trying to say "fructify," but he
means "certify" or "notify")   **124 impertinent** (blunder for "pertinent")
129 defect (blunder for "effect," "purport")

BASSANIO I know thee well; thou hast obtained thy suit.   130
Shylock thy master spoke with me this day,
And hath preferred° thee, if it be preferment
To leave a rich Jew's service to become
The follower of so poor a gentleman.
LANCELOT The old proverb° is very well parted° between my   135
master Shylock and you, sir: you have the grace of God, sir,
and he hath enough.
BASSANIO Thou speak'st it well. Go, father, with thy son.
Take leave of thy old master, and inquire
My lodging out. [*To a Servant*] Give him a livery   140
More guarded° than his fellows'. See it done.
LANCELOT Father, in. I cannot get a service, no! I have ne'er a
tongue in my head, well! [*He looks at his palm.*] If any man
in Italy have a fairer table° which doth offer to swear upon a
book,° I shall have good fortune. Go to,° here's a simple° line   145
of life.° Here's a small trifle of wives! Alas, fifteen wives is
nothing. Eleven widows and nine maids is a simple coming-
in° for one man. And then to scape drowning thrice, and to
be in peril of my life with the edge of a feather bed!° Here
are simple scapes.° Well, if Fortune be a woman,° she's a   150
good wench for this gear.° Father, come. I'll take my leave of
the Jew in the twinkling.
                Exit clown [*Lancelot, with Old Gobbo*]
BASSANIO [*giving Leonardo a list*]
I pray thee, good Leonardo, think on this:
These things being bought and orderly bestowed,°
Return in haste, for I do feast° tonight   155
My best-esteemed acquaintance. Hie thee, go.

---

132 **preferred** recommended   135 **proverb** "he who has the grace of God has enough" | **parted** divided   141 **guarded** trimmed with braided ornament   144 **table** palm of the hand (Lancelot now reads the lines of his palm)   145 **book** Bible (the image is of a hand being laid on the Bible to take an oath) | **Go to** (an expression of impatience) | **simple** unremarkable (said ironically)   145–46 **line of life** curved line at the base of the thumb   147–48 **simple coming-in** modest beginning or income (with sexual suggestion)   149 **feather bed** (suggesting marriage bed or love bed; Lancelot sees sexual adventure and the dangers of marriage in his palm reading)   150 **scapes** (1) adventures (2) transgressions | **Fortune . . . woman** (Fortune was personified as a goddess)   151 **gear** matter   154 **bestowed** stowed on board ship   155 **feast** give a feast for

LEONARDO My best endeavors shall be done herein.

[He starts to leave]

Enter Gratiano

GRATIANO *[to Leonardo]*
Where's your master?

LEONARDO   Yonder, sir, he walks.

Exit Leonardo

GRATIANO Signor Bassanio!

BASSANIO   Gratiano!

GRATIANO I have a suit to you.

BASSANIO   You have obtained it.   160

GRATIANO You must not deny me. I must go with you to Belmont.

BASSANIO Why, then you must. But hear thee, Gratiano;
Thou art too wild, too rude and bold of voice—
Parts° that become thee happily enough,
And in such eyes as ours appear not faults,   165
But where thou art not known, why, there they show
Something too liberal.° Pray thee, take pain
To allay° with some cold drops of modesty°
Thy skipping spirit, lest through thy wild behavior
I be misconstered° in the place I go to   170
And lose my hopes.

GRATIANO   Signor Bassanio, hear me:
If I do not put on a sober habit,°
Talk with respect and swear but now and then,
Wear prayer books in my pocket, look demurely,
Nay more, while grace is saying,° hood mine eyes   175
Thus with my hat, and sigh and say "amen,"
Use all the observance of civility,
Like one well studied in a sad ostent°
To please his grandam,° never trust me more.

BASSANIO Well, we shall see your bearing.   180

GRATIANO Nay, but I bar tonight. You shall not gauge me
By what we do tonight.

BASSANIO   No, that were pity.

---

164 Parts qualities **167 liberal** free of manner (often with sexual connotation)
168 allay temper, moderate | **modesty** decorum **170 misconstered** misconstrued
172 habit demeanor (with a suggestion of "clothes") **175 saying** being said
178 sad ostent grave appearance **179 grandam** grandmother

I would entreat you rather to put on
Your boldest suit of mirth, for we have friends
That purpose merriment. But fare you well;   185
I have some business.
GRATIANO   And I must to Lorenzo and the rest,
But we will visit you at suppertime.

Exeunt

❖

ACT 2
SCENE 3

Location: Venice. Shylock's house

Enter Jessica and [Lancelot] the clown

JESSICA   I am sorry thou wilt leave my father so.
Our house is hell, and thou, a merry devil,
Didst rob it of some taste of tediousness.
But fare thee well. There is a ducat for thee.
                                              [*Giving money*]
And, Lancelot, soon at supper shalt thou see   5
Lorenzo, who is thy new master's guest.
Give him this letter; do it secretly.   [*Giving a letter*]
And so farewell. I would not have my father
See me in talk with thee.
LANCELOT   Adieu! Tears exhibit° my tongue. Most beautiful   10
pagan, most sweet Jew! If a Christian did not play the knave
and get° thee, I am much deceived. But, adieu! These foolish
drops do something drown my manly spirit. Adieu!
JESSICA   Farewell, good Lancelot.   [*Exit Lancelot*]
Alack, what heinous sin is it in me   15
To be ashamed to be my father's child!
But though I am a daughter to his blood,
I am not to his manners. O Lorenzo,
If thou keep promise, I shall end this strife,
Become a Christian and thy loving wife.   20

Exit

---

10 exhibit (blunder for "inhibit," "restrain")   **12 get** beget

❖

ACT 2
SCENE 4

Location: Venice. A street

Enter Gratiano, Lorenzo, Salerio, and Solanio

LORENZO Nay, we will slink away in° suppertime,
Disguise us at my lodging, and return
All in an hour.

GRATIANO We have not made good preparation.

SALERIO We have not spoke us yet of° torchbearers.　　　　5

SOLANIO 'Tis vile, unless it may be quaintly ordered,°
And better in my mind not undertook.

LORENZO 'Tis now but four o'clock. We have two hours
To furnish us.

　　　　　　　　　　Enter Lancelot [with a letter]

　　　　　　　Friend Lancelot, what's the news?

LANCELOT An° it shall please you to break up this,° it shall seem　10
to signify.　　　　　　　　　　　*[Giving the letter]*

LORENZO I know the hand. In faith, 'tis a fair hand,
And whiter than the paper it writ on
Is the fair hand that writ.

GRATIANO　　　　　　　　　Love news, in faith.

LANCELOT By your leave, sir.　　　　*[He starts to leave]*　15

LORENZO Whither goest thou?

LANCELOT Marry, sir, to bid my old master the Jew to sup
tonight with my new master the Christian.

LORENZO
Hold here, take this. *[He gives money.]* Tell gentle Jessica
I will not fail her. Speak it privately.　　　　　　20

　　　　　　　　　　　Exit clown [Lancelot]

Go, gentlemen,
Will you prepare you for this masque tonight?
I am provided of a torchbearer.

---

1 in during　**5 spoke . . . of** yet bespoken, ordered　**6 quaintly ordered** skillfully
and tastefully managed　**10 An** if | **break up this** unseal the letter

SALERIO Ay, marry, I'll be gone about it straight.°
SOLANIO And so will I.
LORENZO   Meet me and Gratiano.   25
  At Gratiano's lodging some hour° hence.
SALERIO 'Tis good we do so.   *Exit [with Solanio]*
GRATIANO Was not that letter from fair Jessica?
LORENZO I must needs° tell thee all. She hath directed
  How I shall take her from her father's house,   30
  What gold and jewels she is furnished with,
  What page's suit she hath in readiness.
  If e'er the Jew her father come to heaven,
  It will be for his gentle° daughter's sake;
  And never dare misfortune cross her foot,°   35
  Unless she° do it under this excuse,
  That she is issue° to a faithless° Jew.
  Come, go with me. Peruse this as thou goest.
                  [He gives Gratiano the letter]
  Fair Jessica shall be my torchbearer.
                                          Exeunt

❖

ACT 2
SCENE 5

Location: Venice. Before Shylock's house

        Enter [Shylock the] Jew and [Lancelot,]
              his man that was, the clown

SHYLOCK Well, thou shalt see, thy eyes shall be thy judge,
  The difference of° old Shylock and Bassanio.—
  What, Jessica!—Thou shalt not gormandize,°
  As thou hast done with me—What, Jessica!—
  And sleep and snore, and rend apparel out—°   5
  Why, Jessica, I say!
LANCELOT   Why, Jessica!

---

24 **straight** at once 26 **some hour** about an hour 29 **must needs** must 34 **gentle** (with pun on "gentile"?) 35 **foot** footpath 36 **she** misfortune 37 **she is issue** Jessica is daughter | **faithless** pagan

2 **of** between 3 **gormandize** eat gluttonously 5 **rend apparel out** wear out your clothes

SHYLOCK Who bids thee call? I do not bid thee call.

LANCELOT Your Worship was wont to tell me I could do nothing without bidding.

Enter Jessica

JESSICA Call you? What is your will?   10

SHYLOCK I am bid forth to supper, Jessica.
There are my keys. But wherefore° should I go?
I am not bid for love—they flatter me—
But yet I'll go in hate, to feed upon
The prodigal Christian. Jessica, my girl,   15
Look to my house. I am right loath° to go.
There is some ill a-brewing towards my rest,
For I did dream of moneybags tonight.°

LANCELOT I beseech you, sir, go. My young master doth expect
your reproach.°   20

SHYLOCK So do I his.

LANCELOT And they have conspired together. I will not say you
shall see a masque, but if you do, then it was not for nothing
that my nose fell a-bleeding on Black Monday° last at six
o'clock i'th' morning, falling out that year on Ash Wednesday   25
was four year in th'afternoon.

SHYLOCK What, are there masques? Hear you me, Jessica:
Lock up my doors, and when you hear the drum
And the vile squealing of the wry-necked° fife,
Clamber not you up to the casements then,   30
Nor thrust your head into the public street
To gaze on Christian fools with varnished faces,°
But stop my house's ears—I mean my casements.
Let not the sound of shallow fopp'ry enter
My sober house. By Jacob's staff° I swear   35
I have no mind of feasting forth tonight.
But I will go.—Go you before me, sirrah.
Say I will come.

---

12 wherefore why **16 right loath** reluctant **18 tonight** last night **20 reproach**
(Lancelot's blunder for "approach"; Shylock takes it in grim humor) **24 Black
Monday** Easter Monday (Lancelot's talk of omens is perhaps intentional gibberish,
a parody of Shylock's fears) **29 wry-necked** played with the musician's head awry,
like a flute (on music in *MV*, see the Contexts materials) [LD] **32 varnished faces**
painted masks **35 Jacob's staff** (see Genesis 32.10 and Hebrews 11.21)

LANCELOT   I will go before, sir. [*aside to Jessica*]
  Mistress, look out at window, for all this;   40
    There will come a Christian by,
    Will be worth a Jewess' eye.   [*Exit*]
SHYLOCK   What says that fool of Hagar's offspring,° ha?
JESSICA   His words were "Farewell, mistress," nothing else.
SHYLOCK   The patch° is kind enough, but a huge feeder,   45
  Snail-slow in profit,° and he sleeps by day
  More than the wildcat. Drones hive not with me;
  Therefore I part with him, and part with him
  To one that I would have him help to waste
  His borrowed purse. Well, Jessica, go in.   50
  Perhaps I will return immediately.
  Do as I bid you. Shut doors after you.
  Fast bind, fast find—°
  A proverb never stale in thrifty mind.   *Exit*
JESSICA   Farewell, and if my fortune be not crossed,   55
  I have a father, you a daughter, lost.

                                                  Exit

❖

ACT 2
SCENE 6

Location: Before Shylock's house, as in 2.5

Enter the masquers, Gratiano and Salerio

GRATIANO   This is the penthouse° under which Lorenzo
  Desired us to make stand.
SALERIO   His hour is almost past.
GRATIANO   And it is marvel he outdwells his hour,°
  For lovers ever run before the clock.   5

---

43 **Hagar's offspring** (Hagar, a gentile and Abraham's servant, gave birth to Ishmael; both mother and son were cast out after the birth of Isaac)   **45 patch** fool   **46 profit** profitable labor   **53 Fast . . . find** keep your property secure and you will always know where it is (proverbial)

1 **penthouse** projecting roof or upper story of a house   4 **it . . . hour** it is surprising that he is late

SALERIO   Oh, ten times faster Venus' pigeons fly
To seal love's bonds new-made than they are wont
To keep obligèd faith unforfeited.°
GRATIANO   That ever holds.° Who riseth from a feast
With that keen appetite that he sits down?   10
Where is the horse that doth untread° again
His tedious measures° with the unbated fire
That he did pace them first? All things that are
Are with more spirit chasèd than enjoyed.
How like a younger° or a prodigal   15
The scarfèd bark° puts from her native bay,
Hugged and embracèd by the strumpet° wind!
How like the prodigal doth she return,
With overweathered ribs° and ragged sails,
Lean, rent,° and beggared by the strumpet wind!   20

                    Enter Lorenzo

SALERIO   Here comes Lorenzo. More of this hereafter.
LORENZO   Sweet friends, your patience° for my long abode;°
Not I, but my affairs, have made you wait.
When you shall please to play the thieves for wives,
I'll watch° as long for you then. Approach;   25
Here dwells my father° Jew.—Ho! Who's within?

          [*Enter*] *Jessica, above* [*in boy's clothes*]

JESSICA   Who are you? Tell me for more certainty,
Albeit I'll swear that I do know your tongue.
LORENZO   Lorenzo, and thy love.
JESSICA   Lorenzo, certain, and my love indeed,   30
For who love I so much? And now who knows
But you,° Lorenzo, whether I am yours?

6–8 Oh, ten . . . unforfeited oh, lovers are ten times quicker in their first pledge of love than in keeping faith in a long-term commitment (**Venus' pigeons** are the doves that draw her chariot) **9 ever holds** always holds true **11 untread** retrace **12 measures** paces **15 younger** younger son, as in the parable of the Prodigal Son (Luke 15); (often emended to *younker*, youth) **16 scarfèd bark** sailing vessel festooned with flags or streamers **17 strumpet** inconsistent, variable (likened metaphorically to the harlots with whom the Prodigal Son wasted his fortune) **19 overweathered ribs** weather-beaten and leaking timbers **20 rent** torn **22 your patience** I beg your patience | **abode** delay **25 watch** keep watch **26 father** father-in-law **32 But you** better than you

LORENZO Heaven and thy thoughts are witness that thou art.

JESSICA [*throwing down a casket*]

Here, catch this casket. It is worth the pains.

I am glad 'tis night, you do not look on me,   35

For I am much ashamed of my exchange.°

But love is blind, and lovers cannot see

The pretty° follies that themselves commit,

For if they could, Cupid himself would blush

To see me thus transformèd to a boy.   40

LORENZO Descend, for you must be my torchbearer.

JESSICA What, must I hold a candle° to my shames?

They in themselves, good sooth, are too too light.°

Why, 'tis an office of discovery,° love,

And I should be obscured.

LORENZO   So are you, sweet,   45

Even in the lovely garnish° of a boy.

But come at once,

For the close° night doth play the runaway,°

And we are stayed° for at Bassanio's feast.

JESSICA I will make fast the doors, and gild° myself   50

With some more ducats, and be with you straight.

                                        [*Exit above*]

GRATIANO Now, by my hood,° a gentle° and no Jew.

LORENZO Beshrew° me but I love her heartily,

For she is wise, if I can judge of her,

And fair she is, if that mine eyes be true,   55

And true she is, as she hath proved herself;

And therefore, like herself, wise, fair, and true,

Shall she be placèd in my constant soul.

                          Enter Jessica [*below*]

What, art thou come? On, gentlemen, away!

Our masquing mates by this time for us stay.°   60

36 **exchange** change of clothes 38 **pretty** ingenious, artful 42 **hold a candle** stand
by and witness (with a play on the idea of acting as torchbearer) 43 **light**
(1) immodest (2) illuminated 44 **'tis . . . discovery** torchbearing is intended to shed
light on matters 46 **garnish** outfit, trimmings 48 **close** dark, secretive | **doth . . .
runaway** is quickly passing 49 **stayed** waited 50 **gild** adorn (literally, cover with
gold) 52 **by my hood** (an asseveration) | **gentle** gracious person (with pun on
"gentile," as at 2.4.34) 53 **Beshrew** a mischief on (a mild oath) 60 **stay** wait
(also in line 64)

Exit [with Jessica and Salerio;
Gratiano is about to follow them]

Enter Antonio

ANTONIO Who's there?
GRATIANO Signor Antonio?
ANTONIO Fie, fie, Gratiano! Where are all the rest?
'Tis nine o'clock; our friends all stay for you.
No masque tonight. The wind is come about;   65
Bassanio presently will go aboard.
I have sent twenty out to seek for you.
GRATIANO I am glad on 't. I desire no more delight
Than to be under sail and gone tonight.

Exeunt

❖

ACT 2
SCENE 7

Location: Belmont. Portia's house

[Flourish of cornets.] Enter Portia, with [the
Prince of] Morocco, and both their trains°

PORTIA Go, draw aside the curtains and discover°
The several° caskets to this noble prince.
Now make your choice.   *[The curtains are drawn]*
MOROCCO The first, of gold, who° this inscription bears,
"Who chooseth me shall gain what many men desire";   5
The second, silver, which this promise carries,
"Who chooseth me shall get as much as he deserves";
This third, dull° lead, with warning all as blunt,°
"Who chooseth me must give and hazard all he hath."
How shall I know if I do choose the right?   10
PORTIA The one of them contains my picture, Prince.
If you choose that, then I am yours withal.°
MOROCCO Some god direct my judgment! Let me see,
I will survey th'inscriptions back again.

0.2 *trains* followers **1 discover** reveal **2 several** different, various **4 who** which
8 dull (1) dull-colored (2) blunt | **all as blunt** as blunt as lead **12 withal** with it

What says this leaden casket? 15
"Who chooseth me must give and hazard all he hath."
Must give—for what? For lead? Hazard for lead?
This casket threatens. Men that hazard all
Do it in hope of fair advantages.
A golden mind stoops not to shows of dross.° 20
I'll then nor give° nor hazard aught for lead.
What says the silver with her virgin hue?
"Who chooseth me shall get as much as he deserves."
As much as he deserves! Pause there, Morocco,
And weigh thy value with an even° hand. 25
If thou be'st rated by thy estimation,°
Thou dost deserve enough; and yet enough
May not extend so far as to the lady;
And yet to be afeard of my deserving
Were but a weak disabling° of myself. 30
As much as I deserve? Why, that's the lady.
I do in birth deserve her, and in fortunes,
In graces, and in qualities of breeding;
But more than these, in love I do deserve.
What if I strayed no farther, but chose here? 35
Let's see once more this saying graved° in gold:
"Who chooseth me shall gain what many men desire."
Why, that's the lady; all the world desires her.
From the four corners of the earth they come
To kiss this shrine, this mortal breathing° saint. 40
The Hyrcanian° deserts and the vasty° wilds
Of wide Arabia are as throughfares now
For princes to come view fair Portia.
The watery kingdom, whose ambitious head
Spits° in the face of heaven, is no bar 45
To stop the foreign spirits,° but they come,
As o'er a brook, to see fair Portia.

---

20 dross worthless matter (literally, the impurities cast off in the melting down of metals) **21 nor give** neither give **25 even** impartial **26 estimation** worth **30 disabling** underrating **36 graved** engraved **40 mortal breathing** living **41 Hyrcanian** (Hyrcania was the country south of the Caspian Sea celebrated for its wildness) | **vasty** vast **45 Spits** (the image is of huge waves breaking at sea) **46 spirits** men of courage

One of these three contains her heavenly picture.
Is't like° that lead contains her? 'Twere damnation
To think so base° a thought; it were too gross   50
To rib her cerecloth in the obscure grave.°
Or shall I think in silver she's immured,°
Being ten times undervalued to tried gold?°
Oh, sinful thought! Never so rich a gem
Was set° in worse than gold. They have in England   55
A coin° that bears the figure of an angel
Stamped in gold, but that's insculped upon;°
But here an angel in a golden bed
Lies all within. Deliver me the key.
Here do I choose, and thrive I as I may!   60
PORTIA   There, take it, Prince; and if my form° lie there,
Then I am yours.
                         [*He unlocks the golden casket*]
MOROCCO   Oh, hell! What have we here?
A carrion Death,° within whose empty eye
There is a written scroll! I'll read the writing.
                                        [*He reads*]
        "All that glisters is not gold;   65
        Often have you heard that told.
        Many a man his life hath sold
        But° my outside to behold.
        Gilded tombs do worms infold.
        Had you been as wise as bold,   70
        Young in limbs, in judgment old,
        Your answer had not been inscrolled.°
        Fare you well; your suit is cold."
Cold, indeed, and labor lost.
Then, farewell, heat, and welcome, frost!   75

---

49 like likely   **50 base** (1) ignoble (2) low in the natural scale, as with lead, a *base*
metal   **50–1 it were . . . grave** it would be too gross an insult to inter her, as it were,
wrapped in a waxed cloth, in a lead casket   **52 immured** enclosed, confined
53 Being . . . gold which has only one-tenth the value of assayed and purified gold
55 set fixed, as a precious stone, in a border of metal   **56 coin** the gold coin known
as the *angel*, which bore the device of the archangel Michael treading on the dragon
57 insculped upon merely engraved upon the surface   **61 form** image   **63 carrion
Death** death's-head   **68 But** only   **72 inscrolled** written on this scroll

Portia, adieu. I have too grieved a heart
To take a tedious leave. Thus losers part.°
                    Exit [with his train. Flourish of cornets]
PORTIA A gentle riddance. Draw the curtains, go.
Let all of his complexion choose me so.
                    [*The curtains are closed, and] exeunt*

❧

ACT 2
SCENE 8

Location: Venice. A street

Enter Salerio and Solanio

SALERIO Why, man, I saw Bassanio under sail.
With him is Gratiano gone along,
And in their ship I am sure Lorenzo is not.
SOLANIO The villain Jew with outcries raised° the Duke,   5
Who went with him to search Bassanio's ship.
SALERIO He came too late. The ship was under sail.
But there the Duke was given to understand
That in a gondola were seen together
Lorenzo and his amorous Jessica.
Besides, Antonio certified the Duke   10
They were not with Bassanio in his ship.
SOLANIO I never heard a passion° so confused,
So strange, outrageous, and so variable
As the dog Jew did utter in the streets:
"My daughter! Oh, my ducats! Oh, my daughter!°   15
Fled with a Christian! Oh, my Christian ducats!
Justice! The law! My ducats, and my daughter!
A sealèd bag, two sealèd bags of ducats,
Of double ducats, stol'n from me by my daughter!
And jewels, two stones, two rich and precious stones,   20
Stol'n by my daughter! Justice! Find the girl!
She hath the stones upon her, and the ducats."

77 **part** depart
4 **raised** roused   12 **passion** passionate outburst   15 (see similar mixed cry in Marlowe's *The Jew of Malta*, p. 146 above) [LD]

SALERIO   Why, all the boys in Venice follow him,
Crying his stones,° his daughter, and his ducats.
SOLANIO   Let good Antonio look he keep his day,°   25
Or he shall pay for this.
SALERIO   Marry, well remembered.
I reasoned° with a Frenchman yesterday,
Who told me, in the narrow seas° that part
The French and English, there miscarrièd
A vessel of our country richly fraught.°   30
I thought upon Antonio when he told me,
And wished in silence that it were not his.
SOLANIO   You were best to tell Antonio what you hear.
Yet do not suddenly, for it may grieve him.
SALERIO   A kinder gentleman treads not the earth.   35
I saw Bassanio and Antonio part.
Bassanio told him he would make some speed
Of his return; he answered, "Do not so.
Slubber not business° for my sake, Bassanio,
But stay the very riping of the time;°   40
And for° the Jew's bond which he hath of me,
Let it not enter in your mind of° love.
Be merry, and employ your chiefest thoughts
To courtship and such fair ostents° of love
As shall conveniently become you there."   45
And even there,° his eye being big with tears,
Turning his face, he put his hand behind him,°
And with affection wondrous sensible°
He wrung Bassanio's hand; and so they parted.
SOLANIO   I think he only loves the world for him.°   50
I pray thee, let us go and find him out

24 stones (in the boys' jeering cry, the *two stones* suggest testicles; see line 20)
25 look . . . day see to it that he repays his loan on time   27 reasoned talked
28 narrow seas English Channel   30 fraught freighted   39 Slubber not business
don't do the business hastily and badly   40 But . . . time pursue your business at
Belmont until it is brought to completion   41 for as for   42 of preoccupied with
44 ostents expressions, shows   46 there thereupon, then   47 behind him (Antonio
turns away in tears while extending his hand back to Bassanio)   48 affection
wondrous sensible wondrously sensitive and keen emotion   50 he . . . him Bassanio
is all he lives for (see Montaigne's essay "Of Friendship" and Shakespeare's sonnets
in the Contexts materials [LD]

And quicken his embracèd heaviness°
With some delight or other.
SALERIO   Do we so.

                                    Exeunt

❖

ACT 2
SCENE 9

Location: Belmont. Portia's house

Enter Nerissa and a Servitor°

NERISSA Quick, quick, I pray thee, draw the curtain straight.°
The Prince of Aragon hath ta'en his oath,
And comes to his election presently.°
                [The curtains are drawn back]

                *[Flourish of cornets.] Enter [the Prince
                of] Aragon, his train, and Portia*

PORTIA Behold, there stand the caskets, noble Prince.
If you choose that wherein I am contained,   5
Straight shall our nuptial rites be solemnized;
But if you fail, without more speech, my lord,
You must be gone from hence immediately.
ARAGON I am enjoined by oath to observe three things:
First, never to unfold° to anyone   10
Which casket 'twas I chose; next, if I fail
Of the right casket, never in my life
To woo a maid in way of marriage;
Lastly,
If I do fail in fortune of my choice,   15
Immediately to leave you and be gone.
PORTIA To these injunctions everyone doth swear
That comes to hazard for my worthless self.
ARAGON And so have I addressed me.° Fortune now
To my heart's hope! Gold, silver, and base lead.   20

---

52 quicken . . . heaviness lighten the sorrow he has embraced
0.1 *Servitor* servant   **1 straight** at once   **3 election presently** choice immediately
10 unfold disclose   **19 addressed me** prepared myself (by this swearing)

"Who chooseth me must give and hazard all he hath."
You shall look fairer ere I give or hazard.
What says the golden chest? Ha, let me see:
"Who chooseth me shall gain what many men desire."
What many men desire! That "many" may be meant   25
By° the fool multitude, that choose by show,
Not learning more than the fond° eye doth teach,
Which pries not to th'interior, but like the martlet°
Builds in° the weather on the outward wall,
Even in the force and road of casualty.°   30
I will not choose what many men desire,
Because I will not jump° with common spirits
And rank me with the barbarous multitudes.
Why then, to thee, thou silver treasure-house!
Tell me once more what title thou dost bear: 35
"Who chooseth me shall get as much as he deserves."
And well said too; for who shall go about
To cozen° fortune, and be honorable
Without the stamp° of merit? Let none presume
To wear an undeservèd dignity.   40
Oh, that estates, degrees,° and offices
Were not derived corruptly, and that clear honor
Were purchased by the merit of the wearer!
How many then should cover that stand bare?°
How many be commanded that command?°   45
How much low peasantry would then be gleaned°
From the true seed of honor,° and how much honor
Picked from the chaff and ruin of the times
To be new-varnished?° Well, but to my choice:
"Who chooseth me shall get as much as he deserves."   50
I will assume desert. Give me a key for this,
And instantly unlock my fortunes here.

       [He opens the silver casket]

---

26 **By** for, to signify 27 **fond** foolish 28 **martlet** swift 29 **in** exposed to 30 **force**
. . . **casualty** power and path of mischance 32 **jump** agree 38 **cozen** cheat
39 **stamp** seal of approval 41 **estates, degrees** status, social rank 44 **cover . . . bare**
wear hats (of authority) who now stand bareheaded 45 **How . . . command?** how
many then should be servants that are now masters? 46 **gleaned** culled out and
discarded 47 **the true seed of honor** persons of noble descent 49 **new-varnished**
having the luster of their true nobility restored to them

PORTIA Too long a pause for that which you find there.
ARAGON What's here? The portrait of a blinking idiot,
Presenting me a schedule!° I will read it.   55
How much unlike art thou to Portia!
How much unlike my hopes and my deservings!
"Who chooseth me shall have as much as he deserves."
Did I deserve no more than a fool's head?
Is that my prize? Are my deserts no better?   60
PORTIA To offend and judge are distinct offices
And of opposèd natures.°
ARAGON   What is here?
                                              [*He reads*]
       "The fire seven times tried this;°
       Seven times tried that judgment is
       That did never choose amiss.   65
       Some there be that shadows° kiss;
       Such have but a shadow's bliss.
       There be fools alive, iwis,°
       Silvered o'er,° and so was this.
       Take what wife you will to bed;   70
       I will ever be your head.°
       So begone; you are sped."°

   Still more fool I shall appear
   By the time I linger here.°
   With one fool's head I came to woo,   75
   But I go away with two.
   Sweet, adieu. I'll keep my oath,
   Patiently to bear my wroth.°
                           [*Exeunt Aragon and train*]
PORTIA Thus hath the candle singed the moth.
   Oh, these deliberate° fools! When they do choose,   80
   They have the wisdom by their wit to lose.

55 schedule written paper   61–2 To offend . . . natures you have no right, having
submitted your case to judgment, to attempt to judge your own case; or, it is not for
me to say, since I've been the indirect cause of your discomfiture   63 The fire . . .
this this silver has been seven times tested and purified   66 shadows illusions   68 iwis
certainly   69 Silvered o'er with silver hair and so apparently wise   71 I . . . head
you will always have a fool's head, be a fool   72 sped done for   73–4 Still . . . here
I shall seem all the greater fool for wasting any more time here   78 wroth sorrow,
unhappy lot (a variant of *ruth*); or, anger   80 deliberate reasoning, calculating

NERISSA The ancient saying is no heresy:
Hanging and wiving goes by destiny.
PORTIA Come, draw the curtain, Nerissa.

[The curtains are closed]

Enter Messenger

MESSENGER Where is my lady?
PORTIA   Here. What would my lord?°   85
MESSENGER Madam, there is alighted at your gate
A young Venetian, one that comes before
To signify th'approaching of his lord,
From whom he bringeth sensible regreets,°
To wit, besides commends° and courteous breath,°   90
Gifts of rich value. Yet° I have not seen
So likely an ambassador of love.
A day in April never came so sweet,
To show how costly° summer was at hand,
As this fore-spurrer° comes before his lord.   95
PORTIA No more, I pray thee. I am half afeard
Thou wilt say anon he is some kin to thee,
Thou spend'st such high-day° wit in praising him.
Come, come, Nerissa, for I long to see
Quick Cupid's post° that comes so mannerly.   100
NERISSA Bassanio, Lord Love, if thy will it be!

Exeunt

❖

ACT 3
SCENE 1

Location: Venice. A street

[Enter] Solanio and Salerio

SOLANIO Now, what news on the Rialto?

---

85 **my lord** (a jesting response to "my lady") 89 **sensible regreets** tangible gifts,
greetings 90 **commends** greetings | **breath** speech 91 **Yet** heretofore 94 **costly**
lavish, rich 95 **fore-spurrer** herald, harbinger 98 **high-day** holiday (extravagant)
100 **post** messenger

SALERIO Why, yet it lives there unchecked° that Antonio hath a
ship of rich lading wrecked on the narrow seas°—the Goodwins,° I think they call the place, a very dangerous flat,° and
fatal, where the carcasses of many a tall° ship lie buried, as   5
they say, if my gossip Report° be an honest woman of her
word.

SOLANIO I would she were as lying a gossip in that as ever
knapped° ginger or made her neighbors believe she wept for
the death of a third husband. But it is true, without any   10
slips of prolixity° or crossing the plain highway of talk,° that
the good Antonio, the honest Antonio—oh, that I had a title
good enough to keep his name company!—

SALERIO Come, the full stop.°

SOLANIO

Ha, what sayest thou? Why, the end is, he hath lost a ship.   15

SALERIO I would it might prove the end of his losses.

SOLANIO Let me say "amen" betimes,° lest the devil cross° my
prayer, for here he comes in the likeness of a Jew.

Enter Shylock

How now, Shylock, what news among the merchants?

SHYLOCK You knew, none so well, none so well as you, of my   20
daughter's flight.

SALERIO That's certain. I for my part knew the tailor that made
the wings she flew withal.°

SOLANIO And Shylock for his own part knew the bird was
fledge,° and then it is the complexion° of them all to leave   25
the dam.°

SHYLOCK She is damned for it.

SALERIO That's certain, if the devil may be her judge.

2 **yet . . . unchecked** a rumor is spreading undenied   3 **the narrow seas** the English
Channel, as at 2.8.28   3–4 **Goodwins** Goodwin Sands, off the Kentish coast near
the Thames estuary   4 **flat** shoal, sandbank   5 **tall** gallant   6 **gossip Report** dame
rumor   9 **knapped** nibbled   11 **slips of prolixity** lapses into long-windedness; or,
long-winded lies; **slips** may be the cuttings or offshoots of tediousness | **crossing . . .
talk** deviating from honest, plain speech   14 **Come . . . stop** finish your sentence;
rein in your tongue as a horse is checked in its manage   17 **betimes** while there is
yet time | **cross** thwart; make the sign of the cross following   23 **the wings . . .
withal** the disguise she escaped in (with a play on *wings* or ornamented shoulder
flaps sewn on garments)   25 **fledge** ready to fly | **complexion** natural disposition
26 **dam** mother

SHYLOCK My own flesh and blood to rebel!

SOLANIO Out upon it, old carrion! Rebels it at these years?° 30

SHYLOCK I say my daughter is my flesh and my blood.

SALERIO There is more difference between thy flesh and hers than between jet° and ivory, more between your bloods than there is between red wine and Rhenish.° But tell us, do you hear whether Antonio have had any loss at sea or no? 35

SHYLOCK There I have another bad match!° A bankrupt, a prodigal, who dare scarce show his head on the Rialto; a beggar, that was used to come so smug upon the mart!° Let him look to his bond. He was wont to call me usurer. Let him look to his bond. He was wont to lend money for a 40 Christian courtesy. Let him look to his bond.

SALERIO Why, I am sure, if he forfeit, thou wilt not take his flesh. What's that good for?

SHYLOCK To bait fish withal. If it will feed nothing else, it will feed my revenge. He hath disgraced me, and hindered me 45 half a million, laughed at my losses, mocked at my gains, scorned my nation, thwarted my bargains, cooled my friends, heated mine enemies; and what's his reason? I am a Jew. Hath not a Jew eyes? Hath not a Jew hands, organs, dimensions, senses, affections, passions? Fed with the same 50 food, hurt with the same weapons, subject to the same diseases, healed by the same means, warmed and cooled by the same winter and summer, as a Christian is? If you prick us, do we not bleed? If you tickle us, do we not laugh? If you poison us, do we not die? And if you wrong us, shall we not 55 revenge? If we are like you in the rest, we will resemble you in that. If a Jew wrong a Christian, what is his humility? Revenge.° If a Christian wrong a Jew, what should his sufferance° be by Christian example? Why, revenge. The villainy

30 Rebels . . . years? (Solanio pretends to interpret Shylock's cry about the rebellion of his own flesh and blood as referring to his own carnal desires, his own erection) 33 jet a black, hard mineral, here contrasted with the whiteness of ivory and Jessica's fair complexion 34 Rhenish a German white wine from the Rhine valley (Salerio seems to prefer the white wine as more refined than the red) 36 match bargain 38 mart marketplace, Rialto 57–8 what . . . Revenge in what spirit does the Christian receive the injury, that of Christian humility? no, he seeks revenge 58–9 his sufferance the Jew's patient endurance

you teach me I will execute, and it shall go hard but° I will   60
better the instruction.

Enter a Man from Antonio

MAN   Gentlemen, my master Antonio is at his house and desires to speak with you both.

SALERIO   We have been up and down° to seek him.

Enter Tubal

SOLANIO   Here comes another of the tribe. A third cannot be   65
matched,° unless the devil himself turn Jew.

Exeunt gentlemen [Solanio, Salerio, with Man]

SHYLOCK   How now, Tubal, what news from Genoa? Hast thou
found my daughter?

TUBAL

I often came where I did hear of her, but cannot find her.

SHYLOCK   Why, there, there, there, there! A diamond gone, cost   70
me two thousand ducats in Frankfort! The curse° never fell
upon our nation till now; I never felt it till now. Two thousand ducats in that, and other   precious, precious jewels. I
would my daughter were dead at my foot, and the jewels in
her ear! Would she were hearsed° at my foot, and the ducats   75
in her coffin! No news of them? Why, so—and I know not
what's spent in the search. Why, thou loss upon loss! The
thief gone with so much, and so much to find the thief, and
no satisfaction, no revenge! Nor no ill luck stirring but what
lights o' my shoulders, no sighs but o' my breathing, no   80
tears but o' my shedding.

TUBAL   Yes, other men have ill luck too. Antonio, as I heard in
Genoa—

SHYLOCK   What, what, what? Ill luck, ill luck?

TUBAL   Hath an argosy cast away,° coming from Tripolis.   85

SHYLCOK   I thank God, I thank God. Is it true, is it true?

TUBAL   I spoke with some of the sailors that escaped the wreck.

SHYLOCK   I thank thee, good Tubal. Good news, good news!
Ha, ha! Heard in Genoa?

---

60 it shall . . . but assuredly; unless difficulties intervene   **64 up and down**
everywhere   **66 matched** found to match them   **71 The curse** God's curse (such as
the plagues visited upon Egypt in Exodus 7–12)   **75 hearsed** coffined   **85 cast
away** shipwrecked

TUBAL Your daughter spent in Genoa, as I heard, one night   90
  fourscore ducats.
SHYLOCK Thou stick'st a dagger in me. I shall never see my
  gold again. Fourscore ducats at a sitting? Fourscore ducats?
TUBAL There came divers of Antonio's creditors in my
  company to Venice that swear he cannot choose but break.°   95
SHYLOCK I am very glad of it. I'll plague him, I'll torture him. I
  am glad of it.
TUBAL One of them showed me a ring that he had of your
  daughter for a monkey.
SHYLOCK Out upon her! Thou torturest me, Tubal. It was my   100
  turquoise; I had it of Leah° when I was a bachelor. I would
  not have given it for a wilderness of monkeys.
TUBAL But Antonio is certainly undone.
SHYLOCK Nay, that's true, that's very true. Go, Tubal, fee° me
  an officer;° bespeak° him a fortnight before. I will have the   105
  heart of him if he forfeit, for were he out of Venice I can
  make what merchandise I will.° Go, Tubal, and meet me at
  our synagogue. Go, good Tubal; at our synagogue, Tubal.

                                        Exeunt [separately]

                        ❖

                     ACT 3
                    SCENE 2

           Location: Belmont. Portia's house

  Enter Bassanio, Portia, Gratiano, [Nerissa,] and all their trains

PORTIA I pray you, tarry. Pause a day or two
  Before you hazard, for in choosing° wrong
  I lose your company. Therefore forbear awhile.
  There's something tells me—but it is not love—
  I would not lose you; and you know yourself   5
  Hate counsels not in such a quality.°
  But lest you should not understand me well—
  And yet a maiden hath no tongue but thought—

---

95 **break** go bankrupt   101 **Leah** Shylock's wife   104 **fee** hire   105 **officer** bailiff
| **bespeak** engage   106–7 **make . . . I will** drive whatever bargains I please
2 **in choosing** if you choose   6 **quality** way, manner

I would detain you here some month or two
Before you venture for me. I could teach you   10
How to choose right, but then I am forsworn.
So° will I never be. So may you miss me.°
But if you do, you'll make me wish a sin,
That I had been forsworn. Beshrew your eyes,
They have o'erlooked° me and divided me!   15
One half of me is yours, the other half yours—
Mine own, I would say; but if mine, then yours,
And so all yours. Oh, these naughty° times
Puts bars° between the owners and their rights!
And so, though yours, not yours.° Prove it so,   20
Let Fortune go to hell for it, not I.°
I speak too long, but 'tis to peise° the time,
To eke it and to draw it out in length,
To stay you from election.°
BASSANIO   Let me choose,
For as I am, I live upon the rack.   25
PORTIA   Upon the rack, Bassanio? Then confess
What treason° there is mingled with your love.
BASSANIO   None but that ugly treason of mistrust,°
Which makes me fear° th'enjoying of my love.
There may as well be amity and life   30
'Tween snow and fire, as° treason and my love.
PORTIA   Ay, but I fear you speak upon the rack,
Where men enforcèd do speak anything.
BASSANIO   Promise me life, and I'll confess the truth.
PORTIA   Well then, confess and live.
BASSANIO   "Confess and love"   35
Had been the very sum of my confession.
Oh, happy torment, when my torturer

---

12 **So forsworn** | **So may . . . me** that being the case, you may fail to win me
15 **o'erlooked** bewitched   18 **naughty** wicked   19 **bars** barriers   20 **though yours, not yours** (I am) yours by right but not by actual possession   20–1 **Prove . . . not I** if it turn out thus (that you are cheated of what is justly yours, of me), let fortune be blamed for it, not I, for I will not be forsworn   22 **peise** retard (by hanging on of weights)   23 **eke it** stretch it out, make it last   24 **election** choice   26–7 **confess What treason** (the rack was used to force traitors to confess)   28 **mistrust** misapprehension   29 **fear** fearful about   31 **as** as between

Doth teach me answers for deliverance!
But let me to my fortune and the caskets.°
PORTIA Away, then! I am locked in one of them.   40
If you do love me, you will find me out.
Nerissa and the rest, stand all aloof.°
Let music sound while he doth make his choice;
Then, if he lose, he makes a swanlike° end,
Fading in music. That the comparison   45
May stand more proper, my eye shall be the stream
And wat'ry deathbed for him. He may win;
And what is music then? Then music is
Even as the flourish° when true subjects bow
To a new-crownèd monarch. Such it is   50
As are those dulcet sounds in break of day
That creep into the dreaming bridegroom's ear
And summon him to marriage. Now he goes,
With no less presence,° but with much more love,
Than young Alcides° when he did redeem   55
The virgin tribute paid by howling° Troy
To the sea monster. I stand for sacrifice;°
The rest aloof are the Dardanian° wives,
With blearèd° visages, come forth to view
The issue° of th'exploit. Go, Hercules!   60
Live thou,° I live. With much, much more dismay
I view the fight than thou that mak'st the fray.

A song, the whilst Bassanio
comments on the caskets to himself

Tell me where is fancy° bred,
Or° in the heart or in the head?

---

39 **fortune . . . caskets** (presumably the curtains are drawn at about this point, as in the previous "casket" scenes, revealing the three caskets) 42 **aloof** apart, at a distance 44 **swanlike** (swans were believed to sing when they came to die) 49 **flourish** sounding of trumpets 54 **presence** noble bearing 55 **Alcides** Hercules (called *Alcides*, as at 2.1.32–5, because he was the grandson of Alcaeus) rescued Hesione, daughter of the Trojan king Laomedon, from a monster to which, by command of Neptune, she was about to be sacrificed; Hercules was rewarded, however, not with the lady's love, but with a famous pair of horses 56 **howling** lamenting 57 **stand for sacrifice** represent the sacrificial victim 58 **Dardanian** Trojan 59 **blearèd** tear-stained 60 **issue** outcome 61 **Live thou** if you live 63 **fancy** love 64 **Or** either

How begot, how nourishèd?   65
Reply, reply.
It is engendered in the eyes,°
With gazing fed, and fancy dies
In the cradle° where it lies.
Let us all ring fancy's knell.   70
I'll begin it—Ding, dong, bell.
ALL   Ding, dong, bell.
BASSANIO   So may the outward shows be least themselves;°
The world is still° deceived with ornament.
In law, what plea so tainted and corrupt   75
But, being seasoned with a gracious voice,
Obscures the show of evil? In religion,
What damnèd error but some sober brow°
Will bless it and approve° it with a text,
Hiding the grossness with fair ornament?   80
There is no vice so simple° but assumes
Some mark of virtue on his° outward parts.
How many cowards, whose hearts are all as false
As stairs° of sand, wear yet upon their chins
The beards of Hercules and frowning Mars,   85
Who, inward searched,° have livers° white as milk?
And these assume but valor's excrement°
To render them redoubted.° Look on beauty,
And you shall see 'tis purchased by the weight,°
Which therein works a miracle in nature,   90
Making them lightest° that wear most of it.
So are those crispèd,° snaky, golden locks,
Which maketh such wanton gambols with the wind
Upon supposèd fairness,° often known

67 **eyes** (love entered the heart especially through the eyes)   69 **In the cradle** in its
infancy, in the eyes   73 **be least themselves** least represent the inner reality   74 **still**
ever   78 **sober brow** solemn-faced clergyman   79 **approve** confirm   81 **simple**
unadulterated   82 **his** its   84 **stairs** steps   86 **searched** surgically probed | **livers**
(the liver was thought to be the seat of courage; for it to be deserted by the blood
would be the condition of cowardice)   87 **excrement** outgrowth, here a beard
88 **redoubted** feared   89 **purchased by the weight** bought (as cosmetics) at so much
per ounce   91 **lightest** most frivolous or lascivious (with pun on the sense of "least
heavy")   92 **crispèd** curly   94 **Upon supposèd fairness** on a woman supposed
beautiful and fair-haired

To be the dowry of a second head,   95
The skull that bred them in the sepulcher.°
Thus ornament is but the guilèd° shore
To a most dangerous sea, the beauteous scarf
Veiling an Indian° beauty; in a word,
The seeming truth which cunning times put on   100
To entrap the wisest. Therefore, thou gaudy gold,
Hard food for Midas,° I will none of thee;
Nor none of thee, thou pale and common drudge
'Tween man and man.° But thou, thou meager° lead,
Which rather threaten'st than dost promise aught,   105
Thy paleness moves me more than eloquence;
And here choose I. Joy be the consequence!
PORTIA *[aside]*   How all the other passions fleet to air,
As° doubtful thoughts, and rash-embraced despair,
And shuddering fear, and green-eyed jealousy!   110
O love, be moderate, allay thy ecstasy,
In measure rain° thy joy, scant° this excess!
I feel too much thy blessing. Make it less,
For fear I surfeit.
BASSANIO *[opening the leaden casket]*
                    What find I here?
Fair Portia's counterfeit!° What demigod°   115
Hath come so near creation? Move these eyes?
Or whether, riding on the balls of mine,
Seem they in motion? Here are severed lips,
Parted with sugar breath; so sweet a bar
Should sunder such sweet friends.° Here in her hairs   120
The painter plays the spider, and hath woven
A golden mesh t'entrap the hearts of men
Faster° than gnats in cobwebs. But her eyes—
How could he see to do them? Having made one,

95–6 To . . . sepulcher to be a wig of hair taken from a woman now dead   97 guilèd
treacherous   99 Indian swarthy, not fair   102 Midas the Phrygian king whose
touch turned everything to gold, including his food   103–4 pale . . . man silver,
used in commerce   104 meager wanting in richness   109 As such as   112 rain
rain down, or perhaps "rein" | scant lessen   115 counterfeit portrait | demigod
the painter as creator   119–20 so . . . friends only so sweet a barrier as her mouth
and breath should be allowed to part such sweet friends as her two lips   123 Faster
(1) more tightly (2) quicker

Methinks it should have power to steal both his   125
And leave itself unfurnished.° Yet look how far°
The substance of my praise doth wrong this shadow°
In underprizing it,° so far° this shadow
Doth limp behind the substance.° Here's the scroll,
The continent° and summary of my fortune.   130
[*He reads*]
    "You that choose not by the view
    Chance as fair,° and choose as true.
    Since this fortune falls to you,
    Be content and seek no new.
    If you be well pleased with this,   135
    And hold your fortune for your bliss,
    Turn you where your lady is
    And claim her with a loving kiss."

A gentle scroll. Fair lady, by your leave,
I come by note,° to give and to receive.   140
Like one of two contending in a prize,°
That thinks he hath done well in people's eyes,
Hearing applause and universal shout,
Giddy in spirit, still gazing in a doubt
Whether those peals of praise be his° or no,   145
So, thrice-fair lady, stand I, even so,
As doubtful whether what I see be true,
Until confirmed, signed, ratified by you.
PORTIA You see me, Lord Bassanio, where I stand,
Such as I am. Though for myself alone   150
I would not be ambitious in my wish
To wish myself much better, yet for you
I would be trebled twenty times myself,
A thousand times more fair, ten thousand times more rich,
That only to stand high in your account°   155
I might in virtues, beauties, livings,° friends,

126 **unfurnished** without a companion | **look how far** however far   127 **shadow** painting, semblance   128 **underprizing it** failing to do it justice | **so far** to a similar extent   129 **the substance** the subject, Portia   130 **continent** container   132 **Chance as fair** take your chances fortunately   140 **by note** by a bill of dues (the scroll); the commercial metaphor continues in *confirmed, signed, ratified* (line 148), *account* (155), *sum* (157), *term in gross* (158), etc.   141 **prize** competition   145 **his** for him   155 **account** estimation   156 **livings** possessions

Exceed account.° But the full sum of me
Is sum of something,° which, to term in gross,°
Is an unlessoned girl, unschooled, unpracticèd;
Happy in this, she is not yet so old   160
But she may learn; happier than this,
She is not bred so dull but she can learn;
Happiest of all is that her gentle spirit
Commits itself to yours to be directed
As from her lord, her governor, her king.   165
Myself and what is mine to you and yours
Is now converted. But now° I was the lord
Of this fair mansion, master of my servants,
Queen o'er myself; and even now, but now,
This house, these servants, and this same myself   170
Are yours, my lord's.° I give them with this ring,
Which when you part from, lose, or give away,
Let it presage the ruin of your love
And be my vantage to exclaim on° you.
                    [*She puts a ring on his finger*]
BASSANIO Madam, you have bereft me of all words.   175
Only my blood speaks to you in my veins,
And there is such confusion in my powers°
As, after some oration fairly spoke
By a belovèd prince, there doth appear
Among the buzzing pleasèd multitude,   180
Where every something being blent together
Turns to a wild of nothing save of joy
Expressed and not expressed.° But when this ring
Parts from this finger, then parts life from hence.
Oh, then be bold to say Bassanio's dead!   185
NERISSA My lord and lady, it is now our time,
That° have stood by and seen our wishes prosper,

---

157 account calculation (playing on *account*, estimation, in line 155) **157–8 But . . .
something** but the full sum of my worth can only be the sum of whatever I am
158 term in gross denote in full **167 But now** a moment ago **171 my lord's**
(under English law, all that a woman previously owned became her husband's upon
marriage; see the Contexts materials on matrimony and women's education) [LD]
174 vantage to exclaim on opportunity to reproach **177 powers** faculties
181–3 Where . . . expressed in which every individual utterance, being blended and
confused, turns into a hubbub of joy **187 That** we who

To cry, "good joy." Good joy, my lord and lady!
GRATIANO My lord Bassanio and my gentle lady,
I wish you all the joy that you can wish—   190
For I am sure you can wish none from me.°
And when Your Honors mean to solemnize
The bargain of your faith, I do beseech you
Even at that time I may be married too.
BASSANIO With all my heart, so° thou canst get a wife.   195
GRATIANO I thank Your Lordship, you have got me one.
My eyes, my lord, can look as swift as yours.
You saw the mistress, I beheld the maid;°
You loved, I loved; for intermission°
No more pertains to me, my lord, than you.   200
Your fortune stood upon the caskets there,
And so did mine too, as the matter falls;°
For wooing here until I sweat again,°
And swearing till my very roof° was dry
With oaths of love, at last, if promise last,°   205
I got a promise of this fair one here
To have her love, provided that your fortune
Achieved her mistress.
PORTIA   Is this true, Nerissa?
NERISSA Madam, it is, so° you stand pleased withal.
BASSANIO And do you, Gratiano, mean good faith?   210
GRATIANO Yes, faith, my lord.
BASSANIO Our feast shall be much honored in your marriage.
GRATIANO
We'll play with them the first boy° for a thousand ducats.
NERISSA What, and stake down?
GRATIANO
No, we shall ne'er win at that sport, and stake down.°   215

---

191 For . . . me I'm sure I can't wish you any more joy than you could wish for
yourselves, or, I'm sure your wishes for happiness cannot take away from my
happiness 195 so provided 198 maid (Nerissa is a lady-in-waiting, not a house
servant) 199 intermission delay (in loving) 202 falls falls out, happens 203 sweat
again sweated repeatedly 204 roof roof of my mouth 205 if promise last if
Nerissa's promise should last, hold out (with a play on *last* and *at last,* "finally")
209 so provided 213 We'll . . . boy we'll wager with them to see who has the first
male heir 215 stake down cash placed in advance (but Gratiano, in his reply, turns
the phrase into a bawdy joke; *stake down* to him suggests a non-erect phallus)

Enter Lorenzo, Jessica, and Salerio, a messenger from Venice

But who comes here? Lorenzo and his infidel?
What, and my old Venetian friend Salerio?
BASSANIO Lorenzo and Salerio, welcome hither,
If that the youth of my new interest° here
Have power to bid you welcome.—By your leave,   220
I bid my very° friends and countrymen,
Sweet Portia, welcome.
PORTIA   So do I, my lord.
They are entirely welcome.
LORENZO I thank Your Honor. For my part, my lord,
My purpose was not to have seen you here,   225
But, meeting with Salerio by the way,
He did entreat me, past all saying nay,
To come with him along.
SALERIO   I did, my lord,
And I have reason for it. Signor Antonio
Commends him° to you.   [*He gives Bassanio a letter*]
BASSANIO   Ere I ope his letter,   230
I pray you tell me how my good friend doth.
SALERIO Not sick, my lord, unless it be in mind,
Nor well, unless in mind. His letter there
Will show you his estate.°   [*Bassanio*] *open[s] the letter*
GRATIANO [*indicating Jessica*]
Nerissa, cheer yond stranger,° bid her welcome.   235
Your hand, Salerio. What's the news from Venice?
How doth that royal merchant,° good Antonio?
I know he will be glad of our success.
We are the Jasons; we have won the fleece.°
SALERIO I would you had won the fleece that he hath lost.   240
PORTIA There are some shrewd° contents in yond same paper
That steals the color from Bassanio's cheek—
Some dear friend dead, else nothing in the world
Could turn so much the constitution

---

219 youth . . . interest newness of my household authority   **221 very** true   **230 Commends him** desires to be remembered   **234 estate** situation   **235 stranger** alien
237 royal merchant chief among merchants   **239 Jasons . . . fleece** (compare with 1.1.170–2)   **241 shrewd** cursed, grievous

Of any constant° man. What, worse and worse?   245
With leave,° Bassanio; I am half yourself,
And I must freely have the half of anything
That this same paper brings you.
BASSANIO   O sweet Portia,
Here are a few of the unpleasant'st words
That ever blotted paper! Gentle lady,   250
When I did first impart my love to you,
I freely told you all the wealth I had
Ran in my veins, I was a gentleman;
And then I told you true. And yet, dear lady,
Rating myself at nothing, you shall see   255
How much I was a braggart. When I told you
My state° was nothing, I should then have told you
That I was worse than nothing; for indeed
I have engaged myself to a dear friend,
Engaged my friend to his mere° enemy,   260
To feed my means. Here is a letter, lady,
The paper as the body of my friend,
And every word in it a gaping wound
Issuing lifeblood. But is it true, Salerio?
Hath all his ventures failed? What, not one hit?°   265
From Tripolis, from Mexico, and England,
From Lisbon, Barbary, and India,
And not one vessel scape the dreadful touch
Of merchant-marring° rocks?
SALERIO   Not one, my lord.
Besides, it should appear that if he had   270
The present° money to discharge° the Jew
He° would not take it. Never did I know
A creature that did bear the shape of man
So keen and greedy to confound° a man.
He plies the Duke at morning and at night,   275
And doth impeach the freedom of the state°

---

245 **constant** settled, not swayed by passion 246 **With leave** with your permission
257 **state** estate 260 **mere** absolute 265 **hit** success 269 **merchant-marring**
capable of damaging a merchant ship 271 **present** available | **discharge** pay off
272 **He** Shylock 274 **confound** destroy 276 **doth . . . state** calls in question the
ability of Venice to defend legally the freedom of commerce of its citizens

If they deny him justice. Twenty merchants,
The Duke himself, and the magnificoes°
Of greatest port° have all persuaded° with him,
But none can drive him from the envious° plea   280
Of forfeiture, of justice, and his bond.

JESSICA   When I was with him I have heard him swear
To Tubal and to Chus,° his countrymen,
That he would rather have Antonio's flesh
Than twenty times the value of the sum   285
That he did owe him; and I know, my lord,
If law, authority, and power deny not,
It will go hard with poor Antonio.

PORTIA [to Bassanio]
Is it your dear friend that is thus in trouble?

BASSANIO   The dearest friend to me, the kindest man,   290
The best-conditioned° and unwearied spirit
In doing courtesies, and one in whom
The ancient Roman honor more appears
Than any that draws breath in Italy.

PORTIA   What sum owes he the Jew?   295

BASSANIO   For me, three thousand ducats.

PORTIA   What, no more?
Pay him six thousand, and deface° the bond;
Double six thousand, and then treble that,
Before a friend of this description
Shall lose a hair through Bassanio's fault.   300
First go with me to church and call me wife,
And then away to Venice to your friend;
For never shall you lie by Portia's side
With an unquiet soul. You shall have gold
To pay the petty debt twenty times over.   305
When it is paid, bring your true friend along.
My maid Nerissa and myself meantime
Will live as maids and widows. Come, away!
For you shall hence upon your wedding day.

---

278 magnificoes chief men of Venice   **279 port** dignity | **persuaded** argued
280 envious malicious   **283 Chus** the Bishops' Bible spelling of *Cush*, son of Ham
and grandson of Noah; *Tubal* was son of Japheth and grandson of Noah (Genesis
10.2, 6)   **291 best-conditioned** best-natured   **297 deface** erase

Bid your friends welcome, show a merry cheer;°   310
Since you are dear bought, I will love you dear.°
But let me hear the letter of your friend.
BASSANIO [*reads*] "Sweet Bassanio, my ships have all mis-
carried, my creditors grow cruel, my estate is very low, my
bond to the Jew is forfeit; and since in paying it, it is im-   315
possible I should live, all debts are cleared between you and
I if I might but see you at my death. Notwithstanding, use
your pleasure. If your love do not persuade you to come, let
not my letter."
PORTIA O love, dispatch all business, and begone!   320
BASSANIO Since I have your good leave to go away,
I will make haste; but till I come again
No bed shall e'er be guilty of my stay,
Nor rest be interposer twixt us twain.

                                                Exeunt

                              ❖

                           ACT 3
                          SCENE 3

                Location: Venice. A street

Enter [Shylock] the Jew and Solanio and Antonio and the Jailer

SHYLOCK Jailer, look to him. Tell not me of mercy.
This is the fool that lent out money gratis.°
Jailer, look to him.
ANTONIO   Hear me yet, good Shylock.
SHYLOCK I'll have my bond. Speak not against my bond.
I have sworn an oath that I will have my bond.   5
Thou called'st me dog before thou hadst a cause,
But since I am a dog, beware my fangs.
The Duke shall grant me justice. I do wonder,
Thou naughty° jailer, that thou art so fond°
To come abroad° with him at his request.   10

---

310 **cheer** countenance 311 **dear . . . dear** at great cost . . . dearly
2 **gratis** free (of interest) 9 **naughty** worthless, wicked | **fond** foolish 10 **abroad** outside

ANTONIO I pray thee, hear me speak.
SHYLOCK I'll have my bond. I will not hear thee speak.
I'll have my bond, and therefore speak no more.
I'll not be made a soft and dull-eyed° fool,
To shake the head, relent, and sigh, and yield   15
To Christian intercessors. Follow not.
I'll have no speaking. I will have my bond.   *Exit Jew*
SOLANIO It is the most impenetrable cur
That ever kept° with men.
ANTONIO   Let him alone.
I'll follow him no more with bootless° prayers.   20
He seeks my life. His reason well I know:
I oft delivered from his forfeitures
Many that have at times made moan to me;
Therefore he hates me.
SOLANIO   I am sure the Duke
Will never grant this forfeiture to hold.   25
ANTONIO The Duke cannot deny the course of law;
For the commodity° that strangers° have
With us in Venice, if it be denied,
Will much impeach the justice of the state,°
Since that° the trade and profit of the city   30
Consisteth of all nations. Therefore go.
These griefs and losses have so bated° me
That I shall hardly spare a pound of flesh
Tomorrow to my bloody creditor.—
Well, jailer, on. Pray God Bassanio come   35
To see me pay his debt, and then I care not.

                                                     Exeunt

                              ❧

14 **dull-eyed** easily duped 19 **kept** associated, dwelt 20 **bootless** unavailing
27 **commodity** facilities or privileges for trading | **strangers** noncitizens, including
Jews 29 **justice . . . state** (on Venice's reputation for justice, see the selection by
Lewkenor and other documents in the Venice section of the Contexts materials) [LD]
30 **Since that** since 32 **bated** reduced

ACT 3
SCENE 4

Location: Belmont. Portia's house

Enter Portia, Nerissa, Lorenzo, Jessica,
and [Balthasar,] a man of Portia's

LORENZO Madam, although I speak it in your presence,
You have a noble and a true conceit°
Of godlike amity,° which appears most strongly
In bearing thus the absence of your lord.
But if you knew to whom you show this honor,°   5
How true a gentleman you send relief,
How dear a lover° of my lord your husband,
I know you would be prouder of the work
Than customary bounty can enforce you.°
PORTIA I never did repent for doing good,   10
Nor shall not now; for in companions
That do converse and waste° the time together,
Whose souls do bear an equal yoke of love,
There must be needs° a like proportion
Of lineaments,° of manners, and of spirit;   15
Which makes me think that this Antonio,
Being the bosom lover° of my lord,
Must needs be like my lord. If it be so,
How little is the cost I have bestowed
In purchasing the semblance of my soul°   20
From out the state of hellish cruelty!°
This comes too near the praising of myself;
Therefore no more of it. Hear other things:
Lorenzo, I commit into your hands
The husbandry and manage° of my house   25
Until my lord's return. For mine own part,
I have toward heaven breathed a secret vow

---

2 **conceit** understanding 3 **amity** friendship and love (see Montaigne "Of
Friendship" in Contexts) [LD] 5 **to whom . . . honor** Antonio, who you honor by
sending money to relieve him 7 **lover** friend 9 **Than . . . you** than ordinary
benevolence can make you 12 **waste** spend 14 **must be needs** must be
15 **lineaments** physical features 17 **bosom lover** dear friend 20 **the semblance of
my soul** Antonio, so like my Bassanio 21 **From . . . cruelty** from the cruel state in
which he presently stands 25 **husbandry and manage** care and management

To live in prayer and contemplation,
Only attended by Nerissa here,
Until her husband and my lord's return.   30
There is a monastery two miles off,
And there we will abide. I do desire you
Not to deny this imposition,°
The which my love and some necessity
Now lays upon you.
LORENZO   Madam, with all my heart,   35
I shall obey you in all fair commands.
PORTIA My people° do already know my mind,
And will acknowledge you and Jessica
In place of Lord Bassanio and myself.
So fare you well till we shall meet again.   40
LORENZO Fair thoughts and happy hours attend on you!
JESSICA I wish Your Ladyship all heart's content.
PORTIA I thank you for your wish and am well pleased
To wish it back on you. Fare you well, Jessica.
                                    Exeunt [Jessica and Lorenzo]
Now, Balthasar,   45
As I have ever found thee honest-true,
So let me find thee still. Take this same letter,
                                    [*Giving a letter*]
And use thou all th'endeavor of a man
In speed to Padua. See thou render this
Into my cousin's hands, Doctor Bellario;   50
And look what° notes and garments he doth give thee,
Bring them, I pray thee, with imagined° speed
Unto the traject,° to the common° ferry
Which trades° to Venice. Waste no time in words,
But get thee gone. I shall be there before thee.   55
BALTHASAR Madam, I go with all convenient speed.   [*Exit*]
PORTIA Come on, Nerissa, I have work in hand
That you yet know not of. We'll see our husbands
Before they think of us.
NERISSA   Shall they see us?

33 **deny this imposition** refuse this charge imposed   37 **people** servants   51 **look what** whatever   52 **imagined** all imaginable   53 **traject** ferry (Italian *traghetto*) |
common public   54 **trades** plies back and forth

PORTIA They shall, Nerissa, but in such a habit°   60
That they shall think we are accomplishèd°
With that° we lack. I'll hold thee any wager,
When we are both accoutered like young men
I'll prove the prettier fellow of the two,
And wear my dagger with the braver grace,   65
And speak between the change of man and boy
With a reed voice, and turn two mincing steps
Into a manly stride, and speak of frays
Like a fine bragging youth, and tell quaint° lies,
How honorable ladies sought my love,   70
Which I denying, they fell sick and died—
I could not do withal!° Then I'll repent,
And wish, for all that, that I had not killed them;
And twenty of these puny° lies I'll tell,
That men shall swear I have discontinued school   75
Above° a twelvemonth.° I have within my mind
A thousand raw tricks of these bragging Jacks,°
Which I will practice.
NERISSA   Why, shall we turn to° men?
PORTIA Fie, what a question's that,
If thou wert near a lewd interpreter!   80
But come, I'll tell thee all my whole device°
When I am in my coach, which stays for us
At the park gate; and therefore haste away,
For we must measure° twenty miles today.

                                              Exeunt

❖

---

60 **habit** apparel, garb   61 **accomplishèd** supplied   62 **that** that which (with a bawdy suggestion)   69 **quaint** elaborate, clever   72 **do withal** help it   74 **puny** childish   75–6 **I . . . twelvemonth** that I am no mere schoolboy   76 **Above** more than   77 **Jacks** fellows   78 **turn to** turn into (but Portia sees the occasion for a bawdy quibble on the idea of "turning toward, lying next to")   81 **device** plan   84 **measure** traverse

ACT 3
SCENE 5

Location: Belmont. Outside Portia's house

Enter [Lancelot the] clown and Jessica

LANCELOT Yes, truly, for look you, the sins of the father are to
be laid upon the children; therefore, I promise° you, I fear
you.° I was always plain with you, and so now I speak my agitation of° the matter. Therefore be o' good cheer, for truly I
think you are damned. There is but one hope in it that can do   5
you any good, and that is but a kind of bastard° hope, neither.°

JESSICA And what hope is that, I pray thee?

LANCELOT Marry, you may partly hope that your father got°
you not, that you are not the Jew's daughter.

JESSICA That were a kind of bastard hope, indeed! So the sins   10
of my mother should be visited upon me.

LANCELOT Truly, then, I fear you are damned both by father
and mother. Thus when I shun Scylla,° your father, I fall into
Charybdis,° your mother. Well, you are gone° both ways.

JESSICA I shall be saved by my husband.° He hath made me a   15
Christian.

LANCELOT Truly, the more to blame he! We were Christians
enough° before, e'en as many as could well live one by another.° This making of Christians will raise the price of hogs.
If we grow all to be pork eaters, we shall not shortly have a   20
rasher° on the coals for money.°

Enter Lorenzo

JESSICA
I'll tell my husband, Lancelot, what you say. Here he comes.

---

2 **promise** assure   2–3 **fear you** fear for you   3–4 **my agitation of** my sense of
agitation about   6 **bastard** unfounded (but also anticipating the usual meaning in
lines 9–10) | **neither** to be sure   8 **got** begot   13, 14 **Scylla, Charybdis** twin
dangers of the *Odyssey*, 12.255, a monster and a whirlpool guarding the straits
presumably between Italy and Sicily (**fall into** plays on the idea of entering the female
sexual anatomy)   14 **gone** done for   15 **I . . . husband** (compare 1 Corinthians
7.14: "the unbelieving wife is sanctified by the husband")   17–18 **We . . . enough**
there were enough of us Christians   18–19 **one by another** (1) as neighbors (2) off
one another   21 **rasher** of bacon | **for money** even for ready money, at any price

LORENZO   I shall grow jealous of you shortly, Lancelot, if you
thus get my wife into corners.

JESSICA   Nay, you need not fear us, Lorenzo. Lancelot and I are   25
out.° He tells me flatly there's no mercy for me in heaven because I am a Jew's daughter; and he says you are no good
member of the commonwealth, for in converting Jews to
Christians you raise the price of pork.

LORENZO [*to Lancelot*]   I shall answer that better to the com-   30
monwealth than you can the getting up of the Negro's belly.
The Moor° is with child by you, Lancelot.

LANCELOT   It is much that the Moor should be more than reason; but if she be less than an honest woman, she is indeed
more than I took her for.°   35

LORENZO   How every fool can play upon the word! I think the
best grace of wit° will shortly turn into silence, and discourse grow commendable in none only but parrots. Go in,
sirrah, bid them prepare for dinner.

LANCELOT   That is done, sir. They have all stomachs.°   40

LORENZO   Goodly Lord, what a wit-snapper are you! Then bid
them prepare dinner.

LANCELOT   That is done too, sir, only "cover"° is the word.

LORENZO   Will you cover° then, sir?

LANCELOT   Not so, sir, neither. I know my duty.°   45

LORENZO   Yet more quarreling with occasion!° Wilt thou show
the whole wealth of thy wit in an instant? I pray thee, understand a plain man in his plain meaning: go to thy fellows,
bid them cover the table, serve in the meat,° and we will
come in to dinner.   50

25–6 are out have fallen out   **32 The Moor** (Lancelot has evidently impregnated
some woman of the household, who, being of African heritage, is referred to as
both "Negro" and "Moor")   **33–5 It is . . . for** it is a matter of concern that the
Moor is larger (being pregnant) than usual, larger than she should be; but if it
turns out that she is less than perfectly chaste, she is something more than I
originally supposed (Lancelot professes to be surprised by what has happened;
with wordplay on *less/more* and *more/Moor*)   **36–7 the best . . . wit** true wittiness
40 They . . . stomachs the guests all have appetites and are prepared in that sense
(Lancelot quibbles with Lorenzo's meaning that the cooks and servants should be
told to get dinner ready)   **43, 44 cover** spread the table for the meal (but in line 52
Lancelot uses the word to mean "put on one's hat")   **45 my duty** my duty to
remain bareheaded   **46 Yet . . . occasion!** still quibbling at every opportunity!
49 meat food

LANCELOT   For° the table,° sir, it shall be served in; for the meat,
sir, it shall be covered;° for your coming in to dinner, sir,
why, let it be as humors and conceits° shall govern.
                                        Exit [Lancelot the] clown
LORENZO   Oh, dear discretion,° how his words are suited!°
The fool hath planted in his memory   55
An army of good words; and I do know
A many° fools, that stand in better place,°
Garnished° like him, that for a tricksy word
Defy the matter.° How cheer'st thou,° Jessica?
And now, good sweet, say thy opinion: 60
How dost thou like the Lord Bassanio's wife?
JESSICA   Past all expressing. It is very meet°
The Lord Bassanio live an upright life,
For, having such a blessing in his lady,
He finds the joys of heaven here on earth;   65
And if on earth he do not merit it,
In reason° he should never come to heaven.
Why, if two gods should play some heavenly match
And on the wager lay° two earthly women,
And Portia one, there must be something else°   70
Pawned° with the other, for the poor rude world
Hath not her fellow.°
LORENZO   Even such a husband
Hast thou of me as she is for a wife.
JESSICA   Nay, but ask my opinion too of that!
LORENZO   I will anon. First let us go to dinner.   75
JESSICA   Nay, let me praise you while I have a stomach.°

51 **For** as for | **table** (here Lancelot quibblingly uses the word to mean the food
itself)   52 **covered** (here used in the sense of providing a cover for each separate
dish)   53 **humors and conceits** whims and fancies   54 **Oh, dear discretion** oh, what
precious discrimination | **suited** suited to the occasion   57 **A many** many | **better
place** higher social station   58 **Garnished** furnished with words, or with garments
58–9 **that . . . matter** who for the sake of ingenious wordplay torture the plain
meaning   59 **How cheer'st thou** what cheer, how are you doing   62 **meet** fitting
67 **In reason** it stands to reason (Jessica jokes that for Bassanio to receive unmerited
bliss on earth—unmerited because no person can earn bliss through his or her
own deserving—is to run the risk of eternal damnation)   69 **lay** stake   70 **else**
more   71 **Pawned** staked, wagered   72 **fellow** equal   76 **stomach** (1) appetite
(2) inclination

LORENZO No, pray thee, let it serve for table talk;
Then, howsome'er thou speak'st, 'mong other things
I shall digest° it.
JESSICA   Well, I'll set you forth.°

Exeunt

❖

ACT 4
SCENE 1

Location: Venice. A court of justice.
Benches, etc., are provided for the justices

Enter the Duke, the Magnificoes, Antonio, Bassanio, [Salerio,]
and Gratiano [with others. The judges take their places]

DUKE What, is Antonio here?
ANTONIO Ready, so please Your Grace.
DUKE I am sorry for thee. Thou art come to answer°
A stony adversary, an inhuman wretch
Uncapable of pity, void and empty   5
From any dram° of mercy.
ANTONIO   I have heard
Your Grace hath ta'en great pains to qualify°
His rigorous course; but since he stands obdurate
And that no lawful means can carry me
Out of his envy's° reach, I do oppose   10
My patience to his fury and am armed
To suffer with a quietness of spirit
The very tyranny° and rage of his.
DUKE Go one, and call the Jew into the court.
SALERIO He is ready at the door. He comes, my lord.   15

Enter Shylock

79 **digest** (1) ponder, analyze (2) "swallow," put up with (with a play also on the gastronomic sense) | **set you forth** (1) serve you up, as at a feast (2) set forth your praises

3 **answer** defend yourself against (a legal term)   6 **dram** sixty grains apothecaries' weight, a tiny quantity   7 **qualify** moderate   10 **envy's** malice's   13 **tyranny** cruelty

DUKE Make room, and let him stand before our° face.—
Shylock, the world thinks, and I think so too,
That thou but leadest this fashion° of thy malice
To the last hour of act,° and then 'tis thought
Thou'lt show thy mercy and remorse° more strange°   20
Than is thy strange° apparent° cruelty;
And where thou now exacts the penalty,
Which is a pound of this poor merchant's flesh,
Thou wilt not only loose° the forfeiture,
But, touched with human gentleness and love,   25
Forgive a moiety° of the principal,
Glancing an eye of pity on his losses
That have of late so huddled on his back—
Enough to press a royal merchant down
And pluck commiseration of° his state   30
From brassy° bosoms and rough hearts of flint,
From stubborn Turks and Tartars never trained
To offices of tender courtesy.
We all expect a gentle answer, Jew.
SHYLOCK I have possessed° Your Grace of what I purpose,   35
And by our holy Sabbath have I sworn
To have the due and forfeit of my bond.
If you deny it, let the danger° light
Upon your charter and your city's freedom!°
You'll ask me why I rather choose to have   40
A weight of carrion flesh than to receive
Three thousand ducats. I'll not answer that,
But say it is my humor.° Is it answered?
What if my house be troubled with a rat
And I be pleased to give ten thousand ducats   45
To have it baned?° What, are you answered yet?
Some men there are love° not a gaping pig,°
Some that are mad if they behold a cat,

16 **our** (the royal plural) 18 **That . . . fashion** that you only maintain this
pretense or form 19 **the last . . . act** the brink of action 20 **remorse** pity |
strange remarkable 21 **strange** unnatural, foreign | **apparent** (1) manifest, overt
(2) seeming 24 **loose** release, waive 26 **moiety** part, portion 30 **of** for 31 **brassy**
unfeeling, hard like brass 35 **possessed** informed 38 **danger** injury 39 **Upon . . .**
freedom (see 3.2.276) 43 **humor** whim 46 **baned** poisoned 47 **love** who love |
gaping pig pig roasted whole with its mouth open

And others, when the bagpipe sings i'th' nose,
Cannot contain their urine; for affection,°   50
Mistress of passion, sways it to the mood
Of what it likes or loathes. Now, for your answer:
As there is no firm reason to be rendered
Why he cannot abide a gaping pig,
Why he a harmless necessary° cat,   55
Why he a woolen° bagpipe, but of force
Must yield to such inevitable shame
As to offend, himself being offended,
So can I give no reason, nor I will not,
More than a lodged° hate and a certain° loathing   60
I bear Antonio, that I follow thus
A losing° suit against him. Are you answered?

BASSANIO This is no answer, thou unfeeling man,
To excuse the current° of thy cruelty.

SHYLOCK I am not bound to please thee with my answers.   65

BASSANIO Do all men kill the things they do not love?

SHYLOCK Hates any man the thing he would not kill?

BASSANIO Every offense is not a hate at first.

SHYLOCK What, wouldst thou have a serpent sting thee twice?

ANTONIO I pray you, think° you question° with the Jew.   70
You may as well go stand upon the beach
And bid the main flood bate his usual height;°
You may as well use question with° the wolf
Why he hath made the ewe bleat for the lamb;
You may as well forbid the mountain pines   75
To wag their high tops and to make no noise
When they are fretten° with the gusts of heaven;
You may as well do anything most hard
As seek to soften that—than which what's harder?—
His Jewish heart. Therefore, I do beseech you,   80
Make no more offers, use no farther means,

---

50 **affection** feeling, desire 55 **necessary** useful for catching rats and mice
56 **woolen** with flannel-covered bag 60 **lodged** settled, steadfast | **certain**
unwavering, fixed 62 **losing** unprofitable 64 **current** flow, tendency 70 **think**
bear in mind | **question** argue 72 **And . . . height** and bid the ocean put an end to
its usual high tide 73 **use question with** interrogate 77 **fretten** fretted, disturbed,
ruffled

But with all brief and plain conveniency
Let me have judgment, and the Jew his will.
BASSANIO [*to Shylock*]
　For thy three thousand ducats here is six.
SHYLOCK　If every ducat in six thousand ducats　　　　　85
　Were in six parts, and every part a ducat,
　I would not draw° them. I would have my bond.
DUKE　How shalt thou hope for mercy, rendering none?
SHYLOCK　What judgment° shall I dread, doing no wrong?
　You have among you many a purchased slave,　　　　90
　Which, like your asses and your dogs and mules,
　You use in abject and in slavish parts,°
　Because you bought them. Shall I say to you,
　"Let them be free, marry them to your heirs!
　Why sweat they under burdens? Let their beds　　　　95
　Be made as soft as yours, and let their palates
　Be seasoned with such viands"?° You will answer
　"The slaves are ours." So do I answer you:
　The pound of flesh which I demand of him
　Is dearly bought, is mine, and I will have it.　　　　100
　If you deny me, fie upon your law!
　There is no force in the decrees of Venice.
　I stand for judgment. Answer: shall I have it?
DUKE　Upon° my power I may dismiss this court,
　Unless Bellario, a learnèd doctor,°　　　　　　105
　Whom I have sent for to determine this,°
　Come here today.
SALERIO　　　　　My lord, here stays without°
　A messenger with letters from the doctor,
　New come from Padua.
DUKE　Bring us the letters. Call the messenger.　[*Exit one*]　110
BASSANIO　Good cheer, Antonio. What, man, courage yet!
　The Jew shall have my flesh, blood, bones, and all,
　Ere thou shalt lose for me one drop of blood.

---

87 **draw** receive　88–9 **mercy . . . judgment** (on the relation of mercy to justice, see
selections from the Play of *The Salutation and Conception* and *Measure for Measure*
in Contexts) [LD]　92 **parts** duties, capacities　97 **such viands** food such as you
eat　104 **Upon** in accordance with　105 **doctor** person of learning (here, of law)
106 **determine this** resolve this legal dispute　107 **stays without** waits outside

ANTONIO I am a tainted wether° of the flock,
Meetest° for death. The weakest kind of fruit   115
Drops earliest to the ground, and so let me.
You cannot better be employed, Bassanio,
Than to live still and write mine epitaph.

Enter Nerissa [dressed like a lawyer's clerk]

DUKE Came you from Padua, from Bellario?
NERISSA From both, my lord. Bellario greets Your Grace.   120
[She presents a letter. Shylock whets his knife on his shoe]
BASSANIO Why dost thou whet thy knife so earnestly?
SHYLOCK To cut the forfeiture from that bankrupt there.
GRATIANO Not on thy sole, but on thy soul, harsh Jew,
Thou mak'st thy knife keen; but no metal can,
No, not the hangman's° ax, bear half the keenness°   125
Of thy sharp envy.° Can no prayers pierce thee?
SHYLOCK No, none that thou hast wit enough to make.
GRATIANO Oh, be thou damned, inexecrable° dog,
And for thy life let Justice be accused!°
Thou almost mak'st me waver in my faith   130
To hold opinion with Pythagoras°
That souls of animals infuse themselves
Into the trunks of men. Thy currish spirit
Governed a wolf who, hanged for human slaughter,°
Even from the gallows did his fell° soul fleet,°   135
And, whilst thou layest in thy unhallowed dam,°
Infused itself in thee; for thy desires
Are wolvish, bloody, starved, and ravenous.
SHYLOCK Till thou canst rail° the seal from off my bond,
Thou but offend'st° thy lungs to speak so loud.   140
Repair thy wit, good youth, or it will fall
To cureless° ruin. I stand here for law.

---

114 **wether** ram, especially a castrated ram 115 **Meetest** fittest 125 **hangman's** executioner's | **keenness** (1) sharpness (2) savagery 126 **envy** malice 128 **inexecrable** thoroughly execrable 129 **And . . . accused!** and may Justice herself be accused for allowing you to live! 131 **Pythagoras** ancient Greek philosopher who argued for the transmigration of souls 134 **hanged for human slaughter** (a possible allusion to the Elizabethan practice of trying and punishing animals for various crimes) 135 **fell** fierce, cruel | **fleet** flit, pass from the body 136 **dam** mother (usually used of animals) 139 **rail** remove by your abusive language 140 **Thou but offend'st** you merely injure 142 **cureless** incurable

DUKE   This letter from Bellario doth commend
A young and learnèd doctor to our court.
Where is he?

NERISSA   He attendeth here hard by   145
To know your answer, whether you'll admit him.

DUKE   With all my heart. Some three or four of you
Go give him courteous conduct to this place.
                                                        [*Exeunt some*]
Meantime the court shall hear Bellario's letter.
[*He reads.*] "Your Grace shall understand that at the receipt   150
of your letter I am very sick; but in the instant that your
messenger came, in loving visitation was with me a young
doctor of Rome. His name is Balthasar. I acquainted him
with the cause in controversy between the Jew and Antonio
the merchant. We turned o'er many books together. He is   155
furnished with my opinion, which, bettered with his own
learning, the greatness whereof I cannot enough commend,
comes with him,° at my importunity,° to fill up Your Grace's
request in my stead. I beseech you, let his lack of years be no
impediment to let him lack° a reverend estimation, for I   160
never knew so young a body with so old a head. I leave him
to your gracious acceptance, whose trial shall better publish
his commendation."°

                    Enter Portia for° *Balthasar* [*dressed
                    like a doctor of laws, escorted*]

You hear the learn'd Bellario, what he writes;
And here, I take it, is the doctor come.—   165
Give me your hand. Come you from old Bellario?

PORTIA
I did, my lord.

DUKE   You are welcome. Take your place.
                                              [*Portia takes her place*]
Are you acquainted with the difference°
That holds this present question in the court?

150 [*He reads*] (in many modern editions, the reading of the letter is assigned to a
clerk, but the original text gives no such indication)   158 **comes with him**
accompanies him in the form of my learned opinion | **importunity** insistence
160 **to let him lack** such as would deprive him of   162–63 **whose . . . commendation** the demonstration of whose excellence will proclaim what is commendable in
him better than my letter can   164.1 *for* disguised as   168 **difference** argument

PORTIA I am informèd throughly° of the cause.°   170
  Which is the merchant here, and which the Jew?
DUKE Antonio and old Shylock, both stand forth.
                          [*Antonio and Shylock stand forth*]
PORTIA Is your name Shylock?
SHYLOCK   Shylock is my name.
PORTIA Of a strange nature is the suit you follow,
  Yet in such rule° that the Venetian law   175
  Cannot impugn° you as you do proceed.—
  You stand within his danger, do you not?
ANTONIO Ay, so he says.
PORTIA   Do you confess the bond?
ANTONIO I do.
PORTIA   Then must the Jew be merciful.
SHYLOCK On what compulsion must I? Tell me that.   180
PORTIA The quality of mercy is not strained.°
  It droppeth as the gentle rain from heaven
  Upon the place beneath. It is twice blest:°
  It blesseth him that gives and him that takes.
  'Tis mightiest in the mightiest; it becomes   185
  The thronèd monarch better than his crown.
  His° scepter shows the force of temporal power,
  The attribute to° awe and majesty,
  Wherein doth sit the dread and fear of kings.
  But mercy is above this sceptered sway;   190
  It is enthronèd in the hearts of kings;
  It is an attribute to God himself;
  And earthly power doth then show likest God's
  When mercy seasons justice. Therefore, Jew,
  Though justice be thy plea, consider this,   195
  That in the course of justice° none of us
  Should see salvation. We do pray for mercy,
  And that same prayer° doth teach us all to render
  The deeds of mercy. I have spoke thus much

---

170 throughly thoroughly | **cause** case **175 rule** order **176 impugn** find fault
with **181 strained** forced, constrained **183 is twice blest** grants a double blessing
187 His the monarch's **188 attribute to** symbol of **196 justice** divine justice
198 that . . . prayer the Lord's Prayer, to forgive others as we would be forgiven by
God (Matthew 6, Luke 11) [LD]

To mitigate the justice of thy plea,°   200
Which if thou follow, this strict court of Venice
Must needs give sentence 'gainst the merchant there.
SHYLOCK My deeds upon my head!° I crave the law,
The penalty and forfeit of my bond.
PORTIA Is he not able to discharge the money?   205
BASSANIO Yes, here I tender it for him in the court,
Yea, twice the sum. If that will not suffice,
I will be bound to pay it ten times o'er,
On forfeit of my hands, my head, my heart.
If this will not suffice, it must appear   210
That malice bears down truth.° And I beseech you,
Wrest once° the law to your authority.
To do a great right, do a little wrong,
And curb this cruel devil of his will.
PORTIA It must not be. There is no power in Venice   215
Can alter a decree establishèd.
'Twill be recorded for a precedent,
And many an error by the same example
Will rush into the state. It cannot be.
SHYLOCK A Daniel° come to judgment! Yea, a Daniel!   220
O wise young judge, how I do honor thee!
PORTIA I pray you, let me look upon the bond.
SHYLOCK [*giving the bond*]
Here 'tis, most reverend doctor, here it is.
PORTIA Shylock, there's thrice thy money offered thee.
SHYLOCK An oath, an oath! I have an oath in heaven.   225
Shall I lay perjury upon my soul?
No, not for Venice.
PORTIA   Why, this bond is forfeit,
And lawfully by this the Jew may claim
A pound of flesh, to be by him cut off
Nearest the merchant's heart.—Be merciful.   230
Take thrice thy money; bid me tear the bond.

---

200 To . . . plea to show the way in which your call for justice needs to be mitigated
or reduced in severity 203 My . . . head! (compare the cry of the crowd at Jesus'
crucifixion: "His blood be on us, and on our children," Matthew 27.25)
211 bears down truth overwhelms righteousness 212 Wrest once for once,
forcibly subject 220 Daniel (in the Apocrypha's story of Susannah and the Elders,
Daniel is the young man who rescues Susannah from her false accusers)

SHYLOCK When it is paid according to the tenor.°
It doth appear you are a worthy judge.
You know the law. Your exposition
Hath been most sound. I charge you by the law,   235
Whereof you are a well-deserving pillar,
Proceed to judgment. By my soul I swear
There is no power in the tongue of man
To alter me. I stay° here on my bond.
ANTONIO Most heartily I do beseech the court   240
To give the judgment.
PORTIA   Why then, thus it is:
You must prepare your bosom for his knife.
SHYLOCK O noble judge! O excellent young man!
PORTIA For the intent and purpose of the law
Hath full relation to° the penalty   245
Which here appeareth due upon the bond.
SHYLOCK 'Tis very true. O wise and upright judge!
How much more elder art thou than thy looks!
PORTIA Therefore lay bare your bosom.
SHYLOCK   Ay, his breast.
So says the bond, doth it not, noble judge?   250
"Nearest his heart," those are the very words.
PORTIA It is so. Are there balance° here
To weigh the flesh?
SHYLOCK   I have them ready.
PORTIA Have by° some surgeon, Shylock, on your charge,°
To stop his wounds, lest he do bleed to death.   255
SHYLOCK Is it so nominated in the bond?
PORTIA It is not so expressed, but what of that?
'Twere good you do so much for charity.
SHYLOCK I cannot find it. 'Tis not in the bond.
PORTIA You, merchant, have you anything to say?   260
ANTONIO But little. I am armed° and well prepared.—
Give me your hand, Bassanio; fare you well!
Grieve not that I am fall'n to this for you,
For herein Fortune shows herself more kind

___

232 **tenor** conditions 239 **stay** stand, insist 245 **Hath . . . to** is fully in accord with 252 **balance** scales 254 **Have by** have ready at hand | **on your charge** at your personal expense 261 **armed** fortified in spirit

Than is her custom. It is still her use°   265
To let the wretched man outlive his wealth
To view with hollow eye and wrinkled brow
An age of poverty; from which ling'ring penance
Of such misery doth she cut me off.
Commend me to your honorable wife.   270
Tell her the process° of Antonio's end,
Say how I loved you, speak me fair° in death;
And, when the tale is told, bid her be judge
Whether Bassanio had not once a love.°
Repent but you° that you shall lose your friend,   275
And he repents not that he pays your debt.
For if the Jew do cut but deep enough,
I'll pay it instantly with all my heart.°

BASSANIO   Antonio, I am married to a wife,
Which is as dear to me as life itself;   280
But life itself, my wife, and all the world
Are not with me esteemed above thy life.
I would lose all, ay, sacrifice them all
Here to this devil, to deliver you.

PORTIA   Your wife would give you little thanks for that, 285
If she were by° to hear you make the offer.

GRATIANO   I have a wife who, I protest, I love;
I would she were in heaven, so she could
Entreat some power to change this currish Jew.

NERISSA   'Tis well you offer it behind her back;   290
The wish would make else an unquiet house.

SHYLOCK   These be the Christian husbands. I have a daughter;
Would any of the stock of Barabbas°
Had been her husband rather than a Christian!—
We trifle° time. I pray thee, pursue° sentence.   295

PORTIA   A pound of that same merchant's flesh is thine.
The court awards it, and the law doth give it.

---

265 still her use commonly Fortune's practice   **271 process** story, manner   **272 speak me fair** speak well of me   **274 a love** a friend's love   **275 Repent but you** grieve only   **278 with . . . heart** (1) wholeheartedly (2) literally, with my heart's blood   **286 by** nearby   **293 Barabbas** a thief whom Pontius Pilate set free instead of Christ in response to the people's demand (see Mark 15); also, the villainous protagonist of Marlowe's *The Jew of Malta* (see selection in the Contexts materials [LD]   **295 trifle** waste | **pursue** proceed with

SHYLOCK Most rightful judge!

PORTIA And you must cut this flesh from off his breast.

The law allows it, and the court awards it.   300

SHYLOCK Most learnèd judge! A sentence!—Come, prepare.

PORTIA Tarry a little; there is something else.

This bond doth give thee here no jot of blood;

The words expressly are "a pound of flesh."

Take then thy bond, take thou thy pound of flesh,   305

But in the cutting it if thou dost shed

One drop of Christian blood, thy lands and goods

Are by the laws of Venice confiscate

Unto the state of Venice.

GRATIANO O upright judge! Mark, Jew. O learnèd judge!   310

SHYLOCK Is that the law?

PORTIA   Thyself shalt see the act;

For, as thou urgest justice, be assured

Thou shalt have justice, more than thou desir'st.

GRATIANO O learnèd judge! Mark, Jew, a learnèd judge!

SHYLOCK I take this offer, then. Pay the bond thrice   315

And let the Christian go.

BASSANIO   Here is the money.

PORTIA Soft!°

The Jew shall have all justice.° Soft, no haste.

He shall have nothing but the penalty.

GRATIANO O Jew! An upright judge, a learnèd judge!   320

PORTIA Therefore prepare thee to cut off the flesh.

Shed thou no blood, nor cut thou less nor more

But just a pound of flesh. If thou tak'st more

Or less than a just pound, be it but so much

As makes it light or heavy in the substance°   325

Or the division° of the twentieth part

Of one poor scruple,° nay, if the scale do turn

But in the estimation of a hair,

Thou diest, and all thy goods are confiscate.

---

317 **Soft!** not so fast! 318 **all justice** precisely what the law provides 325 **substance** mass or gross weight 326 **division** fraction 327 **scruple** twenty grains apothecaries' weight, a small quantity

GRATIANO   A second Daniel,° a Daniel, Jew!   330
Now, infidel, I have you on the hip.°
PORTIA   Why doth the Jew pause? Take thy forfeiture.
SHYLOCK   Give me my principal, and let me go.
BASSANIO   I have it ready for thee. Here it is.
PORTIA   He hath refused it in the open court.   335
He shall have merely justice and his bond.
GRATIANO   A Daniel, still say I, a second Daniel!
I thank thee, Jew, for teaching me that word.
SHYLOCK   Shall I not have barely my principal?
PORTIA   Thou shalt have nothing but the forfeiture,   340
To be so taken at thy peril, Jew.
SHYLOCK   Why, then the devil give him good of it!
I'll stay no longer question.°   [*He starts to go*]
PORTIA   Tarry, Jew!
The law hath yet another hold on you.
It is enacted in the laws of Venice,   345
If it be proved against an alien
That by direct or indirect attempts
He seek the life of any citizen,
The party 'gainst the which he doth contrive
Shall seize one half his goods; the other half   350
Comes to the privy coffer° of the state,
And the offender's life lies in° the mercy
Of the Duke only, 'gainst all other voice.°
In which predicament, I say, thou stand'st;
For it appears, by manifest proceeding,   355
That indirectly and directly too
Thou hast contrived against the very life
Of the defendant; and thou hast incurred
The danger formerly by me rehearsed.°
Down° therefore, and beg mercy of the Duke.   360
GRATIANO   Beg that thou mayst have leave to hang thyself!
And yet, thy wealth being forfeit to the state,

---

330 **Daniel** (see line 220 earlier and note)   331 **on the hip** at a disadvantage (a
phrase from wrestling)   343 **I'll** . . . **question** I'll stay no further pursuing of the
case   351 **privy coffer** private treasury   352 **lies in** lies at   353 **'gainst** . . . **voice**
without appeal   359 **The danger** . . . **rehearsed** the penalty already cited by me
360 **Down** down on your knees

Thou hast not left the value of a cord;
Therefore thou must be hanged at the state's charge.°
DUKE   That thou shalt see the difference of our spirit,   365
I pardon thee thy life before thou ask it.
For° half thy wealth, it is Antonio's;
The other half comes to the general state,
Which humbleness may drive unto a fine.°
PORTIA   Ay, for the state, not for Antonio.°   370
SHYLOCK   Nay, take my life and all! Pardon not that!
You take my house when you do take the prop
That doth sustain my house. You take my life
When you do take the means whereby I live.
PORTIA   What mercy can you render him, Antonio?   375
GRATIANO   A halter° gratis! Nothing else, for God's sake.
ANTONIO   So please my lord the Duke and all the court
To quit the fine for one half of his goods,°
I am content, so° he will let me have
The other half in use,° to render it,   380
Upon his death, unto the gentleman
That lately stole his daughter.
Two things provided more: that for this favor
He presently° become a Christian;
The other, that he do record a gift   385
Here in the court of all he dies possessed°
Unto his son Lorenzo and his daughter.
DUKE   He shall do this, or else I do recant
The pardon that I late° pronouncèd here.
PORTIA   Art thou contented, Jew? What dost thou say?   390
SHYLOCK   I am content.
PORTIA   Clerk, draw a deed of gift.

---

364 **charge** expense   367 **For** as for   369 **which . . . fine** which penitence on your
part may persuade me to reduce to a fine   370 **Ay . . . Antonio** yes, the state's half
may be reduced to a fine, but not Antonio's half   376 **halter** hangman's noose
378 **To . . . goods** to cancel the fine of one-half of Shylock's estate owed to the
state of Venice (line 351)   379 **so** provided that   380 **in use** in trust (until
Shylock's death)   384 **presently** at once   386 **of . . . possessed** what remains of
the portion not placed under Antonio's trust (which will also go to Lorenzo and
Jessica)   389 **late** lately

SHYLOCK I pray you, give me leave to go from hence;
I am not well. Send the deed after me,
And I will sign it.
DUKE   Get thee gone, but do it.
GRATIANO In christening shalt thou have two godfathers.   395
Had I been judge, thou shouldst have had ten more,°
To bring thee to the gallows, not the font.
                                        Exit [Shylock]
DUKE *[to Portia]* Sir, I entreat you home with me to dinner.
PORTIA I humbly do desire Your Grace of pardon.
I must away this night toward Padua,   400
And it is meet° I presently set forth.
DUKE I am sorry that your leisure serves you not.
Antonio, gratify° this gentleman,
For in my mind you are much bound to him.
                          Exeunt Duke and his train
BASSANIO *[to Portia]* Most worthy gentleman, I and my friend   405
Have by your wisdom been this day acquitted
Of grievous penalties, in lieu whereof,°
Three thousand ducats due unto the Jew
We freely cope° your courteous pains withal.
                                        [He offers money]
ANTONIO And stand indebted over and above   410
In love and service to you evermore.
PORTIA He is well paid that is well satisfied,
And I, delivering you, am satisfied,
And therein do account myself well paid.
My mind was never yet more mercenary.   415
I pray you, know me when we meet again.°
I wish you well, and so I take my leave.
                                        [She starts to leave]
BASSANIO Dear sir, of force° I must attempt° you further.
Take some remembrance of us as a tribute,

---

396 ten more to make up a jury of twelve (jurors were colloquially termed
godfathers) **401 meet** necessary, suitable **403 gratify** reward **407 in lieu
whereof** in return for which **409 cope** requite **416 know . . . again** consider our
acquaintance well established (but punning on **know** in the sense of "recognize"
and "have sexual relations with"—meanings that are hidden from Bassanio by
Portia's disguise) **418 of force** of necessity | **attempt** urge

Not as fee. Grant me two things, I pray you: 420
Not to deny me, and to pardon me.°
PORTIA   You press me far, and therefore I will yield.
Give me your gloves,° I'll wear them for your sake.
And, for your love,° I'll take this ring from you.
Do not draw back your hand; I'll take no more,   425
And you in love shall not deny me this.
BASSANIO   This ring, good sir? Alas, it is a trifle!
I will not shame myself to give you this.
PORTIA   I will have nothing else but only this;
And now, methinks, I have a mind to it.   430
BASSANIO   There's more depends on this than on the value.
The dearest° ring in Venice will I give you,
And find it out by proclamation.
Only for this, I pray you, pardon me.
PORTIA   I see, sir, you are liberal° in offers.   435
You taught me first to beg, and now, methinks,
You teach me how a beggar should be answered.
BASSANIO   Good sir, this ring was given me by my wife,
And when she put it on she made me vow
That I should neither sell nor give nor lose it.   440
PORTIA   That 'scuse serves many men to save their gifts.
An if° your wife be not a madwoman,
And know how well I have deserved this ring,
She would not hold out enemy forever
For giving it to me. Well, peace be with you!   445

     Exeunt [Portia and Nerissa]

ANTONIO   My lord Bassanio, let him have the ring.
Let his deservings and my love withal
Be valued 'gainst your wife's commandement.°
BASSANIO   Go, Gratiano, run and overtake him;
Give him the ring, and bring him, if thou canst,   450
Unto Antonio's house. Away, make haste!

     Exit Gratiano [with the ring]

---

421 pardon me pardon my presumption in pressing the matter   **423 gloves** (perhaps Bassanio removes his gloves, thereby revealing the ring that "Balthasar" asks of him)   **424 for your love** for friendship's sake—a polite phrase, but with ironic double meaning as applied to husband and wife   **432 dearest** most expensive **435 liberal** generous   **442 An if** if   **448 commandement** (pronounced in four syllables)

Come, you and I will thither presently,
And in the morning early will we both
Fly toward Belmont. Come, Antonio.

Exeunt

❖

ACT 4
SCENE 2

Location: Venice. A street

Enter [Portia and] Nerissa [still disguised]

PORTIA [*giving a deed to Nerissa*]
Inquire the Jew's house out; give him this deed°
And let him sign it. We'll away tonight
And be a day before our husbands home.
This deed will be well welcome to Lorenzo.

Enter Gratiano

GRATIANO   Fair sir, you are well o'erta'en.°   5
My lord Bassanio upon more advice°
Hath sent you here this ring and doth entreat
Your company at dinner.   [*He gives a ring*]
PORTIA   That cannot be.
His ring I do accept most thankfully,
And so, I pray you, tell him. Furthermore,   10
I pray you, show my youth old Shylock's house.
GRATIANO   That will I do.
NERISSA   Sir, I would speak with you.
[*aside to Portia*] I'll see if I can get my husband's ring,
Which I did make him swear to keep forever.
PORTIA [*aside to Nerissa*]
Thou mayst, I warrant. We shall have old° swearing   15
That they did give the rings away to men;
But we'll outface° them, and outswear them too.—
Away, make haste! Thou know'st where I will tarry.

---

1 this deed the deed of gift   **5 you . . . o'erta'en** I'm happy to have caught up with
you   **6 advice** consideration   **15 old** plenty of   **17 outface** boldly contradict

NERISSA [*to Gratiano*]
Come, good sir, will you show me to this house?
[*Exeunt, Portia separately from the others*]

♣

ACT 5
SCENE 1

Location: Belmont. Outside Portia's house

Enter Lorenzo and Jessica

LORENZO   The moon shines bright. In such a night as this,
When the sweet wind did gently kiss the trees
And they did make no noise, in such a night
Troilus° methinks mounted the Trojan walls
And sighed his soul toward the Grecian tents   5
Where Cressid lay that night.
JESSICA   In such a night
Did Thisbe° fearfully o'ertrip the dew,
And saw the lion's shadow ere himself,
And ran dismayed away.
LORENZO   In such a night
Stood Dido° with a willow° in her hand   10
Upon the wild sea banks, and waft° her love
To come again to Carthage.
JESSICA   In such a night
Medea° gathered the enchanted herbs
That did renew old Aeson.
LORENZO   In such a night
Did Jessica steal° from the wealthy Jew   15

---

4 **Troilus** Trojan prince deserted by his beloved, Cressida, after she had been
transferred to the Greek camp   7 **Thisbe** beloved of Pyramus who, arranging to
meet him by night, was frightened by a lion and fled; the tragic misunderstanding
of her absence led to the suicides of both lovers (see *A Midsummer Night's Dream*,
Act 5)   10 **Dido** Queen of Carthage, deserted by Aeneas | **willow** (a symbol of
forsaken love)   11 **waft** wafted, beckoned   13 **Medea** famous sorceress of
Colchis who, after falling in love with Jason and helping him to gain the Golden
Fleece, used her magic to restore youth to Aeson, Jason's father   15 **steal** (1) escape
(2) rob

And with an unthrift° love did run from Venice
As far as Belmont.

JESSICA   In such a night
Did young Lorenzo swear he loved her well,
Stealing her soul with many vows of faith,
And ne'er a true one.

LORENZO   In such a night   20
Did pretty Jessica, like a little shrew,
Slander her love, and he forgave it her.

JESSICA   I would out-night° you, did nobody come.
But hark, I hear the footing° of a man.

Enter [Stephano,] a messenger

LORENZO   Who comes so fast in silence of the night?   25

STEPHANO   A friend.

LORENZO
A friend? What friend? Your name, I pray you, friend?

STEPHANO   Stephano is my name, and I bring word
My mistress will before the break of day
Be here at Belmont. She doth stray about   30
By holy crosses,° where she kneels and prays
For happy wedlock hours.

LORENZO   Who comes with her?

STEPHANO   None but a holy hermit and her maid.
I pray you, is my master yet returned?

LORENZO   He is not, nor we have not heard from him.   35
But go we in, I pray thee, Jessica,
And ceremoniously let us prepare
Some welcome for the mistress of the house.

Enter [Lancelot, the] clown

LANCELOT   Sola,° sola! Wo ha, ho! Sola, sola!

LORENZO   Who calls?   40

LANCELOT   Sola! Did you see Master Lorenzo? Master Lorenzo,
sola, sola!

LORENZO   Leave holloing, man! Here.

---

16 unthrift prodigal   **23 out-night** outdo in the verbal games we've been playing
24 footing footsteps   **31 holy crosses** wayside shrines   **39 Sola** (imitation of a post
horn)

LANCELOT Sola! Where, where?

LORENZO Here.   45

LANCELOT Tell him there's a post° come from my master, with
his horn° full of good news: my master will be here ere
morning.   [*Exit*]

LORENZO Sweet soul, let's in, and there expect° their coming.
And yet no matter. Why should we go in?   50
My friend Stephano, signify,° I pray you,
Within the house, your mistress is at hand,
And bring your music forth into the air.
                                                              [*Exit Stephano*]
How sweet the moonlight sleeps upon this bank!
Here will we sit and let the sounds of music   55
Creep in our ears. Soft stillness and the night
Become° the touches° of sweet harmony.
Sit, Jessica. [*They sit.*] Look how the floor of heaven
Is thick inlaid with patens° of bright gold.
There's not the smallest orb which thou behold'st   60
But in his motion like an angel sings,
Still choiring° to the young-eyed° cherubins.
Such harmony is in immortal souls,
But whilst this muddy vesture of decay°
Doth grossly close it in,° we cannot hear it.°   65

                                                              [*Enter musicians*]

Come, ho, and wake Diana° with a hymn!
With sweetest touches pierce your mistress' ear
And draw her home with music.   *Play music*

JESSICA I am never merry when I hear sweet music.

---

46 post courier   **47 horn** (Lancelot jestingly compares the courier's post horn to a cornucopia; perhaps too with a glance at the frayed jest about cuckolds' horns) **49 expect** await   **51 signify** make known   **57 Become** suit | **touches** strains, notes (produced by the fingering of an instrument)   **59 patens** thin, circular plates of metal   **62 Still choiring** continually singing | **young-eyed** eternally clear-sighted (in Ezekiel 10.12, the bodies and wings of cherubim are "full of eyes round about") **64 muddy . . . decay** mortal flesh   **65 close it in** enclose the soul | **hear it** hear the music of the spheres (see selections from Boethius and Macrobius in Contexts [LD] **66 Diana** (here, goddess of the moon; compare with 1.2.93)

LORENZO The reason is, your spirits are attentive.°   70
For do but note a wild and wanton herd,
Or race° of youthful and unhandled colts,
Fetching mad bounds, bellowing and neighing loud,
Which is the hot condition of their blood;
If they but hear perchance a trumpet sound,   75
Or any air of music touch their ears,
You shall perceive them make a mutual° stand,
Their savage eyes turned to a modest gaze
By the sweet power of music. Therefore the poet
Did feign that Orpheus° drew° trees, stones, and floods,°   80
Since naught so stockish,° hard, and full of rage
But music for the time doth change his° nature.
The man that hath no music in himself,
Nor is not moved with concord of sweet sounds,
Is fit for treasons, stratagems, and spoils;°   85
The motions of his spirit are dull as night
And his affections dark as Erebus.°
Let no such man be trusted. Mark the music.

Enter Portia and Nerissa

PORTIA That light we see is burning in my hall.
How far that little candle throws his beams!   90
So shines a good deed in a naughty° world.
NERISSA When the moon shone, we did not see the candle.
PORTIA So doth the greater glory dim the less.
A substitute shines brightly as a king
Until a king be by, and then his° state   95
Empties itself, as doth an inland brook
Into the main of waters.° Music! Hark!
NERISSA It is your music, madam, of the house.
PORTIA Nothing is good, I see, without respect.°
Methinks it sounds much sweeter than by day.   100

70 **spirits are attentive** (the spirits would be in motion within the body in merriment, whereas in sadness they would be drawn to the heart and, as it were, busy listening) 72 **race** herd 77 **mutual** common or simultaneous 79 **poet . . . Orpheus** Ovid, in *Metamorphoses*, tells the story of the legendary musician Orpheus [LD] 80 **drew** attracted, charmed I **floods** rivers 81 **stockish** unfeeling 82 **his** its (a tree, a stone, etc.) 85 **spoils** acts of pillage 87 **Erebus** a place of primeval darkness on the way to Hades 91 **naughty** wicked 95 **his** the substitute's 97 **main of waters** sea 99 **respect** comparison, context

NERISSA Silence bestows that virtue on it, madam.
PORTIA The crow doth sing as sweetly as the lark
When neither is attended;° and I think
The nightingale, if she should sing by day,
When every goose is cackling, would be thought   105
No better a musician than the wren.
How many things by season° seasoned are
To their right praise and true perfection!
Peace, ho! The moon sleeps with Endymion°
And would not be awaked.   [*The music ceases*]
LORENZO   That is the voice,   110
Or I am much deceived, of Portia.
PORTIA He knows me as the blind man knows the cuckoo,
By the bad voice.
LORENZO   Dear lady, welcome home.
PORTIA We have been praying for our husbands' welfare,
Which speed, we hope, the better for our words.°   115
Are they returned?
LORENZO   Madam, they are not yet;
But there is come a messenger before,
To signify their coming.
PORTIA   Go in, Nerissa.
Give order to my servants that they take
No note at all of our being absent hence;   120
Nor you, Lorenzo; Jessica, nor you.   [*A tucket° sounds*]
LORENZO Your husband is at hand. I hear his trumpet.
We are no telltales, madam, fear you not.
PORTIA This night, methinks, is but the daylight sick;°
It looks a little paler. 'Tis a day   125
Such as the day is when the sun is hid.

Enter Bassanio, Antonio, Gratiano, and their followers

---

103 attended listened to 107 season fit occasion (but playing on the idea of seasoning, spices) 109 Endymion a shepherd loved by the moon goddess, who caused him to sleep a perennial sleep in a cave on Mount Latmos where she could visit him 115 Which . . . words who prosper and return speedily, we hope, because we prayed for them 121 s.d. tucket flourish on a trumpet 124 sick made pale by the approach of dawn

BASSANIO We should hold day with the Antipodes,
    If you would walk in absence of the sun.°
PORTIA Let me give light, but let me not be light;°
    For a light wife doth make a heavy° husband,   130
    And never be Bassanio so for me.
    But God sort° all! You are welcome home, my lord.
BASSANIO I thank you, madam. Give welcome to my friend.
    This is the man, this is Antonio,
    To whom I am so infinitely bound.   135
PORTIA You should in all sense° be much bound to him,
    For, as I hear, he was much bound° for you.
ANTONIO No more than I am well acquitted of.°
PORTIA Sir, you are very welcome to our house.
    It must appear in other ways than words;   140
    Therefore I scant this breathing courtesy.°
GRATIANO [to Nerissa]
    By yonder moon I swear you do me wrong!
    In faith, I gave it to the judge's clerk.
    Would he were gelt° that had it, for my part,°
    Since you do take it, love, so much at heart.   145
PORTIA A quarrel, ho, already? What's the matter?
GRATIANO About a hoop of gold, a paltry ring
    That she did give me, whose posy° was
    For all the world like cutler's poetry
    Upon a knife, "Love me, and leave me not."   150
NERISSA What talk you of the posy or the value?
    You swore to me, when I did give it you,
    That you would wear it till your hour of death
    And that it should lie with you in your grave.
    Though not for me, yet for your vehement oaths   155
    You should have been respective° and have kept it.

127–8 We . . . sun if you, Portia, like a second sun, would always walk about during the sun's absence, we should never have night but would enjoy daylight even when the Antipodes, those who dwell on the opposite side of the globe, enjoy daylight 129 be light be wanton, unchaste 130 heavy sad (with wordplay on the antithesis of light and heavy) 132 sort decide, dispose 136 in all sense in every way, with every reason 136–7 bound . . . bound Portia plays on (1) obligated (2) indebted and imprisoned 138 acquitted of freed from and amply repaid (by thanks and love) 141 scant . . . courtesy make brief these empty (merely verbal) compliments 144 gelt gelded, castrated | for my part as far as I'm concerned 148 posy a motto on a ring 156 respective mindful, careful

Gave it a judge's clerk! No, God's my judge,
The clerk will ne'er wear hair on 's face that had it.
GRATIANO   He will, an if° he live to be a man.
NERISSA   Ay, if a woman live to be a man.   160
GRATIANO   Now, by this hand, I gave it to a youth,
A kind of boy, a little scrubbèd° boy
No higher than thyself, the judge's clerk,
A prating° boy, that begged it as a fee.
I could not for my heart deny it him.   165
PORTIA   You were to blame—I must be plain with you—
To part so slightly with your wife's first gift,
A thing stuck on with oaths upon your finger,
And so riveted with faith unto your flesh.
I gave my love a ring and made him swear   170
Never to part with it; and here he stands.
I dare be sworn for him he would not leave it,
Nor pluck it from his finger, for the wealth
That the world masters.° Now, in faith, Gratiano,
You give your wife too unkind a cause of grief.   175
An° 'twere to me, I should be mad° at it.
BASSANIO [*aside*]   Why, I were best to cut my left hand off
And swear I lost the ring defending it.
GRATIANO   My lord Bassanio gave his ring away
Unto the judge that begged it and indeed   180
Deserved it too; and then the boy, his clerk,
That took some pains in writing, he begged mine;
And neither man nor master would take aught°
But the two rings.
PORTIA [*to Bassanio*]   What ring gave you, my lord?
Not that, I hope, which you received of me.   185
BASSANIO   If I could add a lie unto a fault,
I would deny it; but you see my finger
Hath not the ring upon it. It is gone.
PORTIA   Even so void is your false heart of truth.
By heaven, I will ne'er come in your bed   190
Until I see the ring!

---

159 an if if   **162 scrubbèd** diminutive   **164 prating** chattering   **174 masters** owns
176 An if | **mad** beside myself   **183 aught** anything

NERISSA [*to Gratiano*]   Nor I in yours
Till I again see mine.
BASSANIO   Sweet Portia,
If you did know to whom I gave the ring,
If you did know for whom I gave the ring,
And would conceive for what I gave the ring,   195
And how unwillingly I left the ring,
When naught would be accepted but the ring,
You would abate the strength of your displeasure.
PORTIA   If you had known the virtue° of the ring,
Or half her worthiness that gave the ring,   200
Or your own honor to contain° the ring,
You would not then have parted with the ring.
What man is there so much unreasonable,
If you had pleased to have defended it
With any terms of zeal, wanted the modesty°   205
To urge° the thing held as a ceremony?°
Nerissa teaches me what to believe:
I'll die for't but some woman had the ring.
BASSANIO   No, by my honor, madam! By my soul,
No woman had it, but a civil doctor,°   210
Which did refuse three thousand ducats of me
And begged the ring, the which I did deny him
And suffered° him to go displeased away—
Even he that had held up the very life
Of my dear friend. What should I say, sweet lady?   215
I was enforced to send it after him.
I was beset with shame and courtesy.
My honor would not let ingratitude
So much besmear it.° Pardon me, good lady!
For by these blessèd candles of the night,°   220
Had you been there, I think you would have begged
The ring of me to give the worthy doctor.
PORTIA   Let not that doctor e'er come near my house.
Since he hath got the jewel that I loved,

---

199 **virtue** moral efficacy   201 **contain** keep safe   205 **wanted the modesty** who
would have been so lacking in consideration as   206 **urge** insist upon receiving |
ceremony something sacred   210 **civil doctor** doctor of civil law   213 **suffered**
allowed   219 **it** my honor   220 **blessèd . . . night** stars

And that which you did swear to keep for me,   225
I will become as liberal° as you:
I'll not deny him anything I have,
No, not my body nor my husband's bed.
Know° him I shall, I am well sure of it.
Lie not a night from° home. Watch me like Argus;°   230
If you do not, if I be left alone,
Now, by mine honor,° which is yet mine own,
I'll have that doctor for my bedfellow.
NERISSA   And I his clerk; therefore be well advised°
How you do leave me to mine own protection.   235
GRATIANO   Well, do you so. Let not me take° him, then!
For if I do, I'll mar the young clerk's pen.°
ANTONIO   I am th'unhappy subject of these quarrels.
PORTIA   Sir, grieve not you; you are welcome notwithstanding.
BASSANIO   Portia, forgive me this enforcèd wrong,   240
And in the hearing of these many friends
I swear to thee, even by thine own fair eyes
Wherein I see myself—
PORTIA   Mark you but that!
In both my eyes he doubly sees himself;
In each eye, one. Swear by your double° self,   245
And there's an oath of credit.°
BASSANIO   Nay, but hear me.
Pardon this fault, and by my soul I swear
I never more will break an oath with thee.
ANTONIO   I once did lend my body for his wealth,°
Which, but for him that had your husband's ring,   250
Had quite miscarried. I dare be bound again,
My soul upon the forfeit,° that your lord
Will nevermore break faith advisedly.°
PORTIA   Then you shall be his surety.° Give him this,
And bid him keep it better than the other.   255

---

226 liberal generous (sexually as well as otherwise)   **229 Know** (with the suggestion of carnal knowledge)   **230 from** away from | **Argus** mythological monster with a hundred eyes   **232 honor** (1) honorable name (2) chastity   **234 be well advised** take care   **236 take** apprehend   **237 pen** (with sexual double meaning)   **245 double** deceitful   **246 of credit** worthy to be believed (said ironically)   **249 wealth** welfare   **252 My . . . forfeit** at the risk of eternal damnation   **253 advisedly** intentionally   **254 surety** guarantor

[*She gives the ring to Antonio, who gives it to Bassanio*]

ANTONIO Here, Lord Bassanio. Swear to keep this ring.

BASSANIO By heaven, it is the same I gave the doctor!

PORTIA I had it of him. Pardon me, Bassanio,
For by this ring the doctor lay with me.

NERISSA And pardon me, my gentle Gratiano,   260
For that same scrubbèd boy, the doctor's clerk,
In lieu of° this last night did lie with me.
                              [*Presenting her ring*]

GRATIANO Why, this is like the mending of highways
In summer, where the ways are fair enough.°
What, are we cuckolds° ere we have deserved it?   265

PORTIA Speak not so grossly. You are all amazed.
Here is a letter; read it at your leisure.
                              [*She gives a letter*]
It comes from Padua, from Bellario.
There you shall find that Portia was the doctor,
Nerissa there her clerk. Lorenzo here   270
Shall witness I set forth as soon as you,
And even but now returned; I have not yet
Entered my house. Antonio, you are welcome,
And I have better news in store for you
Than you expect. Unseal this letter soon.   275
                              [*She gives him a letter*]
There you shall find three of your argosies
Are richly come to harbor suddenly.
You shall not know by what strange accident
I chancèd on this letter.

ANTONIO   I am dumb.°

BASSANIO [*to Portia*] Were you the doctor and I knew you not? 280

GRATIANO [*to Nerissa*]
Were you the clerk that is to make me cuckold?

NERISSA Ay, but the clerk that never means to do it,
Unless he live until he be a man.

BASSANIO Sweet doctor, you shall be my bedfellow.
When I am absent, then lie with my wife.   285

---

262 In lieu of in return for **264 are fair enough** are not in need of repair
265 cuckolds husbands whose wives are unfaithful **279 dumb** at a loss for words

ANTONIO Sweet lady, you have given me life and living;
For here I read for certain that my ships
Are safely come to road.°
PORTIA   How now, Lorenzo?
My clerk hath some good comforts too for you.
NERISSA Ay, and I'll give them him without a fee.   290
                              [*She gives a deed*]
There do I give to you and Jessica,
From the rich Jew, a special deed of gift,
After his death, of all he dies possessed of.
LORENZO Fair ladies, you drop manna° in the way
Of starved people.
PORTIA   It is almost morning,   295
And yet I am sure you are not satisfied
Of these events at full. Let us go in;
And charge us there upon inter'gatories,°
And we will answer all things faithfully.
GRATIANO Let it be so. The first inter'gatory   300
That my Nerissa shall be sworn on is
Whether till the next night she had rather stay°
Or go to bed now, being two hours to day.
But were the day come, I should wish it dark
Till I were couching° with the doctor's clerk.   305
Well, while I live I'll fear no other thing
So sore as keeping safe Nerissa's ring.°

                                        Exeunt

---

288 road anchorage **294 manna** the food from heaven that was miraculously
supplied to the Israelites in the wilderness (Exodus 16) **298 And . . . inter'gatories**
and put questions to us (as in a court of law) **302 stay** wait **305 couching** going
to bed **307 ring** (with sexual suggestion)

CONTEXTS

On the Rialto
and in the Ghetto

Venice

The Venice of Shakespeare's play bears some similarities to the actual island city on the Adriatic. In both there is a Rialto: Shylock asks for news of this meeting place of merchants where Antonio rated him about his money and his usances and "spit upon [his] Jewish gaberdine" (1.3.107). But Shakespeare's Rialto seems to be only a piazza or plaza, not a bridge, an odd omission since the stunning new stone Rialto bridge had been opened in 1591 and must have been the talk of tourists then as now. In both Shakespeare's Venice and the historical one there are Jews, but Shylock's house seems to be in the center of things, to which the Christian revellers carry their torches and from which Lorenzo carries Jessica. Shakespeare's play takes no notice of the ghetto where all of Venice's Jewish population was confined by law. Belmont, where Portia lives, appears on no real map of the Venetian republic's extensive Italian dominions, but the congregation of foreigners there—"For the four winds blow in from every coast / Renownèd suitors" (1.1.168–169)—recalls the cosmopolitan flavor of the historical sixteenth-century Venice itself, one of the greatest centers of international trade. English travel writers of the time invariably commented on Venice's role as crossroads of the world. Thomas Coryate says about the Piazza San Marco, "a man may very properly call it rather *Orbis* than *Urbis forum*, that is, a marketplace of the world, not of the city." And Antonio, in *The Merchant of Venice*, likewise says that "the trade and profit of the city / Consisteth of all nations" (3.3.30–31).

As both Antonio and Shylock know (and as English travelers to Venice regularly commented), a city dependent on global trade requires strong laws to enforce contracts, assure fair dealing, and so on. English traveler Fynes Moryson says that "The Senate of Venice is most reverend for . . . nothing more than [for] their strict observing of justice." An English lover of all things Venetian, such as Lewis

Vittorio Carpaccio (1455–1525), "Healing of the Possessed; or The Miracle of the Relic of the True Cross" (c. 1496). By permission of Scala/Art Resource, NY.

Carpaccio's painting depicts, in the upper left corner, a man being cured of his madness by the miraculous application of a fragment of the True Cross. But the viewer's eye has a hard time focusing on that scene amidst the busy swirl of Venetian life in which Carpaccio sets it. Here is the old, wooden Rialto bridge before it was replaced in 1591 by the great stone arch that now spans the Grand Canal. In the left background, at the foot of the bridge, stand three Muslim men in turbans. The canal is thick with gondolas plying their trade. This is Venice as the busy commercial city that would attract English travelers like Thomas Coryate and Fynes Moryson.

Lewkenor (see his introduction to Contarini's *The Commonwealth and Government of Venice*), found Venetian law to be entirely admirable. But for Shakespeare, nothing—certainly not the endlessly complex question of what constitutes justice—is ever that one-sided. To explain the differences between Venice and the play's Venice, we might simply assume that Shakespeare didn't know very much about the place; it's likely that he had never been there. But there are other ways to explain the oblique relation that Shakespeare's Venice bears to the historical city. As a comedy, however innovative in form, the play foregrounds certain things and puts other things in shadow. In another play he locates in Venice, the tragedy of *Othello*, Shakespeare stages (as he does in *The Merchant*) the judiciousness of the Venetian senatorial apparatus; but *Othello*'s Venice is a more dangerous place, its enemies (Iago; the Turkish navy) more devious even than Shylock. In *Othello*, the outsider's last act is violent death; in *The Merchant* it is enforced conversion (with all its moral violence attached) but followed by a fifth act of music and bawdy humor. The range of possible views of Venice, out of which Shakespeare has created his own extraordinary city, is apparent in the selections that follow, from Lewkenor's insistence that Venice is the virginal city to Coryate's equally over-the-top emphasis on Venice as a city of prostitutes.

Thomas Coryate (1577?–1617)

Thomas Coryate went as far as Turkey, India, and China to make himself a character in his own writing. He was one of the oddest of the numerous Britons whose profession is best described as "traveler." Coryate went first to London, where he became friends with Shakespeare's great contemporary Ben Jonson and other writers who gathered at the Mermaid Tavern. When Coryate later began publishing the story of his travels, Jonson was among those who contributed humorous prefaces that, together with Coryate's idiosyncratic style, created the idea of the writer as an inspired buffoon. In fact, Coryate was a person of enormous curiosity and physical stamina. His first big adventure took him through much of Europe, a trip of 1,975 miles, mostly on foot. The title of his narrative—Coryat's Crudities (i.e., raw, indigestible food) Hastily gobbled up in five months travels . . . Newly digested in the hungry air of Odcombe in the County of Somerset, and now dispersed to the nourishment of the traveling Members of this Kingdom—*catches the spirit of the affair. In his next expedition Coryate covered, again mostly on foot, much of what we now call the Middle East, then spent nine months in Turkey before moving on to Mongolia and India. He died in India in 1617.*

The selections from Coryate's Crudities *presented here reveal the combination of amazement and shrewdness with which he saw Venice. The section on Venice's courtesans betrays the author's almost comical struggle to express both sensual delight and moral condemnation. However peculiar to this singular traveler, Coryate's mixture of wonder and fear, his pleasure and horror as a northerner in danger of being seduced by the sunny south, is typical of many English reactions to Venice and Italy. (The next section of this volume includes selections about Coryate's almost voyeuristic fascination with Jews.)*

from *Crudities*[1]

My observations of the most glorious, peerless, and maiden city of Venice: I call it maiden, because it was never conquered:

I ingenuously confess mine own insufficiency and unworthiness, as being the unworthiest of ten thousand to describe so beautiful, so renowned, so glorious a Virgin (for by that title doth the world most deservedly style her) because my rude and unpolished pen may rather stain and eclipse the resplendent rays of her unparalleled beauty, than add any luster unto it. Yet since I have hitherto continued this slender and naked narration of my observations of five months travels in foreign countries, this noble city doth in a manner challenge this at my hands, that I should describe her also as well as the other cities I saw in my journey, partly because she gave me most loving and kind entertainment for the space of six weeks, which was the sweetest time (I must needs confess) for so much that ever I spent in my life; and partly for that she ministered unto me more variety of remarkable and delicious objects than mine eyes ever surveyed in any city before, or ever shall, if I should with famous Sir John Mandeville,[2] our English Ulysses, spend thirty

---

[1]*Coryat's Crudities* (Glasgow: James MacLehose and Sons, 1905), Volume 1, excerpts from pp. 302–318, 401–407.

[2]Supposed author of an enduringly popular and mostly fictitious book of fabulous travels; the author, whatever his name, was probably French.

whole years together in traveling over most places of the Christian and ethnic[3] world. Therefore omitting tedious introductions, I will descend to the description of this thrice worthy city, the fairest lady, yea the richest paragon and queen[4] of Christendom.

Such is the rareness of the situation of Venice, that it doth even amaze and drive into admiration all strangers that upon their first arrival behold the same. For it is built altogether upon the water in the innermost gulf of the Adriatic Sea which is commonly called Gulfo di Venetia, and is distant from the main sea about the space of three miles. From the which it is divided by a certain great bank called litto maggior, which is at the least fifty miles in length. This bank is so necessary a defense for the city, that it serveth instead of a strong wall to repulse and reverberate the violence of the furious waves of the sea. For were not this bank interposed like a bulwark betwixt the city and the sea, the waves would utterly overwhelm and deface the city in a moment. [. . .]

The first place of Venice that was inhabited is that which now they call the Rialto, which word is derived from rivus altus, that is, a deep river, because the water is deeper there than about the other islands. [. . .] There is only one bridge to go over the great channel,[5] which is the same that leadeth from St. Mark's to the Rialto, and joyneth together both the banks of the channel. This bridge is commonly called Ponte de Rialto, and is the fairest bridge by many degrees for one arch that ever I saw, read, or heard of. For it is reported that it cost about fourscore thousand crowns, which do make four and twenty thousand pound sterling. Truly, the exact view hereof ministered unto me no small matter of admiration to see a bridge of that length (for it is two hundred foot long, the channel being at the least forty paces broad as I have before written) so curiously compacted together with one only arch. [. . .] It was first built but with timber (as I heard diverse Venetian Gentlemen report) but because that was not correspondent to the magnificence of the other parts of the city, they defaced that, and built this most sump-

[3]Heathen, i.e., non-Christian.

[4]Coryate's note: "I call her not thus in respect of any sovereignty that she hath over other nations, in which sense Rome was in former times called queen of the world, but in regard of her incomparable situation, surpassing wealth, and most magnificent buildings."

[5]Canal.

tuous bridge[6] with squared white stone, having two fair rows of pretty little houses for artificers, which are only shops, not dwelling houses. [. . .]

There are in Venice thirteen ferries or passages, which ferries they commonly call traghetti, where passengers may be transported in a gondola to what place of the city they will. Of which thirteen, one is under this Rialto bridge. But the boatmen that attend at this ferry are the most vicious and licentious varlets about all the city. For if a stranger entereth into one of their gondolas, and doth not presently tell them whither he will go, they will incontinently carry him of their own accord to a religious house[7] forsooth, where his plumes shall be well pulled before he cometh forth again. [. . .]

The fairest place of all the city (which is indeed of that admirable and incomparable beauty, that I think no place whatsoever, either in Christendom or Paganism may compare with it) is the Piazza, that is, the marketplace of St. Mark, or (as our English merchants commorant[8] in Venice do call it) the place of St. Mark, in Latin *Forum* or *Platea Di Marci*. Truly such is the stupendious (to use a strange epitheton[9] for so strange and rare a place as this) glory of it, that at my first entrance thereof it did even amaze or rather ravish my senses. For here is the greatest magnificence of architecture to be seen that any place under the sun doth yield. Here you may both see all manner of fashions of attire, and hear all the languages of Christendom, besides those that are spoken by the barbarous ethnics; the frequency of people being so great twice a day, betwixt six of the clock in the morning and eleven, and again betwixt five in the afternoon and eight, that (as an elegant writer saith of it) a man may very properly call it rather *Orbis* than *Urbis forum*, that is, a marketplace of the world, not of the city. [. . .] Part of the Piazza is worthy to be celebrated for that famous concourse and meeting of so many distinct and sundry nations twice a day, betwixt six and eleven of the clock in the morning, and betwixt five in the afternoon and eight, as I have before mentioned, where also the Venetian long-gowned gentlemen do meet together in great

[6]The new, stone Rialto Bridge was completed in 1591.
[7]Whore house.
[8]Dwelling.
[9]Epithet.

troops. For you shall not see as much as one Venetian there of the patrician rank without his black gown and tippet.[10] There you may see many Polonians, Slavonians, Persians, Grecians, Turks, Jews, Christians of all the famousest regions of Christendom, and each nation distinguished from another by their proper and peculiar habits. A singular shew, and by many degrees the worthiest of all the European Countries. [. . .]

[S]ince I have taken occasion to mention some notable particulars of their women, I will insist further upon that matter and make relation of their courtesans also, as being a thing incident and very proper to this discourse, especially because the name of "a courtesan of Venice" is famoused over all Christendom. [. . .]

As for the number of these Venetian courtesans, it is very great. For it is thought there are of them in the whole city and other adjacent places [. . .] at the least twenty thousand, whereof many are esteemed so loose that they are said to open their quivers to every arrow: a most ungodly thing without doubt that there should be a toleration of such licentious wantons in so glorious, so potent, so renowned a city. For methinks that the Venetians should be daily afraid lest their winking at such uncleanness should be an occasion to draw down upon them God's curses and vengeance from heaven and to consume their city with fire and brimstone, as in times past he did Sodom and Gomorrah. But they not fearing any such thing do grant large dispensations and indulgence to them, and that for two causes. First, *ad vitanda majora mala*.[11] For they think that the chastity of their wives would be sooner assaulted and so consequently they should be capricornified[12] (which of all the indignities in the world the Venetians cannot patiently endure) were it not for these places of evacuation. But I marvel how that should be true though[13] these courtesans were utterly rooted out of the city. For the gentlemen do coop up their wives always within the walls of their houses for fear of those inconveniences as much as if there were no courtesans at all in the city, so that you shall seldom see a

---

[10]Strip of velvet at the neck of the gown.

[11]Latin: to avoid greater evil.

[12]Coryate's coinage, from capricorn (the goat), therefore wearing the horns that signify a cuckold.

[13]Would still be the case even if.

Venetian gentleman's wife but either at the solemnization of a great marriage or at the christening of a Jew or late in the evening rowing in a gondola. The second cause is for that the revenues which they pay unto the Senate for their toleration do maintain a dozen of their galleys (as many reported unto me in Venice) and so save them a great charge. [. . .] So infinite are the allurments of these amorous Calypsos[14] that the fame of them hath drawn many to Venice from some of the remotest parts of Christendom to contemplate their beauties and enjoy their pleasing dalliances. And indeed such is the variety of the delicious objects they minister to their lovers that they want nothing tending to delight. For when you come into one of their palaces (as indeed some few of the principalest of them live in very magnificent and portly buildings fit for the entertainment of a great prince) you seem to enter into the paradise of Venus. For their fairest rooms are most glorious and glittering to behold, the walls about being adorned with most sumptuous tapestry and gilt leather. [. . .] Besides you may see the picture of the noble courtesan most exquisitely drawn. As for herself, she comes to thee decked like the queen and goddess of love, insomuch that thou wilt think she made a late transmigration from Paphos, Cnidos, or Cythera, the ancient habitations of Dame Venus. [. . .]

Though these things will at the first sight seem unto thee most delectable allurement, yet if thou shalt rightly weigh them in the scales of a mature judgment thou wilt say with the wise man, and that very truly, that they are like a golden ring in a swine's snout. Moreover she will endeavor to enchant thee partly with her melodious notes that she warbles out upon her lute, which she fingers with as laudable a stroke as many men that are excellent professors in the noble science of music; and partly with that heart-tempting harmony of her voice. Also thou wilt find the Venetian courtesan (if she be a selected woman indeed) a good rhetorician and a most elegant discourser, so that if she cannot move thee with all these foresaid delights, she will assay thy constancy with her rhetorical tongue. And to that end she may minister unto thee the stronger temptations to come to her lure, she will show thee her chamber of recreation where thou shalt see all manner of pleasing objects, as many fair painted coffers wherewith it is granished round about, a curi-

---

[14]In Homer's *Odyssey*, Calypso tempted Odysseus to stay on her island and forsake his voyage home.

ous milk-white canopy of needle work, a silk quilt embroidered with gold, and generally all her bedding sweetly perfumed.

Lewis Lewkenor

Lewis Lewkenor used the introduction to his English translation (1599) of Cardinal Gasparo Contarini's The Commonwealth and Government of Venice *(1551) to praise Venice's government and, obliquely, to suggest a model for England. A member of one of Venice's most influential families, Contarini (1483–1542) served important roles in the city's government. He describes in great detail the structure and workings of what he and many others both in Venice and abroad considered a model of effective government. Although very far from being a democracy, the commonwealth did admit representation from various classes of citizens, and the power of its head, the Duke, was more constrained than the English monarchy's.*

The virtues of a mixed form of government, as opposed to a monarchy, appealed to the translator, Lewkenor, whose lavish praise carries an implicit critique of his own nation's government. In this respect, "To the Reader" qualifies as one of the earliest documents in the tradition of English republicanism. Lewkenor's Venice is the ideal Venice—Venice the Just, a city-state that combines the best elements of all forms of government. This idealization contrasts with other contemporary views of Venice as a place of licentiousness and treachery.

from "To the Reader," the preface to Contarini, *The Commonwealth and Government of Venice*[1]

[Lewkenor has been defending travel writers and travelers to doubters of their tales of foreign wonders. He says that he has taken every opportunity to talk to travelers]

. . . wherein I always especially observed one thing, that whether they with whom I conferred were Englishmen, or Frenchmen, Spaniards, Germans, Polonians, yea or Italians born in the bordering provinces, as of each sort I have been acquainted with many, though sundry of them have been in the farthest parts of Asia and

---

[1]Lewis Lewkenor, "To the Reader," in Gasparo Contarini, *The Commonwealth and Government of Venice*, trans. Lewkenor, London, 1599.

Africa, yet coming once to speak of the city of Venice, they would enforce their speech to the highest of admiration, as being a thing of the greatest worthiness, and most infinitely remarkable, that they had seen in the whole course of their travels.

Some of the youthfuller sort would extol to the skies their humanity towards strangers,[2] the delicacy of their entertainments, the beauty, pomp, and daintiness of their women, and finally the infinite superfluities of all pleasure and delight.

Other of a graver humor would dilate of the greatness of their empire, the gravity of their prince, the majesty of their Senate, the unviolableness of the laws, their zeal in religion, and lastly their moderation and equity, wherein they govern such subjected provinces as are under their dominion, binding them thereby in a faster bond of obedience than all the citadels, garrisons, or whatsoever other tyrannical inventions could ever have brought them unto.

These and such like reports have from time to time kindled within me so great a desire to acquaint myself with the particularities of this famous city, that though during the time of my travel (destinate to more unhappy courses)[3] I was not so fortunate as to be a beholder of the glory thereof, yet I have not omitted from time to time to gather such observations as well by reading the best and choicest authors entreating[4] thereof, as also by conference with sundry well-experienced gentlemen as might not only satisfy the curiosity of my own desire, but also deliver unto other[s] a clear and exact knowledge of every particularity of note, that thereunto appertaineth, which cannot as I imagine (the nobleness of the subject considered) but be pleasing and agreeable to the best conceited spirits, who may out of this commonwealth of Venice gather and comprehend the fruit of all whatsoever other governments throughout the world that are of any fame or excellency: for in the person of the Venetian prince, who sitting at the helm of this city shineth in all exterior ornaments of royal dignity (nevertheless both he and his authority being wholly subjected to the laws) they may see a strange and unusual form of most excellent monarchy.

Then, what more perfect and lively pattern of a well ordered aristocratical government can there in the world be expressed than

[2]Foreigners.
[3]Destined for less fortunate results.
[4]Treating.

that of their Council of Pregati, or Senators, which being the only chief and principal members of all supreme power, yet have not any power, mean[s], or possibility at all to tyrannize, or to pervert their country['s] laws.

Lastly, if they desire to see a most rare and matchless precedent of a democracy or popular estate, let them behold their Great Council, consisting of at least 3000 gentlemen, whereupon the highest strength and mightiness of the estate absolutely relieth, notwithstanding which number all things are ordered with so divine a peaceableness, and so without all tumult and confusion that it rather seemeth to be an assembly of angels than of men.

In fine,[5] whithersoever you turn your eyes, they shall not encounter anything but objects of admiration: their justice is pure and uncorrupted; their penal laws most unpardonably[6] executed; their encouragements to virtue infinite, especially by their distribution of offices and dignities, which is ordered in such so secret, strange, and intricate a sort, that it virtually overreached the subtlety of all ambitious practices, never falling upon any but such as are by the whole assembly allowed for men of greatest wisdom, virtue, and integrity of life. [. . .]

[W]hat is there that can carry a greater disproportion with common rules of experience that unweaponed men in gowns should with such happiness of success give direction and law to many mighty and warlike armies both by sea and land, and that a single city unwalled and alone should command and overtop mighty kingdoms, and such famous far-extended provinces, remaining ever itself invincible; and long-robed citizens to be served, yea and sued unto for entertainment by the greatest princes and peers of Italy. Amidst which infinite affluence of glory and unmeasurable mightiness of power, of which there are in sovereignty partakers about 3000 gentlemen, yet is there not one among them to be found that doth aspire to any greater appellation of honor, or higher title of dignity, than to be called a gentleman of Venice, including in the same the height of all imaginable honor, so dear unto this generous people is the name and love of their country.

And lastly, though not least to be wondered at, they have (as it were entertaining a league and intelligence with the heavenly

[5]In summary.
[6]Strictly.

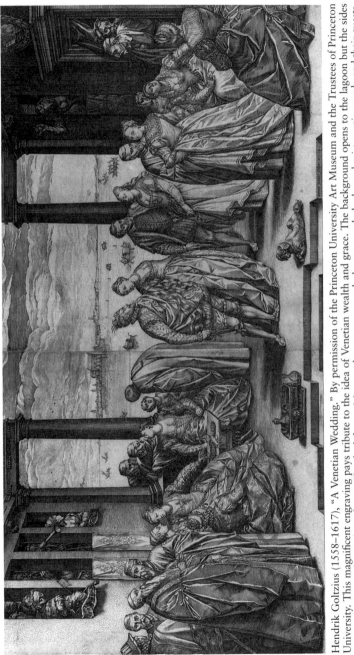

Hendrik Goltzius (1558–1617), "A Venetian Wedding." By permission of the Princeton University Art Museum and the Trustees of Princeton University. This magnificent engraving pays tribute to the idea of Venetian wealth and grace. The background opens to the lagoon but the sides suggest the form of an indoor theater. On the left, musicians and spectators watch the spectacularly dressed aristocratic couple and their guests. Portia and Bassanio might be imagined in such a scene, but there is no place here for Shylock.

powers) preserved this royal city of theirs this thirteen hundred years, since the first foundation thereof, in an estate so perpetually flourishing and unblemished that though sundry and mighty kings and emperors, being enamored with her beauty and goodliness, have with marvelous endeavor and multitude of armies sought to possess themselves of so fair and precious a prey, yet have they hitherto kept her like a pure and untouched virgin, free from the taste or violence of any foreign enforcement. [. . .] The rest of the world honoreth her in the name of a virgin, a name though in all places most sacred and venerable, yet in no place more dearly and religiously to be reverenced than with us,[7] who have thence derived our blessedness, which I beseech God may long continue among us.

Fynes Moryson (1566–1630)

Fynes Moryson (1566–1630) traveled widely in Ireland, Europe, the Middle East, and Asia, sometimes accompanied by his brother, Richard, a high administrator of the English colonial government in Ireland. Fynes Moryson wrote about his travels in a huge work called, for the sake of brevity, An Itinerary (1617). Portions of that work remained unpublished until the twentieth century, when they were edited by Charles Hughes as Shakespeare's Europe *(1903), from which the following selection is drawn. Moryson's attitude toward Venice (and Italy as a whole, with which he frequently conflates Venice) reflects many typical English prejudices of the time: his Italians are lusty, jealous, bloodthirsty—things that a good English Protestant supposedly is not. Moryson's description of Venetian life is a stark contrast to Lewis Lewkenor's idealized portrait.*

from *An Itinerary*[1]

The Justice, Laws, and Judgments in the State of Venice

The Senate of Venice is most reverend for the gray heads, gravity and comeliness of their persons, and their stately habits but for

---

[7]The English, who are ruled by Elizabeth, "the virgin queen."

[1]Fynes Moryson, "Unpublished Chapters from *Itinerary* (1617)," in *Shakespeare's Europe*, ed. Charles Hughes (London: Sherratt and Hughes, 1903), excerpts from pp. 163–165, 405–410, 415, 423–424.

nothing more than their strict observing of justice. They have a law that in time of Carnival or Shrovetide, no man that is masked may wear a sword, because being unknown, he might thereby have means to kill his enemy on the sudden, and while I was in Italy a foreign gentleman upon a fancy to mock the officers of justice, being masked wore a wooden lath like a sword. The officers apprehended him, and finding it to be a lath, yet carried him to the magistrate, who with a grave countenance said to him, *Non burlar' con la Giustitia, Veh*: "Jest not with the Justice, mark me." And he found that he had mocked himself more then the officers, for he paid not a few crowns before he could be freed by mediation of great friends. [. . .]

Adulterers are punished (as other like crimes) according to the civil and canon laws, but the Italians, impatient to bring their honor under public trials, dispatch the punishment of all jealousies by private revenge, killing not only the men so provoking them but their wives' sisters or daughters dishonoring themselves in those kinds. Yea brothers, knowing their sisters to be unchaste when they are married and out of their own house, yet will make this offense known to their husbands, that they may kill them. Whereof examples are frequent, as namely of a Florentine gentleman, who understanding from his wife's brother that she had dishonored them by adultery, took her forth in a coach having only a priest with them, and when they came to a fit place gave her a short time to confess her sins to the priest and then killed her with his own hands. And howsoever in this case it is like she confessed the crime, yet in this and like cases the magistrate useth not to inquire after these revenges, which the Italians' nature hath drawn into custom, besides that many are done secretly without danger to be revealed.

Among other high crimes it is not rare to hear blasphemous speeches in Italy, and the State of Venice is much to be praised for the most severe justice they use against such offenders, having a law to cut out their tongues. Yea while I lived there some roaring boys[2] one night went out upon a wager who should do the greatest villainy, and when they had done most wicked things at last they came all to the window of the Pope's Nuncio,[3] where they sung horrible

[2]Upperclass hoodlums.
[3]Ambassador.

blasphemies against our Lord, his blessed mother, and the apostle St. Peter. The next morning all these rascals (so I call them, whereof most notwithstanding were gentlemen) had escaped out of the city; only two were taken, whom I did see executed in this manner: their hands were cut off in four places where they did the greatest villainies, their tongues were cut out under the window of the Pope's Nuncio, and so they were brought into the marketplace of St. Mark, where upon a scaffold they were beheaded with an axe falling by a pulley, which done, the scaffold and their bodies were burned and the ashes thrown into the sea.

Civil Judgments in the State of Venice

For civil judgments I remember a stone at Padua called *lapis turpitudinis* (that is, the stone of filthiness) because upon market days such were set upon it with naked backsides, as had run into debt having no means to repay it. [. . .] Among other civil judgments they give singular justice in cases of debt and have particular judges over merchants' bankrupting, who give the creditors security to keep them from prison, and cite such bankrupts as fly, selling their goods and dividing them equally among the creditors and preventing all frauds [that] may be used. So as if they find other men's goods deposited in their hands they keep them for the owners. In which case myself when I passed from thence into Turkey, and also my brother, leaving our chests with our apparel and books in the hands of a merchant, who shortly after proved bankrupt, the magistrate kept our goods safe, and when I returned, did restore to me without any charge, not only my own goods, but also my brother's who died in the journey. [. . .]

[T]he Italians, above all other nations, most practice revenge by treasons, and especially are skillful in making and giving poisons. [. . .]

For fleshly lusts, the very Turks (whose carnal religion alloweth them)[4] are not so much transported therewith as the Italians are (in their restraint of civil laws and the dreadful law of God). A man of these northerly parts[5] can hardly believe without the testimony of

[4]According to Moryson, the Turks' religion is fleshly, not spiritual, and permits sexual licentiousness.

[5]England.

his own eyes and ears how chastity is laughed at among them and hissed out of all good company, or how desperate adventures they will make to achieve disordinate[6] desire in these kinds. [. . .] In Italy marriage is indeed a yoke, and that not easy, but so grievous, as brethren nowhere better agreeing yet contend among themselves to be free from marriage, and he that of free will or by persuasion will take a wife to continue their posterity, shall be sure to have his wife and her honor as much respected by the rest, as if she were their own wife or sister, beside their liberal contribution to maintain her, so as themselves may be free to take the pleasure of women at large.[7] By which liberty (if men only respect this world) they live more happily than other nations. For in those frugal commonwealths the unmarried live at a small rate of expenses and they make small conscience of fornication, esteemed a small sin and easily remitted by confessors. Whereas other nations will live at any charge to be married and will labor and suffer wants, yea beg with a wife, rather then have the sting of conscience and infamy by whoring. The women of honor in Italy, I mean wives and virgins, are much sooner inflamed with love, be it lawful or unlawful, than the women of other nations. For being locked up at home and covered with veils when they go abroad[8] and kept from any conversation with men and being wooed by dumb[9] signs, as walking twice a day by their houses kissing of the posts thereof and like fopperies, they are more stirred up with the sight and much more with the flattering and dissembling speeches of men, and more credulous in flattering their own desires, by thinking the said poor actions of wooing to be signs of true love, than the women of other nations having free conversation with men. In general the men of all sorts are carried with fierce affections to forbidden lusts, and to those most which are most forbidden, most kept from them, and with greatest cost and danger to be obtained. And because they are barred not only the speech and conversation but the least sight of their love (all which are allowed men of other nations), they are carried rather with a blind rage of passion and a strong imagination of their own

[6]Inordinate.
[7]Commit adultery.
[8]In public.
[9]Silent.

brain [rather] than with true contemplation of virtues, or [with] the power of beauty to adore them as images rather than love them as women. And as now they spare no cost, and will run great dangers to obtain their lustful desires, so would they pursue them to very madness had they not the most natural remedy of this passion ready at hand to allay their desires, namely harlots, whom they call courtesans, having beauty and youth and whatsoever they can imagine in their mistress, besides the pleasure of change more to delight them, so driving out love with love, as one nail with another. [. . .]

In Italy as adultery seldom or never falls within the punishment of the law, because the Italians' nature carries them to such an high degree of private revenge as the law cannot inflict greater (which private revenge by murder upon just grounds of jealousy is commonly taken secretly, and if known, yet winked at and favored by the magistrate, in his own nature approving as well the revenge as the secrecy thereof for avoiding shame) so fornication in Italy is not a sin winked at, but rather may be called an allowed trade. For princes and states raise great tributes[10] from it. [. . .] At Venice the tribute to the state from courtesans was thought to exceed three hundred thousand crowns yearly. And the Pope's holiness made no less gain from this fair trade at Rome. [. . .]

[10]Taxes.

Jews in England and Venice

The easiest way for an Englishman of Shakespeare's time to meet a Jew was to travel abroad. Officially all Jews had been banished in 1290. Before that, Jews were permitted to live in England as long as they served the crown's economic purpose: they were forced into the role of financiers, only to be milked of their profits by their royal patron. The Jews' special status with the king made them more than usually hated by the king's political and economic rivals. When royal greed bankrupted the Jewish community and made them useless for extortion, King Edward I took the popular and holy course of expelling them. In the diaspora that followed, some English Jews went to Spain, which banished them in 1492 if they were not willing to convert to Christianity. Others joined the Jewish populations in Italy and eastern Europe. Muslim countries were relatively more welcoming than Christian countries, and many of the displaced European Jews found homes in the Ottoman Empire, which stretched from the Balkans to the Turkish capital in Constantinople (now Istanbul) through the coastal Middle East and north Africa. Despite their banishment, a very few Jews still lived in England, but they led secret lives, often as nominal converts, always fearful of being outed by their Christian neighbors. For most Englishmen, Jews existed more as a nasty rumor or an ethnic joke than as ordinary people. The repository of ancient fears and fantasies, they supposedly had brought upon themselves the status of permanent outsider.

Shakespeare's decision to create the vividly peculiar character of Shylock is therefore remarkable. Scholars have speculated that current events may have motivated him. In 1594, Roderigo Lopez, a Portuguese physician of Jewish descent, was executed for supposedly plotting the murder of his patient, Queen Elizabeth. Christopher Marlowe's *The Jew of Malta* was revived that same year; its unusual success may have owed something to the Lopez affair, and some scholars speculate that it may have prompted Shakespeare to write his (very different) play. And Shakespeare may have heard or read accounts of Venetian Jews, like those by

Thomas Coryate. But none of these speculations can "explain" *The Merchant of Venice*. Nor can Christian theology, although it is necessary for understanding the play. Shylock's faith in the efficacy of "the law" ("My deeds upon my head! I crave the law" [4.1.203]) and Portia's appeal to the quality of what she calls "mercy" reflect a Christian understanding of the difference between the Old Testament and the New. Under God's law, humanity stood condemned by Adam's original fault, but Christ's sacrifice fulfilled the requirements of that law and created the possibility of salvation through faith in God's mercy. The romance plot of *The Merchant of Venice* is shadowed by a dramatization of the inevitable tension between the principles of justice and mercy. But just as it is often difficult in real-life judicial decisions to balance the competing demands of strict law and the desire for forgiveness, so in Shakespeare's play the strain of the comic resolution remains troublingly evident. Shylock's human claims on us are too great—he refuses to be merely a symbol rather than a person—and the lessons of history are too powerful for any allegorical scheme to stabilize the volatile compound of Shakespeare's play.

The selections that follow begin in history, with accounts of the expulsion of Jews and of the Lopez affair; move to writings about Jews by Shakespeare's contemporaries and then to excerpts from two very different "Jew" plays; and conclude with dramas of justice and mercy.

Raphael Holinshed (d. 1580)

Chronicles of England, Scotland, and Ireland was published in 1578 and reissued, with enlargements, in 1587. Raphael Holinshed and his contributing authors created a year-by-year record of events (and myths and moralized stories), serving in part to justify the Protestant reigns of Henry VIII and his daughter Elizabeth. At the same time, the Chronicles *are remarkable for the extent to which they acknowledge uncertainty and admit competing interpretations. (Notice in the excerpt, for instance, in the story of the ship's master who drowned his cargo of Jews, that "some have written" he was rewarded "but others affirm" he was hanged.) Holinshed's* Chronicles *were well known to Shakespeare, who drew on them for his English history plays.*

The following selections recount events leading up to the expulsion of the Jews in 1290. The first one may seem surprisingly sympathetic to the "sore impoverished" Jews, but the context is a broader denunciation of Edward's rapacity toward all his subjects. The second selection recounts the apocryphal story of the martyrdom of little Hugh of Lincoln. It is one of a remarkably large repertory of stories about ritual murders of Christian children. In Chaucer's Canterbury Tales *the Prioress tells a story set vaguely in "Asia" about a little boy murdered by Jews as he goes through the ghetto singing a holy song; at the end of the tale, the Prioress mentions Hugh of Lincoln "slain by cursed Jews only a little while ago." Such stories, absurd as they are, still have, even in our own times, the power to inflame irrational prejudice.*

from *Chronicles of England, Scotland, and Ireland*[1]

Thirty-ninth year of the reign of Henry III (1255)

"The king demandeth money of the Jews"[2]

[W]hereas he stood in great need of money, he required by way of a tallage[3] eight thousand marks of the Jews, charging them on pain of hanging not to defer that payment. The Jews, sore impoverished with grievous and often payments, excused themselves by the pope's usurers[4] and reproved plainly the king's excessive taking of money, as well of his Christian subjects as of them. The king, on the other side, to let it be known that he taxed not his people without just occasion and upon necessity that drove him

---

[1] Raphael Holinshed, *Chronicles of England, Scotland, and Ireland*. London, 1587, pp. 251–252, 285.

[2] Holinshed's marginal note.

[3] Tax.

[4] Meaning unclear: possibly, they excused themselves because the pope's usurers had taken too much business from them; or they suggested that the king get money from the pope's usurers instead of them.

thereto, confessed openly that he was indebted in his bonds obligatory[5] in three hundred thousand marks; and again, the yearly revenues assigned to his son Prince Edward arose to the sum of fifteen thousand marks and above, where the revenues that belonged unto the crown were greatly diminished, in such wise that without the aid of his subjects he should never be able to come out of debt. To be short, when he had fleeced the Jews to the quick, he set them to farm unto his brother,[6] Earl Richard, that he might pull off skin and all; but yet considering their poverty, he spared them and, nevertheless, to relieve his brother's necessity, upon a pawn he lent him an huge mass of money.[7] These shifts did the king use from time to time, not caring with what huge exactions and impositions he burdened the inhabitants of his land, whereby he procured to himself the name of an oppressor and covetous scraper. [. . .]

Fortieth year of the reign of Henry III (1256)

"Jews accused and executed for crucifying
a child at Lincoln named Hugh"[8]

[U]pon the two and twentieth of November were brought unto Westminster a hundred and two Jews from Lincoln that were accused for the crucifying of a child in the last summer, in despight[9] of Christ's religion. They were upon their examination sent to the Tower. The child which they had so crucified was named Hugh, about an eight years of age. They kept him ten days after they got him into their hands, sending in the mean time unto diverse other places of the realm for others of their nation to be present at the crucifying of him. The murder came out by

---

[5]He owed money on outstanding bonds.

[6]He gave his brother the right to take a percentage of all the Jews' earnings.

[7]The king, having taxed everyone on the grounds that he was impoverished, lent his brother money in exchange for a guarantee, or pawn, in case his brother did not repay.

[8]Holinshed's marginal note.

[9]Out of contempt for.

the diligent search made by the mother of the child, who found his body in a well on the back side of the Jew's house where he was crucified; for she had learned that her son was lastly seen playing with certain Jews' children of like age to him before the door of the same Jew. The Jew that was owner of the house was apprehended, and being brought before Sir John de Lexinton, upon promise of pardon confessed the whole matter. For they used yearly (if they could come by their prey) to crucify one Christian child or other. The king, upon knowledge had hereof, would not pardon this Jew that had so confessed the matter but caused him to be executed at Lincoln, who coming to the place where he should die, opened more matter concerning such as were of counsel and present at the crucifying of the poor innocent. Whereupon at length also eighteen of them that were so brought to London were convinced, adjudged, and hanged, the others remaining long in prison.

Eighteenth year of the reign of Edward I (1290)

"The Jews banished out of England"[10]

In [this] year was a parliament holden[11] at Westminster, wherein [. . .] it was also decreed that all the Jews should avoid out of the land, in consideration whereof a fifteenth was granted to the king,[12] and so hereupon were the Jews banished out of all the king's dominions, and never since could they obtain any privileges to return hither again. All their goods not moveable were confiscated, with their taillies and obligations[13]; but all other their goods that were moveable, together with their coin of gold and silver, the king licensed them to have and convey to them. A sort of the richest of them, being shipped with their treasure in a mighty tall ship which they had hired, when the same was under sail and got down the Thames toward the mouth of the river beyond Quinborough, the master mariner bethought him of a

---

[10]Holinshed's marginal note.

[11]Held.

[12]A tax of fifteen percent (presumably to reward the king for banishing the Jews).

[13]The estates that were legally due them (entailled) and the debts that were owed to them.

wile and caused his men to cast anchor, and rode at the same till the ship by ebbing of the stream remained on the dry sands. The master herewith enticed the Jews to walk out with him on land for recreation. And at length, when he understood the tide to be coming in, he got him back to the ship, whither he was drawn up by a cord. The Jews made not so much haste as he did because they were not aware of the danger. But when they perceived how the matter stood they cried to him for help; howbeit he told them that they ought to cry rather unto Moses, by whose conduct their fathers passed through the Red Sea, and therefore, if they would call to him for help he was able enough to help them out of those raging floods which now came in upon them. They cried indeed but no succor appeared, and so they were swallowed up in water. The master returned with the ship and told the king how he had used the matter, and had both thanks and reward, as some have written. But others affirm (and more truly as should seem) that diverse of those mariners which dealt so wickedly against the Jews were hanged for their wicked practice, and so received a just reward for their fraudulent and mischievous dealing.

Martin Luther (1483–1546)

This brief selection is an extreme statement of the anti-Semitism so common throughout the Europe of Shakespeare's time. By comparison, Gratiano's taunting and Antonio's spitting on Shylock's Jewish gaberdine seem mild expressions of distaste. What makes the selection historically interesting is that its author is one of the towering figures of western religious thought. Martin Luther was a German monk who grew increasingly incensed at the corruption of the Roman Catholic Church. The "Ninety-Five Theses" he posted on the door of the church in Wittenberg, where he was a professor of theology, gave the major impetus to the protest movement that became the Protestant Reformation. Luther's book-length screed against Jews is a minuscule part of his enormous body of theological work. It should be read in historical context. Unfortunately, that context is not only the sixteenth century but all the centuries when these violent ideas have been repeated in one language or another.

from *On the Jews and Their Lies*, trans. Martin H. Bertram[1]

We Christians must not tolerate that they [deny Christ's divinity] in their public synagogues, in their books, and in their behavior, openly under our noses, and within our hearing, in our own country, houses, and regimes. If we do, we together with the Jews and on their account will lose God the Father and his dear Son, who purchases us at such cost with his holy blood, and we will be eternally lost, which God forbid!

Accordingly, it must and dare not be considered a trifling matter but a most serious one to seek counsel against this and to save our souls from the Jew, that is, from the devil and from eternal death. My advice is:

First, that their synagogues be burned down, and that all who are able toss in sulphur and pitch: it would be good if someone could also throw in hellfire. [. . .] Second, that all their books—their prayer books, their Talmudic writings, also the entire Bible—be taken from them, not leaving them one leaf, and that these be preserved for those who may be converted. [. . .] Third, that they be forbidden on pain of death to praise God, to give thanks, to pray, and to teach publicly among us and in our country. [. . .] Fourth, that they be forbidden to utter the name of God within our hearing. [. . .]

But what will happen even if we do burn down the Jews' synagogues and forbid them publicly to praise God, to pray, to teach, to utter God's name? They will still keep doing it in secret. If we know that they are doing this in secret, it is the same as if they were doing it publicly. For our knowledge of their secret doings and our toleration of them implies that they are not secret after all, and thus our conscience is encumbered with it before God. So let us beware. In my opinion the problem must be resolved thus: If we wish to wash our hands of the Jews' blasphemy and not share in their guilt, we have to part company with them. They must be driven from our country. Let them think of their fatherland; then they need no longer wail and lie before God against us that we are holding them captive, nor need we then any longer complain that they are burdening us with their blasphemy and their usury. This is the most natural and the best course of action, which will safeguard the interest of both parties.

[1]Martin Luther, *On the Jews and Their Lies* (1543), trans. Martin H. Bertram, in *Luther's Works*. Philadelphia: Fortress Press, 1971, pp. 137–306 (excerpt from pp. 285–288).

William Camden (1551–1623)

This excerpt is about the execution of Roderigo Lopez for conspiracy to murder Queen Elizabeth. William Camden was a prolific and influential English historian; his major work, Britannia, *was published (in Latin) in 1586. Also originally in Latin was* Annals, or The History of the Most Renowned and Victorious Princess Elizabeth, Late Queen of England. *The English translation was printed in 1630 after Camden's death. The fact that Dr. Lopez came from a Jewish family figures prominently in most contemporary accounts of the scandal, although the alleged plot was hatched on behalf of Catholic Spain. The laughter in the last line of the selection is a noteworthy detail.*

from *Annals, or The History of the Most Renowned and Victorious Princess Elizabeth, Late Queen of England* (1630)[1]

[1594] As these learned English fugitives[2] studied to advance the Infanta of Spain[3] to the scepter of England by writing, so others of their number secretly attempted the same by the sword, sending privily certain murderers to kill Queen Elizabeth, and some Spaniards attempted it by poison. The Spaniards suspecting the fidelity of the English in a matter of so great weight, used the help of Roderigo Lopez of the Jewish sect, the Queen's physician for her household, and of Stephen Ferreira Gama and Emmanuel Loisie, [Portuguese] (for many [Portuguese] in those days crept into England as retainers to the exiled Don Antonio[4]),who by means of letters intercepted, being apprehended, were about the end of February arraigned in Guild Hall at London and charged by their own confessions to have conspired to make away the Queen by poison. Lopez, having been for a long time a man of noted fidelity, was not once suspected (save that outlandish[5] physicians may by bribes and corruption be easily made poisoners and traitors). He confessed that he was drawn by Andrada, a Por-

---

[1]William Camden, *Annals, or The History of the Most Renowned and Victorious Princess Elizabeth, Late Queen of England*, trans. Robert Norton, 3rd ed. London, 1635.

[2]Camden has been talking about English Catholics who plotted against Elizabeth from abroad.

[3]Daughter of the Spanish King Philip II.

[4]Claimant to the throne of Portugal against Philip II of Spain.

[5]Foreign.

tug[uese], to employ his best and secret service for the King of Spain; that he had received from his most inward counselor, Christopher Moro,[6] a rich jewel; that he had diverse times advertised[7] the Spaniard of such things as he could learn; that at length upon a contract for 50,000 ducats he had promised to poison the Queen. [. . .]

At the bar, Lopez spake not much but cried out that Ferreira and Emmanuel were wholly composed of fraud and lying; that he intended no hurt against the Queen, but hated the gifts of a tyrant; that he had given that jewel to the Queen which was sent to him from the Spaniard; and that he had no other meaning but to deceive the Spaniard and wipe him of his money. [. . .]

The rest spake nothing from themselves, many times accusing Lopez. They were all of them condemned and after three months put to death at Tyburn, Lopez affirming that he had loved the Queen as he loved Jesus Christ, which from a man of the Jewish profession was heard not without laughter.

Thomas Coryate (1577–1617)

In Venice and Constantinople, Thomas Coryate made special efforts to meet the Jewish people he could not meet at home. (For Coryate, see p. 97.) Standing in the ghetto trying to convince the Jews of their theological errors, he may seem comical, but he is also admirable in his relative openness to experience. He is warmly grateful to Amis, the Jew who is his host in Constantinople, although it is not likely that he would have called Amis his "countryman" had he met him in England. Coryate's fascination with Jewish worship, the rite of circumcision, the observation of the holiday of Succoth, and so on is less a sign of premature multiculturalism than an attempt to discover how accurately modern Jews conform to biblical practice as Coryate understands it.

[6]The Spanish secretary of state.
[7]Advised.

from *Crudities*[1]

[Coryate and the Jews of Venice]

I was at a place where the whole fraternity of the Jews dwelleth together, which is called the ghetto, being an island, for it is enclosed round about with water. It is thought there are of them in all betwixt five and six thousand. They are distinguished and discerned from the Christians by their habits[2] on their heads; for some of them do wear hats and those red, only those Jews that are born in the western parts of the world, as in Italy etc., but the eastern Jews, being otherwise called the Levantine[3] Jews, which are born in Jerusalem, Alexandria, Constantinople, etc., wear turbans upon their heads as the Turks do; but the difference is this: the Turks wear white, the Jews yellow. By that word *turban* I understand a roll of fine linen wrapped together upon their heads, which serveth them instead of hats, whereof many have been often worn by the Turks in London.

They have divers synagogues in their ghetto, at the least seven, where all of them, both men, women and children, do meet together upon their Sabbath, which is Saturday, to the end to do their devotion, and serve God in their kind, each company having a several synagogue. In the midst of the synagogue they have a round seat made of wainscot, having eight open spaces therein, at two whereof, which are at the sides, they enter into the seat as by doors. The Levite[4] that readeth the law to them, hath before him at the time of divine service an exceeding long piece of parchment,[5] rolled up upon two wooden handles, in which is written the whole sum and contents of Moses' law in Hebrew: that doth he (being discerned[6] from the lay people only by wearing of a red cap, whereas the others do wear red hats) pronounce before the congregation not

[1]Thomas Coryate, *Coryat's Crudities*. Glasgow: James MacLehose and Sons, 1905, pp. 370–376.

[2]Garments.

[3]Coryate's note: "They are so called from the Latin word *levare*, which sometimes signifieth as much as *elevare*, that is to elevate or lift up. Because the sun elevateth and raiseth it self in height every morning in the East herehence also cometh the Levant sea, for the Eastern Sea."

[4]Member of the priestly tribe of Levi.

[5]The Torah.

[6]Differentiated.

by a sober, distinct, and orderly reading, but by an exceeding loud yelling, undecent roaring, and as it were a beastly bellowing of it forth; and that after such a confused and huddling manner, that I think the hearers can very hardly understand him. Sometimes he cries out alone, and sometimes again some others, serving as it were his clerks hard without his seat and within, do roar with him, but so that his voice (which he straineth so high as if he sung for a wager) drowneth all the rest. Amongst others that are within the room with him, one is he that cometh purposely thither from his seat, to the end to read the law, and pronounce some part of it with him, who when he is gone, another riseth from his seat, and cometh thither to supply his room. This order they keep from the beginning of service to the end.

One custom I observed amongst them very irreverent and profane, that none of them, either when they enter the synagogue, or when they sit down in their places, or when they go forth again, do any reverence or obeisance answerable to such a place of the worship of God, either by uncovering their heads, kneeling, or any other external gesture, but boldly dash into the room with their Hebrew books in their hands, and presently sit in their places, without any more ado. Every one of them whatsoever he be, man or child, weareth a kind of light yellowish veil made of linsey-woolsey[7] (as I take it) over his shoulders, something worse than our courser holland, which reacheth a little beneath the middle of their backs.[8] They have a great company of candlesticks in each synagogue made partly of glass and partly of brass and pewter, which hang square about their synagogue, for in that form is their synagogue built; of their candlesticks I told above sixty in the same synagogue.

I observed some few of those Jews, especially some of the Levantines, to be such goodly and proper men, that then I said to myself our English proverb "to look like a Jew" (whereby is meant sometimes a weather beaten warp-faced fellow, sometimes a frenetic and lunatic person, sometimes one discontented) is not true. For indeed I noted some of them to be most elegant and sweet featured persons, which gave me occasion the more to lament their religion. [. . .] In the room wherein they celebrate their divine ser-

---

[7]Coarse woolen material.

[8]Coryate refers to the prayer shawl, the *tallith* or *talles*.

vice, no women sit, but have a loft or gallery proper to themselves only, where I saw many Jewish women, whereof some were as beautiful as ever I saw, and so gorgeous in their apparel, jewels, chains of gold, and rings adorned with precious stones, that some of our English countesses do scarce exceed them, having marvelous long trains like princesses that are borne up by waiting women serving for the same purpose: an argument to prove that many of the Jews are very rich.

One thing they observe in their service which is utterly condemned by our Savior Christ, that is a very tedious babbling, and an often repetition of one thing, which cloyed mine ears so much that I could not endure them any longer, having heard them at least an hour; for their service is almost three hours long. They are very religious in two things only, and no more, in that they worship no images, and that they keep their sabbath so strictly, that upon that day they will neither buy nor sell, nor do any secular, profane, or irreligious exercise (I would to God our Christians would imitate the Jews herein); no, not so much as dress their victuals, which is always done the day before, but dedicate and consecrate themselves wholly to the strict worship of God.

Their circumcision they observe as duly as they did any time betwixt Abraham (in whose time it was first instituted) and the incarnation of Christ. For they use to circumcise every male child when he is eight days old, with a stony knife. But I had not the opportunity to see it. Likewise they keep many of those ancient feasts that were instituted by Moses. Amongst the rest the feast of tabernacles is very ceremoniously observed by them. From swine's flesh they abstain as their ancient forefathers were wont to do, in which the Turks do imitate them at this day. Truly it is a most lamentable case for a Christian to consider the damnable estate of these miserable Jews, in that they reject the true Messias[9] and Savior of their souls, hoping to be saved rather by the observation of those Mosaical ceremonies (the date whereof was fully expired at Christ's incarnation) than by the merits of the Savior of the world, without whom all mankind shall perish. And as pitiful it is to see that few of them living in Italy are converted to the Christian religion. For this I understand is the main impediment to their conversion: All their

[9]Messiah.

goods are confiscated as soon as they embrace Christianity; and this I heard is the reason: because whereas many of them do raise their fortunes by usury, in so much that they do not only shear, but also flay many a poor Christian's estate by their griping extortion, it is therefore decreed by the Pope, and other free Princes in whose territories they live, that they shall make a restitution of all their ill gotten goods, and so disclog their souls and consciences, when they are admitted by holy baptism into the bosom of Christ's church. Seeing then when their goods are taken from them at their conversion, they are left even naked and destitute of their means of maintenance, there are fewer Jews converted to Christianity in Italy, than in any country of Christendom.

[Coryate argues theology in the ghetto]

But now I will make relation of that which I promised in my treatise of Padua, I mean my discourse with the Jews about their religion. For when as walking in the court of the ghetto, I casually met with a certain learned Jewish rabbi that spake good Latin, I insinuated myself after some few terms of complement into conference with him, and asked him his opinion of Christ, and why he did not receive him for his Messias. He made me the same answer that the Turk did at Lyons, of whom I have before spoken, that Christ forsooth was a great prophet, and in that respect as highly to be esteemed as any prophet amongst the Jews that ever lived before him; but derogated altogether from his divinity, and would not acknowledge him for the Messias and Savior of the world, because he came so contemptibly, and not with that pomp and majesty that beseemed the redeemer of mankind. I replied that we Christians do, and will even to the effusion of our vital blood, confess him to be the true and only Messias of the world, seeing he confirmed his doctrine while he was here on earth with such an innumerable multitude of divine miracles which did most infallibly testify his divinity; and that they themselves, who are Christ's irreconcilable enemies, could not produce any authority, either out of Moses, the Prophets, or any other authentic author, to strengthen their opinion concerning the temporal kingdom of the Messias, seeing it was foretold to be spiritual; and told him, that Christ did as a spiritual king reign over his subjects in conquering their spiritual enemies the flesh, the world, and the devil. Withal I added that the predictions and sacred oracles both of Moses and all the holy Prophets of God aimed altogether at Christ as their only mark, in regard he was the full consummation of the Law and the Prophets, and I urged a place of Isaiah[10] unto him concerning the name Emanuel, and a virgin's conceiving and bearing of a son; and at last descended to the persuasion of him to abandon and renounce his Jewish religion and to undertake the Christian faith, without the which he should be eternally damned. He again replied that we Christians do misinterpret the Prophets, and very perversely wrest them to our own sense, and for his own part he had confidently resolved to live and die in his Jewish faith, hoping to be saved by the observations of Moses' law. In the end he seemed to be somewhat exasperated against me, because I sharply taxed their superstitious ceremonies. For many of them are such refractory people that they cannot endure to hear any reconciliation to the Church of Christ, in regard they esteem him but for a carpenter's son, and a silly poor wretch that once rode upon an ass, and most unworthy to be the Messias whom they expect to come with most pompous magnificence and imperial royalty, like a peerless monarch, guarded with many legions of the gallantest worthies and most eminent personages of the whole world, to conquer not only their old country Judea and all those opulent and flourishing kingdoms, which heretofore belonged to the four ancient monarchies (such is their insupportable pride) but also all the nations generally under the cope of heaven, and make the king of Guiana and all other princes whatsoever dwelling in the remotest parts of the habitable world his tributary vassals. Thus hath God justly infatuated their understandings, and given them the spirit of slumber (as Saint Paul speaketh out of the Prophet Isaiah[11]), eyes that they should not see, and ears that they should not hear unto this day.

But to shut up this narration of my conflict with the Jewish rabbi, after there had passed many vehement speeches to and fro betwixt us, it happened that some forty or fifty Jews more flocked about me, and some of them began very insolently to swagger with me, because I durst reprehend their religion. Whereupon fearing least they would have offered me some violence, I withdrew myself

[10]Isaiah 7.14.
[11]Romans 11.8, citing Isaiah 6.9.

by little and little towards the bridge at the entrance into the ghetto, with an intent to fly from them, but by good fortune our noble ambassador Sir Henry Wotton[12] passing under the bridge in his gondola at that very time espied me somewhat earnestly bickering with them, and so incontinently[13] sent unto me out of his boat one of his principal gentlemen, who conveyed me safely from these unchristian miscreants, which perhaps would have given me just occasion to forswear any more coming to the ghetto.

Thus much for the Jewish ghetto, their service, and my discourse with one of their rabbis.

from "Constantinopolitan Observations"[1]

[Coryate is present at a Jewish circumcision in Constantinople]

The seventh of August being Saturday, my courteous friend Master William Pearch being desirous to gratify me in a matter for the which I had often before solicited him, invited me and Master William Ford, preacher to our nation, to the house of a certain English Jew, called Amis, born in the Crooked Friars in London, who hath two sisters more of his own Jewish religion, commorant in Galata,[2] who were likewise born in the same place; to this man's house, I say, we came the foresaid day about nine of the clock in the morning, to see a matter which in my former travels I wished to have seen, especially in Venice, but never till then had the opportunity to attain unto, namely a circumcision. It was done in a private house, according to the custom of the Jews resident in Constantinople, and not in a synagogue, as it is with the Jews in other countries. This aforesaid Amis, for the love he bore to our English nation, in the which he lived till he was thirty years of age, being at the time of my residence in Constantinople sixty, as also for his good will sake,

---

[12]Wotton (1568–1639), diplomat and man of letters, was appointed ambassador to Venice by King James in 1604.

[13]Immediately.

---

[1]Thomas Coryate, "Master Thomas Coryate's Travels to and Observations in Constantinople," in Samuel Purchas, *Hakluytus Posthumus or Purchase His Pilgrims* (1625). Glasgow: James MacLehose and Sons, 1905, pp. 427–428, 431–433.

[2]Dwelling in Galata, a section of Constantinople (modern Istanbul) inhabited by foreign merchants.

which he bore to my foresaid friend Master William Pearch, received us with very courteous entertainment, presenting unto us at a table in a fine little room where he placed us diverse delicate dishes and fruits with a cup of most excellent wine, often welcoming us with many hearty and well-wishing speeches. While we were at breakfast, diverse Jews came into the room, and sung certain Hebrew songs; after which the child was brought to his father, who sat down in a chair, and placed the child, being now eight days old, in his lap. The whole company being desirous that we Christians should observe their ceremony, called us to approach near to the child. And when we came, a certain other Jew, drawing forth a little instrument made not unlike those small scissors that our ladies and gentlewomen do much use, did with the same cut off the prepuce or foreskin of the child, and after a very strange manner unused (I believe) of the ancient Hebrews, did put his mouth to the child's yard,[3] and sucked up the blood. All his privities (before he came into the room) were besprinkled with a kind of powder, which after the circumciser had done his business, was blowed away by him, and another powder cast on immediately. After he had dispatched his work, the same also after his work was done, took a little strong wine that was held in a goblet by a fellow that stood near him, and poured it into the child's mouth to comfort him in the midst of his pains, who cried out very bitterly. The pain being for the time very bitter indeed, though it will be (as they told me) cured in the space of four and twenty hours. But those of any riper years that are circumcised (as it too often cometh to pass, that Christians which turn Turks)[4] as at forty or fifty years of age, do suffer great pain for the space of a month. The prepuce that was cut off was carried to the mother, who keepeth it very preciously as a thing of worth.

[Coryate at a Succoth celebration]

The twentieth of September being Monday, the Jews of Constantinople and Galata began their Feast of Tabernacles,[5] which lasted till the eight and twentieth of the same month, that is just nine days, in which they differ from the ancient Jews who were commanded by

[3]Penis.
[4]Convert to Islam.
[5]Jewish festival of Succoth that begins five days after Yom Kippur.

Almighty God to spend only eight days in the celebration of their feast. I talked with a Jew concerning the reason of this their difference, who told me that it was because being so far from Jerusalem, as in Constantinople they did not altogether so certainly know the first day according to the course of the moon, as those Jews that live in Jerusalem, and therefore for the better assurance of this matter, they add a day to the number that God limited and appointed their forefathers; whereas the Jews that live in Jerusalem, and the parts of the Holy Land, near thereabout, by the course of the moon more certainly knowing the precise time of the beginning, do spend only eight days in their feast and no more. Again, they do in another respect differ from God's institution. For he commanded only two days to be more solemnly celebrated then the rest, that is, the first and the last, but they celebrate two at the beginning and two also at the last. But as of the former two, the first day is the chiefest, being kept with more solemnity than the second: so also of the two later, the last of all is more ceremoniously observed than the former. In this space they are much given to holiness, resting from all labor during the whole nine days, and they sometimes eat and drink in their tabernacles,[6] which are made partly in their private houses, or the corner of some gallery belonging thereto, at the least if they have any, and partly near to their synagogues. They make the sides of their tabernacles of reeds of bulrushes, and cover them at the top with bays. It was my hap to be in one of them that was made near to a synagogue.

Also the ninth day, which was the last of their feast, about four of the clock in the afternoon, I was at their liturgy in one of their synagogues, being admitted to sit down among them. I find the irreverence of the Jews in Venice and of those of Constantinople to be like in the service of God. They neither uncover nor kneel the whole time of their prayer; sometimes they stand altogether, and sometimes they sit altogether. For some quarter of an hour after the beginning of the reading of their Law, they wear nothing over their back, but their ordinary apparel, but then all of them put on their ephod[7] both men and children; which ephod is made of the same white stuff, as the Turkish turbans are; these hang over their backs and reach down

---

[6]Temporary constructions built to memorialize the tent-like dwellings used by the ancient Jews during the exodus from Egypt.

[7]Jewish priestly garment.

to the middle part of their bodies, after a looser manner than I think the ancient Jews were wont to wear them, for I read in the 2. Sam. the 6. Chapter, and 14. Verse, that King David girt it about his middle when he danced before the Ark; but they hang it loose about their bodies. This ephod many of them carried in a little scrip from their houses, and back again after the end of their liturgy. When they sat at their devotion they used a most ridiculous and unseemly gesture; for they always moved their bodies up and down very strangely, the head being in a continual motion without any cessation. After that they move their right side then their left and lastly their forepart forward; which kind of wagging of their bodies by interchangeable turns they use during the whole time of their service.

Fynes Moryson (1566–1630)

Moryson's report of his travels includes the following "discourse" about the status of Jews in various European countries. (For information about Moryson, see p. 107.) Like other writers of the time, he blames the Jews themselves for the fact that they are "despised" by both Christians and Muslims. His word choice spins the facts. In countries that have not banished them, the Jews are "allowed" (rather than forced) to live under harsh conditions. In Italy, he claims, Jews are "permit[ted]" to function as money-lenders by princes who use them to extort money from their subjects. The "miserable" condition in which they live throughout the diaspora is, he claims, the "curse" for their refusal to recognize Christ as the Messiah. The unself-conscious conflation of theological and economic explanations is common in early-modern anti-Jewish polemics. A similar conflation can occasionally be found in the rhetoric of Christian characters in The Merchant of Venice.

from *An Itinerary*[1]

A general and brief discourse of the Jews

The Jews are a nation incredibly despised among all Christians, and of the Turks also, and were dispersed throughout the face of the

---

[1]Fynes Moryson, "Unpublished Chapters from *Itinerary*," in *Shakespeare's Europe*, ed. Charles Hughes. London: Sherrett and Hughes, 1903, pp. 487–489.

world, save that they have been long banished out of some Christian kingdoms, as England, France, and Netherlands, where notwithstanding they lurk disguised though they be not allowed any habitation by the state. And where they are allowed to dwell, they live upon usury and selling of frippery wares, as brokers therein permitted by Christian princes for private gain to use horrible extortions upon their subjects, but are not allowed to buy any lands, houses, or stable inheritances, neither have they any coin of their own, but use the coins of princes where they live. The ten tribes of the kingdoms of Israel were long since carried captive and dispersed in the furthest East, and are not known where they live, having no commerce with the Jews known to us.

Touching those of the kingdoms they had at Jerusalem, they are thought to be mingled in their tribes and families, but the general opinion is that those of the Tribe of Judah live in Turkey, and those of the Tribe of Benjamin live in Italy, Germany, and Poland. They are a miserable nation and most miserable in that they cannot see the cause thereof, being the curse of the blood of their Messiah, which they took upon themselves and their children, whose coming they still expect, saying it is thus long deferred for their sins but they look for his coming from the East before and towards the end of the world. At Prague under the Emperor of Germany they are allowed a little city to dwell in, with gates whereof they keep the keys and walled round about for their safety. The Emperor also allows them to dwell in two cities of Silesia and diverse villages of Moravia, being provinces of the kingdom of Bohemia. In Germany they have only a street allowed them to dwell in at Frankfort (famous for the yearly marts). In Poland, at Crakow they have a little city wherein were about 700 familes which paid yearly to the king 500 guldens, beside the tribute upon occasions imposed of a gulden for each head and their obligation to lend the king money upon his occasions. They have also habitation in other towns of Poland, and myself passed a village only inhabited by Jews. Besides the great men there entertain Jews to be their baillies[2] to order and gather their rents, finding them very useful in all services of profit and wherein wit is required. [. . .]

[2]Agents, managers.

In Italy [. . .] the Jews live in no respect, no, not the most learned or richest of them, but in less contempt of the people[3]; and the princes who extort upon their own subjects do also for gain admit the Jews into their cities and permit them to use horrible extortion upon their subjects in the lending of money and in selling or letting out by the day or week upon use[4] both men's and women's apparel and furnitures for horses, and all kinds of frippery wares. Thus at Venice they have a courtyard closed with gates and capable of great numbers, wherein they dwell. At Rome they have whole streets allowed for their habitation, and live there in great number, paying their tribute to the Pope at Shrovetide when they are allowed to shew public games. They are allowed to live in all cities of Italy and have greater privileges in Piedmont than in other parts, but in all these places they are tied to wear a red or yellow cap, or more commonly a little bonnet or hat.

Robert Wilson (d. 1600)

Robert Wilson was a colleague of Shakespeare in the Lord Chamberlain's theater company. Like Shakespeare he was both an actor and a playwright, although the similarity stops there. Wilson practiced on older dramaturgy. It is allegorical; its characters' names tell us what they represent (Lucre, Simplicity, Merchant); it directly treats contemporary social issues in moral and satirical terms. We do not look to The Three Ladies of London *(1584) for depth of character—for that we look to* The Merchant of Venice. *Nor do we look for Shakespeare's supple command of verse and prose: Wilson writes in jingly rhymes. But his play is full of outrageous comedy, and the two selections in this volume overlap with issues dramatized in* The Merchant of Venice. *The section presented here deals in a surprising manner with the relations between a Christian merchant and a Jewish money-lender.*

[3]By the common people.
[4]For interest (as in usury).

from *The Three Ladies of London*[1]

Enter [in Turkey] Mercadorus[2] the Merchant [speaking in a heavy stage version of an Italian accent] and Gerontus[3] a Jew.

GERONTUS. But Signior Mercadorus tell me, did ye serve me well or
    no?
    That having gotten my money would seem the country to
      forgo:
    You know I lent you two thousand ducats for three months'
      space,
    And ere the time came you got another thousand by flattery
      and your smooth face.
    So when the time came that I should have received my money,
    You were not to be found but was fled out of the country:
    Surely if we that be Jews should deal so one with an other,
    We should not be trusted again of our own brother.
    But many of you Christians make no conscience to falsify your
    faith and break your day. I should have been paid at the month's
    end, and now it is two year you have been away. Well I am glad
    you be come again to Turkey, now I trust I shall receive the
    interest of you so well as the principal.
MERCADOR. A good a maister Geronto, pray hartly bare a me a little
    while,
    And me shall pay ye all without any deceit or guile:
    Me have a much business for by pretty knacks to send to Eng-
      land,
    Good a sir, bare a me four or five days, me'll dispatch your
      money out of hand.
GERONTUS. Signior Mercador, I know no reason why, because you
    have dealt with me so ill,
    Sure you did it not for need, but of set purpose and will:
    And I tell ye to bear with ye four or five days goes sore against
      my mind,

---

[1]Robert Wilson, *A Right Excellent and Pleasant Comedy Called The Three Ladies of London.* London, 1584.

[2]In other parts of the play, the name is usually Mercador (meaning "merchant"); in this section, the name usually takes the Latin form Mercadorus, probably to chime with the Jew's name, Gerontus.

[3]Probably "old man" but possibly also an allusion to Gernutus, in the old ballad "Gernutus the Jew of Venice," who pledges a pound of his own flesh.

Lest you should steal away and forget to leave my money behind.

MERCADOR. Pray hartly do tink a no such ting, my good friend a me,
Be me trot and fait' me'll pay you all every penny.

GERONTUS. Well I'll take your faith and troth once more, I'll trust to your honesty
In hope that for my long tarrying you will deal well with me:
Tell me what ware you would buy for England, such necessaries as they lack.

MERCADOR. O no lack some pretty fine toy or some fantastic new knack,
For da gentlewomans in England buy much tings for fantasy:
You pleasure a me sir, what me mean a dere buy.[4]

GERONTUS. I understand you sir, but keep touch with me, and I'll bring you to great store,
Such as I perceive you came to this country for:
As musk, amber, sweet powders, fine odors, pleasant perfumes, and many such toys,
Wherein I perceive consisteth that country gentlewoman's joys.
Besides I have diamonds, rubies, emeralds, saphires, smaradines,[5] opals, onacles,[6] jasinths, agates, turquoise, and almost of all kind of precious stones: And many moe fit thinges to suck away money from such green-headed[7] wantons.

MERCADOR. Fait' a my good friend, me tank you most hartly alway,
Me shall a content your debt within dis two or tree day.

GERONTUS. Well look you do keep your promise, and another time you shall command me:
Come, go we home where our commodities you may at pleasure see.

[. . .]

*Enter Mercadorus reading a letter to himself, and let
Gerontus the Jew follow him, and speak as followeth.*

[4]Please tell me what I should buy (in order to sell) there.
[5]A light green semi-precious stone.
[6]Onyx.
[7]Gullible.

GERONTUS. Signior Mercador, why doe you not pay me? Think you I
will bee mocked in this sort?
This is three times you have flouted me; it seems you make
thereat a sport.
Truly pay me my money, and that even now presently,
Or by mighty Mahomet[8] I swear, I will forthwith arrest ye.
MERCADOR. Ha pray a bare wit me tre or four days, me have much
business in hand:
Me be troubled with letters you see here, dat comes from Eng-
land.
GERONTUS. Tush this is not my matter, I have nothing therewith to do;
Pay me my money or I'll make you, before to your lodging you
go.
I have officers stand watching for you, so that you cannot pass
by,
Therefore you were best to pay me, or else in prison you shall
lie.
MERCADOR. Arrest me dou scall[9] knaue, marry do and if thou dare,
Me will not pay de one penny, arrest me, do, me do not care.
Me will be a Turk, me came hedar[10] for dat cause,
Darefore me care not for de so mush as two straws.
GERONTUS. This is but your words, because you would defeat me;
I cannot think you will forsake your faith so lightly.
But seeing you drive me to doubt, I'll try your honesty:
Therefore be sure of this, I'll go about it presently.

Exit.

MERCADOR. Marry farewell and be hanged, sitten scald[11] drunken
Jew.
I warrant ye me shall be able very vell to pay you.
My Lady Lucre have sent me here dis letter,
Praying me to cozen de Jew for love a her.
Darefore me'll go to get a some Turk's apparell,
Dat me may cozen da Jew and end dis quarrell.   *Exit.*

---

[8]Mahomet, or Mohammed. It was not unusual in this period for fictional Jews to
swear by the Muslim prophet.
[9]Thou scabby.
[10]Hither (in a stage-Italian accent).
[11]Shit-covered and scabby.

Enter the Judge of Turkey, with Gerontus and Mercadorus.

JUDGE. Sir Gerontus, because you are the plaintiff, you first your
  mind shall say;
  Declare the cause you did arrest this merchant yesterday.
GERONTUS. Then learned Judge attend. This Mercadorus whom you
  see in place,
  Did borrow two thousand ducats of me, but for a five weeks'
    space.
  Then Sir, before the day came, by his flattery he obtained one
    thousand more,
  And promised me at two months end I should receive my store:
  But before the time expired, he was closely[12] fled away,
  So that I never heard of him at least this two years' day:
  Till at the last I met with him, and my money did demand,
  Who sware to me at five days' end, he would pay me out of
    hand.
  The five days came, and three days more, then one day he
    requested;
  I perceiving that he flouted me, have got him thus arrested.
  And now he comes in Turkish weeds[13] to defeat me of my
    money,
  But I trow[14] he will not forsake his faith, I deem he hath more
    honesty.
JUDGE. Sir Gerontus you know, if any man forsake his faith, king,
  country, and become a Mahomet[15]
  All debts are paid; 'tis the law of our realm, and you may not
    gainsay it.
GERONTUS. Most true (reverend Judge) we may not, nor I will not,
  against our laws grudge.
JUDGE. Signior Mercadorus is this true that Gerontus doth tell?
MERCADOR. My Lord Judge, de matter and de circumstance be true
  me know well.
  But me will be a Turk, and for dat cause me came here.

---

[12]Secretly.
[13]Clothes.
[14]Believe.
[15]Muslim.

JUDGE. Then it is but a folly to make many words. Senior Mercadorus
draw near.

Lay your hand upon this book, and say after me.

MERCADOR. With a good will, my Lord Judge, me be all ready.

GERONTUS. Not for any devotion, but for lucre's sake of my money.

JUDGE AND MERCADOR. Say "I, Mercadorus, do utterly renounce
before all the world, my duty to my Prince, my honor to my
parents, and my good will to my country: Furthermore I protest
and swear to be true to this country during life, and thereupon I
forsake my Christian faith."

GERONTUS. Stay there, most puissant Judge. Senior Mercadorus,
consider what you do.

Pay me the principal; as for the interest, I forgive it you:

And yet the interest is allowed amongst you Christians, as well
as in Turkey,

Therefore respect your faith, and do not seem to deceive me.

MERCADOR. No point da interest, no point da principal.

GERONTUS. Then pay me the one half, if you will not pay me all.

MERCADOR. No point da half, no point denier,[16] me will be a Turk I
say,

Me be weary of my Christ's religion, and for dat me come
away.

GERONTUS. Well seeing it is so, I would be loath to hear the people
say, it was long of[17] me.

Thou forsakest thy faith, wherefore I forgive thee frank and
free,

Protesting before the Judge, and all the world, never to demand
penny nor halfpenny.

MERCADOR. O Sir Gerontus, me take a your proffer, and tank you
most hartily.

JUDGE. But Signior Mercadorus, I trow[18] ye will be a Turk for all
this.

MERCADOR. Signior no, not for all da good in da world, me forsake a
my Christ.

[16]A small coin.
[17]Because of.
[18]Trust.

JUDGE. Why then it is as Sir Gerontus said, you did more for the
greediness of the money,
Than for any zeal or good will you bare to Turkey.
MERCADOR. Oh Sir, you make a great offence,
You must not judge a my conscience.
JUDGE. One may judge and speak truth, as appears by this,
Jews seek to excel in Christianity, and Christians in
Jewishness.[19]

Exit.

MERCADOR. Vell vell, but me tank you, Sir Gerontus, with all my
very hart.
GERONTUS. Much good may it do you sir, I repent it not for my part.
But yet I would not have this bolden you to serve another so,
Seek to pay and keep day with men, so a good name on you
will go. *Exit.*
MERCADOR. You say vel Sir: it dus me good, dat me have cozened
de Jew;
Faith I would my Lady Lucre de whole matter now knew:
What is dat me will not do for her sweet sake.
But now me will provide my journey toward England to take.
'Me be a Turk? No, it will make my Lady Lucre to smile,
When she knows how me did da scall[20] Jew beguile. *Exit.*

Christopher Marlowe (1564–1593)

In The Jew of Malta *(c. 1590), Christopher Marlowe created the other
most compelling Jewish character in Elizabethan drama besides Shylock. But Marlowe's play is very different from Shakespeare's. It is a
sardonic satire on universal human greed and treachery. On Malta, as
we hear about the victims in its slave market, "everyone's price is written on his back": everyone can be bought or sold, and Barabas the Jew
is less hypocritical than the mealy-mouthing governor, who cunningly
destroys both the Jew who has offered to help him and the Turks to*

---

[19]Jews try harder to uphold Christian virtues, and Christians try to do worse than
Jews are supposed to do.
[20]Scurvy, miserable.

whom he owes allegiance, and ends the play giving praise to heaven. Barabas has none of Shylock's plausible humanity; he is cartoon-like in his over-the-top, gleeful villainy. Marlowe was born the same year as Shakespeare and was murdered at the age of twenty-nine. In his spectacular brief career, during which he influenced Shakespeare just as Shakespeare was influencing him, he wrote, among other astounding works, the two-part Tamburlaine, *the tragedy* Doctor Faustus, *and the tragic history play* Edward II.

from *The Jew of Malta*[1]

Act One

Enter Barabas[2] in his counting house, with heaps of gold before him.

BARABAS. So that of thus much that return was made;
And of the third part of the Persian ships
There was the venture summed and satisfied.[3]
As for those Samnites and the men of Uz[4]
That bought my Spanish oils and wines of Greece,
Here have I pursed their paltry silverlings.
Fie, what a trouble tis to count this trash!
Well fare the Arabians, who so richly pay
The things they traffic for with wedge of gold,
Whereof a man may easily in a day
Tell[5] that which may maintain him all his life.
The needy groom, that never fingered groat[6]
Would make a miracle of thus much coin,
But he whose steel-barred coffers are crammed full,
And all his lifetime hath been tired

---

[1]Christopher Marlowe, *The Famous Tragedy of the Rich Jew of Malta.* London, 1633.

[2]Barabas (prounounced with the accent on the first syllable) suggests the name Barabbas, the thief whom Pontius Pilate released instead of Jesus.

[3]Accounted for and paid up.

[4]The place names conjure up a vast, vaguely biblical-sounding world; Job came from "the land of Uz"(Job 1.1).

[5]Count.

[6]A small coin.

Wearying his fingers ends with telling it,
Would in his age be loath to labor so,
And for a pound to sweat himself to death.
Give me the merchants of the Indian mines
That trade in metal of the purest mold;
The wealthy Moor, that in the eastern rocks
Without control can pick his riches up
And in his house heap pearl like pebble-stones,
Receive them free and sell them by the weight,
Bags of fiery opals, sapphires, amethysts,
Jacinths, hard topaz, grass green emeralds,
Beauteous rubies, sparkling diamonds,
And seld-seen costly stones of so great price
As one of them, indifferently rated
And of a carat of this quantity,
May serve in peril of calamity
To ransom great kings from captivity.
This is the ware wherein consists my wealth.
And thus methinks should men of judgment frame
Their means of traffic from the vulgar trade,
And, as their wealth increaseth, so enclose
Infinite riches in a little room.
But now how stands the wind?
Into what corner peers my halcyon's bill?[7]
Ha! to the east? Yes; see how stand the vanes—
East and by south. Why then I hope my ships
I sent for Egypt and the bordering isles
Are gotten up by Nilus winding banks.
Mine argosy from Alexandria,
Loaden with spice and silks, now under sail,
Are smoothly gliding down by Candy[8] shore
To Malta, through our Mediterranean sea. [. . .]
Thus trowls our fortune in by land and sea,
And thus are we on every side enriched.
These are the blessings promised to the Jews,

[7]Weather vane.
[8]Crete.

And herein was old Abram's happiness.[9]
What more may heaven do for earthly man
Than thus to pour out plenty in their laps,
Ripping the bowels of the earth for them,
Making the seas their servant, and the winds
To drive their substance with successful blasts?
Who hateth me but for my happiness?
Or who is honored now but for his wealth?
Rather had I, a Jew, be hated thus,
Than pitied in a Christian poverty;
For I can see no fruits in all their faith
But malice, falsehood, and excessive pride,
Which methinks fits not their profession.
Haply some hapless man[10] hath conscience,
And for his conscience lives in beggary.
They say we are a scattered nation:
I cannot tell, but we have scrambled up
More wealth by far than those that brag of faith.
There's Kirriah Jairim, the great Jew of Greece,
Obed in Bairseth, Nones in Portugal,[11]
Myself in Malta, some in Italy,
Many in France, and wealthy every one,
Ay, wealthier far than any Christian.
I must confess we come not to be kings.
That's not our fault. Alas, our number's few,
And crowns come either by succession
Or urged by force, and nothing violent,
Oft have I heard tell, can be permanent.
Give us a peaceful rule; make Christians kings,
That thirst so much for principality.
I have no charge, nor many children,
But one sole daughter, whom I hold as dear

---

[9]God's covenant with Abraham (Abram) was that his seed would be fruitful and multiply, and that the Jews' days of living as strangers in another people's land would come to an end (Genesis 15). Barabas misinterprets these "blessings" as a promise of mere wordly wealth.

[10]Perhaps some unlucky man.

[11]Fictitious names designed to give the sense of a global network.

As Agamemnon did his Iphigen;[12]
And all I have is hers. [. . .]

[Representatives of the Turkish Sultan have arrived at Malta to demand that the Knights of Malta pay him the tribute money they owe. Ferneze, the governor, decides that the money for the Turks must be paid by the Jews of Malta.]

Enter Barabas and three Jews.

FIRST KNIGHT. Have you determined what to say to them?

FERNEZE. Yes; give me leave—and, Hebrews, now come near.
From the Emperor of Turkey is arrived
Great Selim-Calymath, his highness' son,
To levy of us ten years' tribute past.
Now, then, here know that it concerneth us.

BARABAS. Then, good my lord, to keep your quiet still,
Your lordship shall do well to let them have it.

FERNEZE. Soft, Barabas, there's more 'longs to't than so.
To what this ten years' tribute will amount,
That we have cast,[13] but cannot compass[14] it
By reason of the wars that robbed our store;
And therefore are we to request your aid.

BARABAS. Alas, my lord, we are no soldiers,
And what's our aid against so great a prince?

FIRST KNIGHT. Tut, Jew, we know thou art no soldier:
Thou art a merchant and a moneyed man,
And 'tis thy money, Barabas, we seek.

BARABAS. How, my lord! My money?

FERNEZE. Thine and the rest;
For, to be short, amongst you't must be had.

FIRST JEW. Alas, my lord, the most of us are poor.

FERNEZE. Then let the rich increase your portions.

BARABAS. Are strangers[15] with your tribute to be taxed?

SECOND KNIGHT. Have strangers leave with us to get their wealth?
Then let them with us contribute.

---

[12]Agamemnon sacrificed Iphegenia in order to be allowed to sail to Troy.
[13]Reckoned.
[14]Encompass, reach.
[15]Foreigners.

BARABAS. How? equally?

FERNEZE. No, Jew, like infidels;
For through our sufferance of your hateful lives,
Who stand accursed in the sight of heaven,
These taxes and afflictions are befallen,
And therefore thus we are determined.
Read there the articles of our decrees.

OFFICER. [*reads*] "First, the tribute money of the Turks shall all be levied amongst the Jews, and each of them to pay one half of his estate."

BARABAS. How, half his estate? I hope you mean not mine.

FERNEZE. Read on.

OFFICER. "Secondly, he that denies to pay shall straight become a Christian."

BARABAS. How! a Christian! Hum, what's here to do?

OFFICER. "Lastly, he that denies this, shall absolutely lose all he has."

ALL THREE JEWS. Oh, my lord, we will give half.

BARABAS. Oh, earth-mettled[16] villains, and no Hebrews born!
And will you basely thus submit yourselves
To leave your goods to their arbitrament?[17]

FERNEZE. Why, Barabas, wilt thou be christened?

BARABAS. No, Governor, I will be no convertite.

FERNEZE. Then pay thy half.

BARABAS. Why, know you what you did by this device?
Half of my substance is a city's wealth.
Governor, it was not got so easily,
Nor will I part so slightly therewithal.

FERNEZE. Sir, half is the penalty of our decree.
Either pay that or we will seize on all.

BARABAS. Corpo di Dio![18] Stay: you shall have half.
Let me be used but as my brethren are.

FERNEZE. No, Jew, thou hast denied the articles,
And now it cannot be recalled.

---

[16]Made of base material.

[17]Decision.

[18]Body of God (Italian).

BARABAS. Will you then steal my goods?
Is theft the ground of your religion?
FERNEZE. No, Jew; we take particularly thine
To save the ruin of a multitude;
And better one want[19] for a common good
Than many perish for a private man.[20]
Yet, Barabas, we will not banish thee,
But here in Malta, where thou gott'st thy wealth,
Live still, and, if thou canst, get more.
BARABAS. Christians, what or how can I multiply?
Of nought is nothing made.
FIRST KNIGHT. From nought at first thou cam'st to little wealth,
From little unto more, from more to most.
If your first curse fall heavy on thy head,
And make thee poor and scorned of all the world,
'Tis not our fault, but thy inherent sin.
BARABAS. What, bring you scripture to confirm your wrongs?[21]
Preach me not out of my possessions.
Some Jews are wicked, as all Christians are;
But say the tribe that I descended of
Were all in general cast away for sin,
Shall I be tried for their transgression?
The man that dealeth righteously shall live.
And which of you can charge me otherwise?
FERNEZE. Out, wretched Barabas!
Sham'st thou not thus to justify thyself,
As if we knew not thy profession?[22]
If thou rely upon thy righteousness,
Be patient, and thy riches will increase.
Excess of wealth is cause of covetousness,
And covetousness, oh, 'tis a monstrous sin.

---

[19]Lack.
[20]A sly allusion to John 12.50, where the high priest of the Pharisees says concerning Jesus that "it is expedient for us that one man should die for the people" (King James version).
[21]Barabas responds to Ferneze's charge that the Jews are damned because they denied Jesus.
[22]Religious affiliation; also career as a money-man.

BARABAS. Ay, but theft is worse. Tush, take not from me then,
    For that is theft; and, if you rob me thus,
    I must be forced to steal and compass more.
FIRST KNIGHT. Grave Governor, list not to his exclaims.
    Convert his mansion to a nunnery;
    His house will harbor many holy nuns. [. . .]

Act Two

Enter Barabas, with a light.

BARABAS. Thus like the sad presaging raven that tolls
    The sick man's passport[23] in her hollow beak,
    And in the shadow of the silent night
    Doth shake contagion from her sable wings,
    Vexed and tormented runs poor Barabas
    With fatal curses towards these Christians.
    The uncertain pleasures of swift-footed time
    Have ta'en their flight, and left me in despair,
    And of my former riches rests no more
    But bare remembrance, like a soldier's scar
    That has no further comfort for his maim.
    O thou that with a fiery pillar led'st
    The sons of Israel through the dismal shades,
    Light Abraham's offspring; and direct the hand
    Of Abigail this night, or let the day
    Turn to eternal darkness after this.
    No sleep can fasten on my watchful eyes
    Nor quiet enter my distempered thoughts,
    Till I have answer of my Abigail.

Enter Abigail, above.

ABIGAIL. Now have I happily espied a time
    To search the plank my father did appoint,[24]
    And here, behold, unseen, where I have found
    The gold, the pearls, and jewels, which he hid.

---

[23]Admission to the land of death.
[24]The floorboard my father designated.

BARABAS. Now I remember those old women's words,
  Who, in my wealth, would tell me winter's tales,
  And speak of spirits and ghosts that glide by night
  About the place where treasure hath been hid;
  And now methinks that I am one of those,
  For whilst I live, here lives my soul's sole hope,
  And when I die, here shall my spirit walk.
ABIGAIL. Now that[25] my father's fortune were so good
  As but to be about this happy place!
  'Tis not so happy.[26] Yet when we parted last,
  He said he would attend me in the morn.
  Then, gentle sleep, where'er his body rests,
  Give charge to Morpheus[27] that he may dream
  A golden dream, and of the sudden [wake]
  Come, and receive the treasure I have found.
BARABAS. *Bueno para todos mi ganado no era.*[28]
  As good go on, as sit so sadly thus.
  But stay! what star shines yonder in the east?
  The loadstar of my life, if Abigail.
  Who's there?
ABIGAIL. Who's that?
BARABAS. Peace, Abigail, 'tis I.
ABIGAIL. Then, father, here receive thy happiness.
BARABAS. Hast thou't?

[Abigail] throws down bags.

ABIGAIL. Here. Hast thou't? There's more, and more, and more.
BARABAS. O my girl,
  My gold, my fortune, my felicity,
  Strength to my soul, death to mine enemy.
  Welcome the first beginner of my bliss.
  Oh Abigail, Abigail, that I had thee here too,
  Then my desires were fully satisfied.

---

[25]Would that.
[26]Lucky.
[27]Classical god of dreams.
[28]My flock is not good for everybody (Spanish).

But I will practise thy enlargement thence:
Oh girl, oh gold, oh beauty, oh my bliss![29] [. . . .]

[*A slave market on Malta, where "Everyone's price is written
on his back." Barabas has just purchased Ithamore.*]

BARABAS. Now let me know thy name, and therewithal
Thy birth, condition, and profession.[30]
ITHAMORE. Faith, sir, my birth is but mean: my name's
Ithamore, my profession what you please.
BARABAS. Hast thou no trade? Then listen to my words,
And I will teach thee that shall stick by thee.
First, be thou void of these affections:
Compassion, love, vain hope, and heartless fear.
Be moved at nothing. See thou pity none,
But to thyself smile when the Christians moan.
ITHAMORE. Oh, brave master! I worship your nose for this.
BARABAS. As for myself, I walk abroad a-nights
And kill sick people groaning under walls.
Sometimes I go about and poison wells,
And now and then, to cherish[31] Christian thieves,
I am content to lose some of my crowns[32]
That I may, walking in my gallery,
See 'em go pinioned[33] along by my door.
Being young, I studied physic,[34] and began
To practise first upon the Italian.
There I enriched the priests with burials
And always kept the sexton's arms in ure[35]
With digging graves and ringing dead men's knells.

---

[29]Compare with Solanio's imitation of Shylock, "'My daughter! Oh, my ducats! Oh, my daughter!'" (*Merchant* 2.8.15).

[30]Religion.

[31]Make bold.

[32]Coins.

[33]Chained (Barabas lets them steal so that he can have the pleasure of watching them get caught).

[34]Medicine.

[35]Use.

And after that was I an engineer,
And in the wars 'twixt France and Germany,
Under pretence of helping Charles the Fifth,[36]
Slew friend and enemy with my stratagems.
Then after that was I an usurer,
And with extorting, cozening, forfeiting,
And tricks belonging unto brokery,
I filled the jails with bankrupts in a year,
And with young orphans planted hospitals,
And every moon made some or other mad,
And now and then one hang himself for grief,
Pinning upon his breast a long great scroll
How I with interest tormented him.
But mark how I am blest for plaguing them.
I have as much coin as will buy the town.
But tell me now, how hast thou spent thy time?
ITHAMORE. Faith master,
In setting Christian villages on fire,
Chaining of eunuchs, binding galley slaves.
One time I was an hostler[37] at an inn,
And in the night time secretly would steal
To travelers' chambers, and there cut their throats.
Once at Jerusalem, where the pilgrims kneeled,
I strewed powder on the marble stones,
And therewithal their knees would rankle so,
That I have laughed a-good to see the cripples
Go limping home to Christendom on stilts.
BARABAS. Why, this is something. Make account of me
As of thy fellow; we are villains both.
Both circumcised; we hate Christians both.
Be true and secret; thou shalt want no gold.

---

[36]King of Spain and so-called Holy Roman Emperor (1500–1558).
[37]Stable-man.

Anonymous (15th Century)

> *Two potentially conflicting values—justice and mercy—meet in the courtroom scene of* The Merchant of Venice. *In the Christian theology of Shakespeare's age, such a conflict was seen in the difference between the Old and New Testaments. According to that doctrine, Christ took upon himself the penalty for man's sin, thus fulfilling the law of the Old Testament and offering believers the means for salvation. The demands of justice and mercy are both met in Christ's sacrifice. One form of the conflict and its divine resolution is dramatized in the fifteenth-century play of* The Salutation and Conception, *one of a linked group of religious plays. sometimes called the Coventry or N-Town cycle, which were performed on the Feast of Corpus Christi. It is an allegorical elaboration of a single verse of Psalm 85, "Mercy and truth have met together; righteousness [justice] and peace have kissed." The four qualities are personified as God's daughters, who debate how the Father should deal with His guilty human creatures. The debate, sometimes referred to as "The Parliament of Heaven," was a motif in late Medieval art and literature; it appears in the great Middle English poem* Piers Plowman. *The excerpt from the play begins with Contemplation, followed by The Virtues (one of the angelic orders), begging God to intervene for suffering humanity.*

from the Play of *The Salutation and Conception,* "The Parliament of Heaven"[1]

CONTEMPLATION. Four thousand six hundred four, I tell,[2]
>   Man for his offence and foul folly
> Hath lain years in the pains of hell,
>   And were worthy to lie therein endlessly;
> But then should perish your great mercy.
>   Good Lord, have on man pity,
> Have mind of the prayer said by Isaiah,
>   Let mercy meke[3] thine highest majesty. [. . .]

> Ah! woe to us wretches that wretched be,
>   For God hath added sorrow to sorrow.

---

[1]Adapted from *Ludus Coventriae,* ed. James Orchard Halliwell. London, 1841.
[2]Reckon, count (the number of years since the fall of man).
[3]Soften, make meek.

I pray thee, Lord, thy souls come see,
　　How they lie and sob for sickness and sorrow.
With thy blessed blood from bales them borrow,[4]
　　Thy careful[5] creatures crying in captivity:
Ah! tarry not, gracious Lord, till it be tomorrow.
　　The devil hath deceived them by his iniquity. [. . .]

Man is cumbered in sin, I cry to thy sight,
　　Gracious Lord, gracious Lord , gracious Lord, come down!

VIRTUES. Lord, pleaseth it[6] thine high domination,
　　On man that thou made to have pity.
Patriarchs and prophets have made supplication;
　　Our office is to present their prayers to thee.
Angels, archangels, we three
　　That be in the first hierarchy,
For man to thine high majesty
　　Mercy, mercy, mercy, we cry! [. . .]

THE FATHER. For the wretchedness of the needy,
　　And the poor's lamentation,
Now shall I rise that am Almighty:[7]
　　Time is come of reconciliation.
My prophets with prayers have made supplication,
　　My contrite creatures cry all for comfort,
All mine angels in heaven, without cessation,
　　They cry that grace to man might exort.[8]

TRUTH. Lord, I am thy daughter, Truth:
　　Thou wilt see I be not lore;[9]

[4]From suffering (bales) redeem them.
[5]Full of care.
[6]Let it please.
[7]These lines (translating lines in Latin that have been omitted here) paraphrase Psalm 12.5.
[8]Spring up, issue forth.
[9]Missing.

Thine unkind creatures to save were rewth:[10]
   The offense of man hath grieved thee sore.
When Adam had sinned, thou saidest thore[11]
   That he should die and go to hell;
And now to bliss him to restore—
   Two contraries may not together dwell.

Thy truth, Lord, shall last without end,
   I may in no wise from thee go.
That wretch that was to thee so unkind
   He may not have too much woe;
He despised thee and pleased thy foe.
   Thou art his creator and he is thy creature.
Thou hast loved truth, it is said ever more,
   Therefore in pains let him evermore endure.

MERCY. O Father of Mercy and God of comfort,
   That counsel us in each tribulation,
Let your daughter Mercy to you resort,
   And on man that is mischieved[12] have compassion.
Him grieveth full greatly his transgression;[13]
   All heaven and earth cry for mercy;
Me seemeth there should be no exception,[14]
   Their prayers been[15] offered so specially. [. . .]

JUSTICE. Mercy, me marveleth what you moveth.[16]
   Ye know well I am your sister Righteouness;
God is rightful and rightfulness loveth.
   Man offended Him that is endless,
Therefore his endless punishment may never cease;
   Also he forsook his maker that made him of clay,

[10]Would be cause for regret.
[11]There, at that point.
[12]Hurt.
[13]His transgression grieves him.
[14]Objection.
[15]Have been.
[16]I am surprised at what you propose.

And the devil to his master he chose.
Should he be saved? Nay, nay, nay! [. . .]

MERCY. Sister Rightousness, ye are too vengeable.[17]
Endless sin God endless may restore:
Above all his works, God is merciable.[18]
Though he forsook God by sin, by faith he forsook him
never the more.
And though he presumed never so sore,
Ye must consider the frailness of mankind.
Learn and ye list, this is God's lore:[19]
The mercy of God is without end.

PEACE. To spare your speeches, sisters, is fit;
It is not honest in Virtues to be in dissension:
The peace of God overcometh all wit.[20]
Thou, Truth and Right, say great reason,
Yet Mercy sayeth best to my pleson;[21]
For if man's soul should abide in hell,
Between God and man ever should be division,
And then might not I, Peace, dwell.

Therefore me seemeth best ye thus accord,
Then heaven and earth ye shall [gratify];
Put both your sentence in our Lord[22]
And in his wisdom let him deem—
This is most fitting me should seem—
And let see how we four may all abide.
That man's soul it should perish, it were [pity],
Or that any of us from other should divide.

[17]Inclined to vengeance.
[18]Merciful.
[19]Learn if you will that this is God's teaching.
[20]Passes all understanding.
[21]Pleases me best.
[22]Both of you put your opinions before God ("sentence" = opinion, judgment).

TRUTH. In truth hereto I consent,
   I will pray our Lord it may so be.

JUSTICE. I, Righteousness, am well content,
   For in him is very equity.

MERCY. And I, Mercy, from this counsel will not flee,
   Till Wisdom hath said I shall cease.

PEACE. Here is God now, here is unity,
   Heaven and earth is pleased with peace.

THE SON. I think the thoughts of peace and naught of wickedness.
   This I deem to cease your controversy:
If Adam had not died, perished had Righteousness,[23]
   And also Truth had been lost thereby:
Truth and Right would chastise folly;[24]
   If another death come not, Mercy should perish,
Then Peace were exiled finally:
   So twain deaths must be, you four to cherish.[25]
But he that shall die, ye must know
   That in him may be no iniquity,
That hell may hold him by no law,
   But that he may pass at his liberty.
Where such a one is, [go before] and see,
   And his death for man's death shall be redemption.
All heaven and earth seek now ye,
   Pleaseth it you this conclusion.[26] [. . .]

A counsel of the Trinity must be had,[27]
   Which of us shall man restore.

---

[23]Justice (righteousness) would have perished.

[24]It is in the nature of truth and justice to punish folly.

[25]So there must be two deaths to encourage (be kind to) all four of you (God's daughters).

[26]If this conclusion pleases you.

[27]In two omitted stanzas, God's daughters say that they can find no one adequate to die for mankind and that only God himself is sufficient; therefore the Son says there must be a meeting of the Trinity—God the Father, the Son, and the Holy Spirit—to decide the matter.

THE FATHER. In your wisdom, Son, man was made thore,[28]
And in wisdom was his temptation;
Therefore, Son, sapience ye must ordain[29] herefore,
And see how of man may be salvation.

THE SON. Father, he that shall do this must be both God and man.
Let me so how I may wear that weed;[30]
And sith[31] in my wisdom he began,
I am ready to do this deed.

THE HOLY SPIRIT. I, the Holy Ghost, of you twain do proceed,
This charge I will take on me:
I, Love, to your lover shall you lead:
This is the assent of our unity.

MERCY. Now is the loveday made of us four finally,
Now may we live in peace as we were wont:
Misericordia et Veritas obviauerunt sibi,
Justicia et Pax osculata sunt.[32]
Et hic osculabunt pariter omnes.[33]

William Shakespeare (1564–1616)

In this scene from Shakespeare's city comedy Measure for Measure,
Isabella (a young woman devoted to virginity and the life of a nun)
comes to Angelo (the deputy to the absent Duke of Vienna) to plead for
the life of her brother, Claudio, who has been condemned for fornica-
tion, impregnating his fiancée. Isabella urges mercy while Angelo insists
upon the letter of the law. In this tense scene of outer debate and inner
turmoil, Angelo, the spokesman for law, recognizes his own uncontrol-
lable sexual passion and his hypocrisy; while Isabella, pleading for

[28]There, at that point.

[29]You must provide wisdom.

[30]Garment.

[31]Since.

[32]Mercy and truth have met together; righteousness and peace have kissed (Psalm 85.10).

[33]And here they kiss each other. (In the stanzas that complete the play, the angel Gabriel descends to Mary to announce Christ's conception.)

mercy, finds herself defending a brother whose sexual license she abhors.
Isabella's defense of what Portia, in The Merchant of Venice, *calls "the*
quality of mercy" is the best contemporary analogue to one of the Venet-
ian play's central themes, the opposition between the supposedly Old
Testament principle of law and the New Testament principle of mercy.

from *Measure for Measure*, Act 2, Scene 2[1]

ACT 2, SCENE 2

Enter Provost [and a] Servant.

SERVANT
He's hearing of a cause; he° will come straight.
I'll tell him of you.
PROVOST   Pray you, do. [*Exit Servant.*] I'll know
His pleasure; may be he will relent. Alas,
He° hath but as offended in a dream!
All sects, all ages smack of this vice—and he   5
To die for 't!

Enter Angelo.

ANGELO   Now, what's the matter, Provost?
PROVOST
Is it your will Claudio shall die tomorrow?
ANGELO
Did not I tell thee yea? Hadst thou not order?
Why dost thou ask again?
PROVOST
Lest I might be too rash.   10
Under your good correction,° I have seen
When, after execution, judgment hath
Repented o'er his doom.°

---

[1]From *The Complete Works of William Shakespeare*, ed. David Bevington (New York: Harper Collins, 1992).

---

1 he i.e., Angelo, deputy to the Duke.   **4 He** i.e., Claudio, brother of Isabella.
11 Under . . . correction i.e., allow me to say.   **13 doom** sentence.

ANGELO
Go to; let that be mine.
Do you your office, or give up your place,   15
And you shall well be spar'd.
PROVOST
I crave your honor's pardon.
What shall be done, sir, with the groaning Juliet?
She's very near her hour.
ANGELO   Dispose of her
To some more fitter place, and that with speed.   20

[*Enter Servant.*]

SERVANT
Here is the sister of the man condemn'd
Desires access to you.
ANGELO   Hath he a sister?
PROVOST
Ay, my good lord; a very virtuous maid,
And to be shortly of a sisterhood,
If not already.
ANGELO   Well, let her be admitted.   25

[*Exit Servant.*]

See you the fornicatress be remov'd.
Let her have needful, but not lavish, means;
There shall be order for 't.

        Enter Lucio and Isabella.

PROVOST   Save° your honor!
ANGELO
Stay a little while. [*To Isabella.*] Y' are welcome.
What's your will?   30
ISABELLA
I am woeful suitor to your honor,

28 **Save** God save.

Please but your honor hear me.

ANGELO   Well; what's your suit?

ISABELLA

There is a vice that most I do abhor,

And most desire should meet the blow of justice,

For which I would not plead, but that I must;   35

For which I must not plead, but that I am

At war 'twixt will and will not.

ANGELO   Well; the matter?

ISABELLA

I have a brother is condemn'd to die.

I do beseech you, let it be his fault,°

And not my brother.

PROVOST [*Aside*]   Heaven give thee moving graces!   40

ANGELO

Condemn the fault, and not the actor of it?

Why, every fault's condemn'd ere it be done.

Mine were the very cipher of a function,

To fine the faults whose fine° stands in record,

And let go by the actor.   45

ISABELLA

O just but severe law!

I had a brother, then. Heaven keep your honor!

LUCIO [*Aside to Isabella*]

Give't° not o'er so. To him again, entreat him!

Kneel down before him, hang upon his gown.

You are too cold. If you should need a pin,°   50

You could not with more tame a tongue desire it.

To him, I say!

ISABELLA

Must he needs die?

ANGELO   Maiden, no remedy.

ISABELLA

Yes; I do think that you might pardon him,

And neither heaven nor man grieve at the mercy.   55

---

38 let . . . fault i.e., let the fault die. 44 fine . . . fine punish . . . penalty. 48 Give 't . . .
so don't give up so soon. 50 need a pin i.e., ask for the smallest trifle.

ANGELO
I will not do 't.

ISABELLA   But can you, if you would?

ANGELO
Look what° I will not, that I cannot do.

ISABELLA
But might you do 't, and do the world no wrong,
If so your heart were touch'd with that remorse°
As mine is to him?

ANGELO   He's sentenc'd; 'tis too late.   60

LUCIO [*Aside to Isabella*]
You are too cold.

ISABELLA
Too late? Why, no; I, that do speak a word,
May call it back again. Well, believe this,
No ceremony that to great ones 'longs,
Not the king's crown, nor the deputed sword,°   65
The marshal's truncheon,° nor the judge's robe,
Become them with one half so good a grace
As mercy does
If he had been as you and you as he,
You would have slipp'd like him; but he, like you,   70
Would not have been so stern.

ANGELO   Pray you be gone.

ISABELLA
I would to heaven I had your potency,
And you were Isabel! Should it then be thus?
No; I would tell what 'twere to be a judge,
And what a prisoner.

LUCIO [*Aside to Isabella*]
            Ay, touch him; there's the vein.   75

ANGELO
Your brother is a forfeit of the law,
And you but waste your words.

ISABELLA   Alas, alas!

---

57 Look what whatever.   **59 remorse** pity.   **65 deputed sword** sword of justice
entrusted by God to his deputy.   **66 truncheon** staff borne by military officers.

Why, all the souls that were were forfeit once,
And He that might the vantage best have took
Found out the remedy°. How would you be,   80
If He, which is the top of judgment,° should
But judge you as you are? O, think on that,
And mercy then will breathe within your lips,
Like man new made.°

ANGELO   Be you content, fair maid.
It is the law, not I, condemn your brother.   85
Were he my kindman, brother, or my son,
It should be thus with him. He must die tomorrow.

ISABELLA
Tomorrow! O, that's sudden! Spare him, spare him!
He's not prepar'd for death. Even for our kitchens
We kill the fowl of season.° Shall we serve heaven   90
With less respect than we do minister
To our gross selves? Good, good my lord, bethink
    you:
Who is it that hath died for this offense?
There's many have committed it.

LUCIO [*Aside to Isabella*]   Ay, well said.

ANGELO
The law hath not been dead, though it hath slept.   95
Those many had not dar'd to do that evil
If the first that did th' edict infringe
Had answer'd for his deed. Now 'tis awake,
Takes note of what is done, and like a prophet
Looks in a glass° that shows what future evils,   100
Either now, or by remissness new-conceiv'd,°
And so in progress° to be hatch'd and born,

78–80 **Why . . . remedy** (A reference to the Redemption, despite man's sinfulness which would have justified God's destruction of humankind.)   81 **top of judgment** supreme judge.   84 **new made** i.e., new created by salvation, born again.   90 **of season** that is in season and properly mature.   100 **glass** magic crystal.   101 **Either . . . new-conceiv'd** i.e., both evils already hatched and those that would be encouraged by continued laxity of enforcement.   102 **in progress** in the course of time.

Are now to have no successive degrees,°
But here° they live, to end.

ISABELLA   Yet show some pity.

ANGELO

I show it most of all when I show justice;   105
For then I pity those I do not know,
Which a dismiss'd° offense would after gall,°
And do him right° that, answering one foul wrong,
Lives not to act another. Be satisfied;
Your brother dies tomorrow. Be content.   110

ISABELLA

So you must be the first that gives this sentence,
And he, that suffers. O, it is excellent
To have a giant's strength, but it is tyrannous
To use it like a giant.

LUCIO [*Aside to Isabella*]   That's well said.

ISABELLA

Could great men thunder   115
As Jove himself does, Jove would never be quiet,°
For every pelting,° petty officer
Would use his heaven for thunder,
Nothing but thunder! Merciful Heaven,
Thou rather with thy sharp and sulphurous bolt   120
Splits the unwedgeable and gnarled oak
Than the soft myrtle; but man, proud man,
Dress'd in a little brief authority,
Most ignorant of what he's most assur'd,°
His glassy essence,° like an angry ape,   125
Plays such fantastic tricks before high heaven
As makes the angels weep; who, with our spleens,°
Would all themselves laugh mortal.°

---

103 **successive degrees** successors.   104 **here** i.e., in potential offenders.   107 **dismiss'd** forgiven. | **gall** irritate, injure.   108 **right** justice.   116 **be quiet** have any quiet.   117 **pelting** paltry.   124 **assur'd** assured of (by God's merciful promises).   125 **glassy essence** i.e., his soul, which is reflected from God; "glassy" refers to a mirror. | **angry ape** i.e., ludicrous buffoon.   127 **with our spleens** i.e., if they laughed at folly as we do.   128 **themselves laugh mortal** i.e., laugh as though they were mortal.

LUCIO [*Aside to Isabella*]
O, to him, to him, wench! He will relent.
He's coming. I perceive 't.
PROVOST [*Aside*]   Pray heaven she win him!   130
ISABELLA
We cannot weigh our brother with ourself.°
Great men may jest with saints; 'tis wit in them,
But in the less° foul profanation.
LUCIO [*Aside to Isabella*]
Thou 'rt i' th' right, girl; more o' that.
ISABELLA
That in the captain's but a choleric word,°   135
Which in the soldier is flat blasphemy.°
LUCIO [*Aside to Isabella*]
Art avis'd° o' that? More on 't.
ANGELO
Why do you put these sayings upon me?°
ISABELLA
Because authority, though it err like others,
Hath yet a kind of medicine in itself,   140
That skins the vice o' th' top.° Go to your bosom;
Knock there, and ask your heart what it doth know
That's like my brother's fault. If it confess
A natural guiltiness such as is his,
Let it not sound a thought upon your tongue   145
Against my brother's life.
ANGELO [*Aside*]
She speaks, and 'tis such sense
That my sense° breeds with it. —Fare you well.
                                                [*He starts to go.*]
ISABELLA
Gentle my lord,° turn back.

131 cannot . . . ourself cannot judge our fellow men by the same standards we use in judging ourselves (because we are so blinded to justice).   **133 in the less** in men of lesser rank (it is).   **135 That . . . word** i.e., we treat the abusive language a general uses in anger merely as an outburst; we are indulgent toward the failings of great men.   **136 blasphemy** defamation.   **137 avis'd** informed, aware.   **138 put . . . me** apply these sayings to me.   **141 skins . . . top** covers over the sore with skin, leaving it unhealed. (The *medicine* of l. 139 is thus only a palliative.)   **147–148 sense . . . sense** import . . . sensuality.   **149 Gentle my lord** my noble lord.

ANGELO
I will bethink me. Come again tomorrow.   150
ISABELLA
Hark how I'll bribe you. Good my lord, turn back.
ANGELO
How? Bribe me?
ISABELLA
Ay, with such gifts that° heaven shall share with
    you.
LUCIO [*Aside to Isabella*]
You had marr'd all else.°
ISABELLA
Not with fond° sicles° of the tested° gold,   155
Or stones whose rate° are either rich or poor
As fancy values them, but with true prayers
That shall be up at heaven and enter there
Ere sunrise—prayers from preserved° souls,
From fasting maids whose minds are dedicate   160
To nothing temporal.
ANGELO   Well, come to me tomorrow.
LUCIO [*Aside to Isabella*]
Go to; 'tis well. Away!
ISABELLA
Heaven keep your honor safe!
ANGELO [*Aside*]   Amen!
For I am that way going to temptation,
Where prayers cross.°
ISABELLA   At what hour tomorrow   165
Shall I attend your lordship?
ANGELO
At any time 'fore noon.
ISABELLA
Save your honor!
                    [*Exeunt Isabella, Lucio, and Provost.*]
ANGELO   From thee, even from thy virtue!
What's this, what's this? Is this her fault or mine?

---

153 that as. **154 else** otherwise. **155 fond** i.e., foolishly valued. | **sicles** shekels. |
tested purest, tested by the touchstone. **156 rate** values. **159 preserved** protected
(from the world). **165 cross** are at cross purposes.

The tempter or the tempted, who sins most, ha?   170
Not she, nor doth she tempt; but it is I
That, lying by the violet in the sun,
Do as the carrion does, not as the flow'r,
Corrupt with virtuous season.° Can it be
That modesty may more betray our sense°   175
Than woman's lightness? Having waste ground enough,
Shall we desire to raze the sanctuary
And pitch our evils there?° O, fie, fie, fie!
What dost thou, or what are thou, Angelo?
Dost thou desire her foully for those things   180
That make her good? O, let her brother live!
Thieves for their robbery have authority
When judges steal themselves. What, do I love her,
That I desire to hear her speak again,
And feast upon her eyes? What is't I dream on?   185
O cunning enemy that, to catch a saint,
With saints dost bait thy hook! Most dangerous
Is that temptation that doth goad us on
To sin in loving virtue. Never could the strumpet,
With all her double vigor, art,° and nature,°   190
Once stir my temper;° but this virtuous maid
Subdues me quite. Ever till now,
When men were fond,° I smil'd and wond'red how.
                                                                Exit.

---

174 Corrupt . . . season i.e., putrify while all else flourishes.   175 sense sensual
nature.   178 pitch our evils there i.e., erect a privy not on *waste ground* (l. 176) but
on sanctified ground.   190 art artifice. | nature sensual nature.   191 temper mental
balance, temperament.   193 fond foolishly in love.

Usury

You needn't owe a pound of flesh—a credit card debt at twenty-four percent will do—to appreciate some of the emotions attached in *The Merchant of Venice* to the subject of money-lending. But what seems normal within a fully developed capitalist economy was surrounded with prohibition, fear, and mystery within the emergent economic system of Shakespeare's time. Usury (i.e., lending at interest whether within legal limits or, as Shakespeare calls it in Sonnet 6, "forbidden usury") was, despite attempts to wish it away, a fact of life. Farmers needed to borrow to buy seed for next year's crops; merchants needed to borrow to buy merchandise; and, as some of the selections presented in this section recognize, without the incentive of interest, the flow of capital would dry up. Money-lending was widely practiced. The historian William Harrison, in his *Description of England* (1587), calls usury "a practice brought in by the Jews, now perfectly practiced almost by every Christian and so commonly that he is accounted but for a fool that doth lend his money for nothing." But scripture seemed to forbid the practice of usury (see the biblical citations in the selection from Philip Stubbes's *Anatomy of Abuses*), and ancient ideals of friendship and hospitality were opposed to it. Deeper feelings that there was something unnatural in, as Antonio puts it, making barren metal breed more metal as if it were alive also made interest on loans seem, to conservative writers, a wicked practice. (Possibly that is a reason why the ancient association of Jews and money-lending persisted in an England virtually depopulated of Jews. Since Christians were theoretically forbidden from doing it, and yet it was widely done, then it must follow as the night the day that usurers, despite all evidence to the contrary, are Jews.) Parliament sought to forbid usury by statute in 1552, but the law was impossible to enforce, and in 1571 the statute was revised to allow a ten percent ceiling on interest.

Shakespeare takes this urgent historical issue into the realm of myth by literalizing the metaphor that likens debt to taking the heart out of a man. (Technically, Shylock's bond is not a loan for interest but a penalty for nonperformance, but the horror that underlies some of the following selections also underlies Shakespeare's disturbing equation of money with flesh and blood.)

The selections here begin with a widely known ancient text by Seneca, which sets out a social ideal based on the free circulation of "benefits." Philip Stubbes, in *The Anatomy of Abuse*, and Robert Wilson, in the selection from his play *The Three Ladies of London*, represent the conservative side of the issue; Thomas Wilson's *Discourse upon Usury* at least makes it debatable, while Francis Bacon's essay "Of Usury" takes a more modern and tolerant view.

Seneca (c. 4 BCE–AD 65)

First-century Stoic philosopher, politician, and playwright Lucius Annaeus Seneca was tutor to the Emperor Nero and under him exercised great political influence. Seneca addressed his discourse On Mercy to Nero, who later ordered Seneca, when he had fallen out of favor, to kill himself. Dying obediently, Seneca showed that he had learned his own lessons about self-control and fearlessness. Seneca's writing influenced the early Church fathers, and his influence continued into the Renaissance. Shakespeare might well have known the selection presented here. Shakespeare also knew Seneca's rhetorically elaborate and deliberately shocking plays, which were published in English in 1581. Their influence is evident in the first wave of Elizabethan tragedies, including Shakespeare's Titus Andronicus.

Seneca's treatise On Benefits, the opening of which appears here, makes gift-giving, gift-receiving, and gift-returning the beating heart of civil society. He envisages the circulation of benefits as a process binding giver and receiver in the kind of dance symbolized by the figures of the Three Graces. The Merchant of Venice is full of benefits bestowed, returned, and refused. Shylock gives to Antonio only on the promise of precise return, but Antonio gives freely to Bassanio, and Portia assures the benefit's return. The episode of the rings reads like a comic version of the Senecan ideal of giving, receiving, and giving again.

from *On Benefits*[1]

Among the numerous faults of those who pass their lives recklessly and without due reflection [. . .] I should say that there is hardly any one so hurtful to society as this, that we neither know how to bestow or how to receive a benefit. [. . .] A benefit is received in the same temper in which it is given, and ought not, therefore, to be given carelessly, for a man thanks himself for that which he receives without the knowledge of the giver. Neither ought we to give after long delay, because in all good offices the will of the giver counts for much, and he who gives tardily must long have been unwilling to give at all. Nor, assuredly, ought we to give in an offensive manner, because human nature is so constituted that insults sink deeper than kindnesses; the remembrance of the latter soon passes away, while that of the former is treasured in the memory; so what can a man expect who insults while he obliges? All the gratitude which he deserves is to be forgiven for helping us. [. . .]

The man who while he gives thinks of what he will get in return, deserves to be deceived. But what if the benefit turns out ill? Why, our wives and our children often disappoint our hopes, yet we marry and bring up children, and are so obstinate in the face of experience that we fight after we have been beaten, and put to sea after we have been shipwrecked. How much more constancy ought we to show in bestowing benefits! If a man does not bestow benefits because he has not received any, he must have bestowed them in order to receive them in return, and he justifies ingratitude, whose disgrace lies in not returning benefits when able to do so. [. . .] As it is, virtue consists in bestowing benefits for which we are not certain of meeting with any return, but whose fruit is at once enjoyed by noble minds. So little influence ought this to have in restraining us from doing good actions, that even though I were denied the hope of meeting with a grateful man, yet the fear of not having my benefits returned would not prevent my bestowing them, because he

[1]L. Annaeus Seneca, *On Benefits*, trans. Aubrey Stewart. London: George Bell and Sons, 1900, pp. 1–11.

who does not give, forestalls the vice of him who is ungrateful. I will explain what I mean. He who does not repay a benefit, sins more, but he who does not bestow one, sins earlier.

[. . .] The book-keeping of benefits is simple: it is all expenditure; if any one returns it, that is pure profit; if he does not return it, it is not lost, since I gave it for the sake of giving. No one writes down his gifts in a ledger or like a grasping creditor demands repayment to the day and hour. A good man never thinks of such matters, unless reminded of them by some one returning his gifts; otherwise they become like debts owing to him. It is a base usury to regard a benefit as an investment. [. . .]

He who is quick to believe that he has thrown away his benefits, does really throw them away; but he who presses on and adds new benefits to his former ones, forces out gratitude even from a hard and forgetful breast. In the face of many kindnesses, your friend will not dare to raise his eyes; let him see you whithersoever he turns himself to escape from his remembrance of you; encircle him with your benefits. As for the power and property of these, I will explain it to you if first you will allow me to glance at a matter which does not belong to our subject, as to why the Graces are three in number, why they are sisters, why hand in hand, and why they are smiling and young, with a loose and transparent dress. Some writers think that there is one who bestows a benefit, one who receives it, and a third who returns it; others say that they represent the three sorts of benefactors, those who bestow, those who repay, and those who both receive and repay them. But take whichever you please to be true; what will this knowledge profit us? What is the meaning of this dance of sisters in a circle, hand in hand? It means that the course of a benefit is from hand to hand, back to the giver; that the beauty of the whole is lost if the course is anywhere broken, and that it is fairest when it proceeds in unbroken regular order. In the dance there is one esteemed beyond the others, who represents the givers of benefits. Their faces are cheerful, as those of men who give or receive benefits are wont to be. They are young, because the memory of benefits ought not to grow old. They are virgins, because benefits are pure and untainted, and held holy by all; in benefits there should be no strict or binding conditions, therefore the Graces wear loose flowing tunics, which are transparent, because benefits love to be seen. [. . .]

Sandro Botticelli (1444–1510), *Primavera* (c. 1477), detail of the Three Graces. By permission of Scala/Art Resource, NY.

In *On Benefits*, Seneca interprets the mythological figures of the Three Graces to symbolize a social ideal in which gifts, or benefits, circulate in an endless round of giving, receiving, and giving again. The three women, dancing hand in hand, were a favorite subject for painters and sculptors from the late classical period through the Renaissance. The Florentine artist Sandro Botticelli placed them among other figures in *Primavera* (Spring), painted in 1477–1478 to hang in a villa of his patrons, the Medici family. (The painting is now in the Uffizi Gallery, Florence.) Scholars disagree about the precise interpretation of *Primavera*, but a celebration of marriage and fruitful sexuality seems to be one of the things intended by this great painting of graceful sensuality.

Men must be taught to give willingly, to receive willingly, and to return willingly; and to place before themselves the high aim, not merely of equalling, but even of surpassing those to whom they are indebted, both in good offices and in good feeling. [. . .] Do then teach me how I may bestow more good things, and be more grateful to those who have earned my gratitude, and how the minds of both parties may vie with one another, the giver in forgetting, the receiver in remembering his debt. [. . . T]he first thing which we have to learn is, what we owe in return for a benefit received. One man says that he owes the money which he has received, another that he owes a consulship, a priesthood, a province, and so on. These, however, are but the outward signs of kindnesses, not the kindnesses themselves. A benefit is not to be felt and handled, it is a thing which exists only in the mind. There is a great difference between the subject-matter of a benefit, and the benefit itself. Wherefore neither gold, nor silver, nor any of those things which are most highly esteemed, are benefits, but the benefit lies in the goodwill of him who gives them. The ignorant take notice only of that which comes before their eyes, and which can be owned and passed from hand to hand, while they disregard that which gives these things their value. The things which we hold in our hands, which we see with our eyes, and which our avarice hugs, are transitory, they may be taken from us by ill luck or by violence; but a kindness lasts even after the loss of that by means of which it was bestowed; for it is a good deed, which no violence can undo. [. . .]

What, then, is a benefit? It is the art of doing a kindness which both bestows pleasure and gains it by bestowing it, and which does its office by natural and spontaneous impulse. It is not, therefore, the thing which is done or given, but the spirit in which it is done or given, that must be considered, because a benefit exists, not in that which is done or given, but in the mind of the doer or giver. How great the distinction between them is, you may perceive from this, that while a benefit is necessarily good, yet that which is done or given is neither good nor bad. The spirit in which they are given can exalt small things, can glorify mean ones, and can discredit great and precious ones; the objects themselves which are sought after have a neutral nature, neither good nor bad; all depends upon the direction given them by the guiding spirit from which things receive their shape.

Philip Stubbes (fl. 1583–1591

A puritan and a pamphleteer, Stubbes vigororously condemned what he saw as the "abuses"—and they were legion—of the place he calls "Ailgna" (Anglia spelled backwards). Stubbes is most often remembered for his attack on "filthy plays and bawdy interludes," which despite itself pays backhanded compliment to the vigor of Shakespeare's theater. The following selection is a condemnation of moneylending; another selection about the danger of music appears later. Elsewhere in The Anatomy of Abuses *Stubbes acknowledges that the laws of Ailgna allow lending at interest (he has in mind the actual statute of 1571, which set a limit of ten percent), but here, through biblical citation and a stirring appeal to emotion, he manages to condemn the practice without overtly condemning English law.*

from *The Anatomy of Abuses*[1]

Great Usury in Ailgna

It is as impossible for a man to borrow money there (for the most part) without usury, interest, and loan, or without some good hostage, gage, or pledge, as it is for a dead man to speak with audible voice. [. . .]

Our Savior Christ willeth us to be so far from covetousness and usury, as he sayth, "Give to him that asketh thee, and from him that would borrow turn not away thy face."[2] Again, "Lend of thy goods to them who are not able to pay thee again, and thy reward shall be great in heaven."[3] If we must lend our goods then to them that are not able to pay us again, no not so much as the bare thing lent, where is the interest, the usury, the gain and the overplus, which we fish for so much? Therefore our Savior Christ saieth, *Beatius est dare potius accipere*—it is more blessed to give than to receive. In the 22 of Exodus, Deut[eronomy] 24:23, Leviticus 25, Nehe[miah] 5, Ezechi[el] 22:18, and many other places, we are forbidden to use any kind of usury or interest, or to receive any overplus besides the

---

[1]Philip Stubbes, *The Anatomy of Abuses*, 2nd ed. London, 1585, pp. 74–78.

[2]Matthew 5.6 (Stubbes's note).

[3]Stubbes cites Luke 6; he is probably thinking of verse 30, which in the Geneva Bible reads, "Give to every man that asketh of thee: and him that taketh away thy goods ask them not again."

principal, either in money, coin, wine, oil, beasts, cattle, meat, drink, cloth, or anything else whatsoever. [. . .]

Believe me, it grieveth me to hear (walking in the streets) the pitiful cries and miserable complaints of poor prisoners in durance for debt, and like so to continue all their life, destitute of liberty, meat, drink (though of the meanest sort), and clothing to their backs, lying in filthy straw and loathsome dung, worse than any dog, void of all charitable consolation and brotherly comfort in this world, wishing and thirsting after death to set them at liberty and loose them from their shackles, gyves, and iron bands. Notwithstanding, these merciless tigers are grown to such barbarous cruelty that they blush not to say, "Tush, he shall either pay me whole or else lie there till his heels rot from his buttocks, and, before I will release him, I will make dice of his bones." But take heed, thou devil (for I dare not call thee a Christian), lest the Lord say to thee, as he said to that wicked servant (who, having great sums forgiven him, would not forgive his brother his small debt, but, catching him by the throat, said, Pay that thou owest), "Bind him hands and feet, and cast him into utter darkness, where shall be weeping and gnashing of teeth."[4]

An usurer is worse than a thief, for the one stealeth but for need, the other for covetousness and excess; the one stealeth but in the night commonly, the other daily and hourly, night and day, at all times indifferently.

An usurer is worse than Judas, for he betrayed Christ but once, made restitution, and repented (though his repentance sprang not of faith but of despair); but these usurers betray Christ in his members daily and hourly, without any remorse or restitution at all.

They are worse than hell itself, for it punisheth but only the wicked and reprobate;[5] but the usurer maketh no difference of any but punisheth all alike.

They are crueller than death, for it destroyeth but the body and goeth no further, but the usurer destroyeth both the body and soul forever. And to be brief, the usurer is worse than the devil himself,

---

[4]Stubbes adds the detail about weeping and gnashing to Christ's parable of forgiveness (Matthew 18.23–35).

[5]According to the doctrine of reprobation, which was central to Stubbes's Calvinist theology, God has deprived certain people (the reprobate) of the possibility of salvation.

for the devil plagueth but only those that are in his hands, or else those whom God permitteth him; the usurer plagueth not only those that are within his jurisdiction already, but even all other, without compassion of any.

Francis Bacon (1561–1626)

Both in his life and in the afterlife of reputation, Francis Bacon excited strong and contradictory responses. The forward-thinking philosopher who inculcates a "new science" of inductive reasoning unobscured by prejudice is also the self-seeking politician who rose on the fallen body of his patron, the Earl of Essex, to become, in 1618, King James's lord chancellor—only to fall precipitously in 1621, charged with the tawdry crime of accepting bribes. He published his Essays *between 1597 and 1625. The opening line of his essay "Of Truth" ("'What is truth?' said jesting Pilate, and would not stay for an answer") is typical of his style of daring, dramatic intellectual boldness; so too is the cool, confident, Olympian manner in which he categorizes and dissects his often very hot subjects. In "Of Usury" Bacon writes with analytical detachment which is at an opposite pole from the hysterical manner of many contemporary diatribes against usury.*

from "Of Usury"[1]

Many have made witty invectives against usury. They say that it is a pity the devil should have God's part, which is the tithe.[2] That the usurer is the greatest Sabbath-breaker, because his plough goeth every Sunday. That the usurer is the drone that Virgil speaketh of, *Ignavum fucos pecus a praesepibus arcent.*[3] That the usurer breaketh the first law that was made for mankind after the fall, which was, *in sudore vultus tui comedes panem tuum*; not, *in sudore vultus alieni.*[4] That usurers should have orange-tawny bon-

---

[1]Francis Bacon, *The Essays or Counsels, Civil and Moral of Francis, Lord Verulam, Viscount St. Alban.* London, 1629, pp. 239–243.

[2]Ten percent.

[3]The unhelpful drone seats himself at someone else's table (*Georgics* 4:244).

[4]In the sweat of thy face shalt thou eat bread (Genesis 3.17), not in the sweat of someone else's.

nets, because they do judaize.[5] That it is against nature for money to beget money;[6] and the like. [. . .] But few have spoken of usury usefully. It is good to set before us the incommodities and commodities of usury, that the good may be either weighed out or culled out; and warily to provide, that while we make forth to that which is better, we meet not with that which is worse.

The discommodities of usury are, First, that it makes fewer merchants. For were it not for this lazy trade of usury, money would not lie still, but would in great part be employed upon merchandizing; which is the *vena porta*[7] of wealth in a state. The second, that it makes poor merchants. For, as a farmer cannot husband his ground so well if he sit at a great rent,[8] so the merchant cannot drive his trade so well, if he sit at great usury. The third is incident to the other two; and that is the decay of customs[9] of kings or states, which ebb or flow with merchandizing. The fourth, that it bringeth the treasure of a realm or state into a few hands. For the usurer being at certainties, and others at uncertainties, at the end of the game most of the money will be in the box; and ever a state flourisheth when wealth is more equally spread. The fifth, that it beats down the price of land, for the employment of money is chiefly either merchandiing or purchasing, and usury waylays both. The sixth, that it doth dull and damp all industries, improvements, and new inventions, wherein money would be stirring, if it were not for this slug. The last, that it is the canker and ruin of many men's estates, which in process of time breeds a public poverty.

On the other side, the commodities of usury are, first, that howsoever usury in some respect hindereth merchandizing, yet in some other it advanceth it; for it is certain that the greatest part of trade is driven by young merchants, upon borrowing at interest; so as if the usurer either call in or keep back his money, there will ensue, presently, a great stand[10] of trade. The second is, that were it not for

[5]Act like a Jew.
[6]Compare the dispute between Antonio and Shylock about breeding barren metal: 1.3.89–90, 127–129.
[7]Major artery.
[8]The high rent he pays on his land diminishes a farmer's profits.
[9]Duties, taxes.
[10]Halt.

this easy borrowing upon interest, men's necessities would draw upon them a most sudden undoing, in that they would be forced to sell their means (be it lands or goods) far under foot;[11] and so, whereas usury doth but gnaw upon them, bad markets would swallow them quite up. As for mortgaging or pawning, it will little mend the matter, for either men will not take pawns without use;[12] or if they do, they will look precisely for the forfeiture. I remember a cruel moneyed man in the country, that would say, "The devil take this usury, it keeps us from forfeitures of mortgages and bonds." The third and last is, that it is a vanity to conceive that there would be ordinary borrowing without profit; and it is impossible to conceive the number of inconveniences that will ensue if borrowing be cramped. Therefore to speak of the abolishing of usury is idle. All states have ever had it, in one kind or rate, or other. So as that opinion must be sent to Utopia.

To speak now of the reformation, and reiglement,[13] of usury; how the discommodities of it may be best avoided, and the commodities retained: It appears, by the balance of commodities and discommodities of usury, two things are to be reconciled. The one, that the tooth of usury be grinded, that it bite not too much; the other, that there be left open a means to invite moneyed men to lend to the merchants, for the continuing and quickening of trade. This cannot be done except you introduce two several sorts of usury, a less and a greater. For if you reduce usury to one low rate, it will ease the common borrower, but the merchant will be to seek[14] for money. And it is to be noted, that the trade of merchandize, being the most lucrative, may bear usury at a good rate; other contracts not so. To serve both intentions, the way would be briefly thus: That there be two rates of usury: the one free and general for all; the other under license only to certain persons and in certain places of merchandizing. First, therefore, let usury in general be reduced to five in the hundred; and let that rate be proclaimed to be free and current; and let the state shut itself[15] out to take any penalty for the

---

[11]At a large loss.
[12]Interest.
[13]Regulation.
[14]Have to seek.
[15]Prohibit itself.

same. This will preserve borrowing from any general stop or dryness. This will ease infinite borrowers in the country. This will, in good part, raise the price of land, because land purchased at sixteen years' purchase will yield six in the hundred, and somewhat more; whereas this rate of interest yields but five. This by like reason will encourage and edge industrious and profitable improvements; because many will rather venture in that kind than take five in the hundred, especially having been used to greater profit. Secondly, let there be certain persons licensed to lend to known merchants upon usury at a higher rate; and let it be with the cautions following: Let the rate be, even with the merchant himself, somewhat more easy than that he used formerly to pay; for by that means, all borrowers shall have some ease by this reformation, be he merchant or whosoever. Let it be no bank or common stock, but every man be master of his own money. Not that I altogether mislike banks, but they will hardly be brooked,[16] in regard of certain suspicions. Let the state be answered some small matter[17] for the license, and the rest left to the lender; for if the abatement[18] be but small, it will no whit discourage the lender. For he, for example, that took before ten or nine in the hundred, will sooner descend to eight in the hundred than give over his trade of usury, and go from certain gains to gains of hazard. [. . .]

If it be objected that this doth in a sort authorize usury, which before was in some places but permissive, the answer is, that it is better to mitigate usury by declaration than to suffer it to rage by connivance.

Robert Wilson (d. 1600)

The following selection from Wilson's play The Three Ladies of London *(see p. 131), puts the figure of Usury on stage with his friends Fraud, Simony, and Dissimulation. Among other things, we see Usury's*

---

[16]Tolerated. (Bacon favors an extreme of economic individualism, because of the suspicions that attach to organized money markets.)

[17]Be granted a small fee.

[18]Lowering of the interest.

part in dispossessing Hospitality, as the rogues (accompanied by the Italian merchant, Mercador) do everthing they can to serve Lady Lucre, the embodiment of the unprincipled pursuit of money.

from *The Three Ladies of London*[1]

[Dissimulation, Fraud, and Simplicity are on stage, as] Enter Simony[2] and Usury hand in hand.

SIMONY. Friend Usury, I think we are well near at our journey's end:
But knowest thou whom I have espied?
USURY. No.
SIMONY. Fraud our great friend.
USURY. And I see another that is now come into my remembrance.
SIMONY. Who is that?
USURY. Marry,[3] Master Davy Dissimulation, a good helper, and our old acquaintance.
SIMPLICITY. Now all the cards in the stock are dealt about,
The four knaves[4] in a cluster comes ruffling out.
SIMONY. What, Fraud and Dissimulation, happily found out!
I marvel what piece of work you two go about.
FRAUD. Faith, sir, we met by chance, and towards London are bent,
USURY. And to London we hie; it is our chiefest intent
To see if we can get entertainment of[5] the ladies or no.
DISSIMULATION. And for the self same matter even thither we go.
SIMONY. Then we are luckily well met, and seeing we wish all for one thing,
I would we our wills and wishing might win.
SIMPLICITY. Yes they will be sure to win the Devil and all,
Or else they'll make a man to spew out his gall.
Oh that vile Usury, he lent my father a little money, and for breaking one day
He took the fee-simple of his house and mill quite away:

[1]Robert Wilson, *A Right Excellent and Pleasant Comedy Called The Three Ladies of London*. London, 1584.
[2]Simony is the practice of using the Church for personal profit.
[3]A common expression of surprise or intensity, from Mary.
[4]Fraud, Dissimulation, Simony, Usury.
[5]Positions as servants from.

And yet he borrowed not half a quarter so much as it cost;
But I think if he had had but a shilling it had been lost.
So he killed my father with sorrow, and undid me quite,
And[6] you deal with him, sirs, you shall find him a knave full of
    spight.
And Simony, I per se I,[7] Simony too he is a knave for the
    nonce.[8]
He loves to have twenty livings[9] at once,
And if he let an honest man, as I am, to have one,
He'll let it[10] so dear that he shall be undone.
And he seeks to get parsons' livings into his hand,
And puts in some odd dunce that to his payment will stand:
So if the parsonage be worth forty or fifty pound a year,
He will give one twenty nobles to mumble service once a
    month there.

SIMONY AND USURY BOTH. What rascal is he that speaketh by us
    such villainy?

DISSIMULATION.
    Sirs, he was at us erewhile too; it is no matter, it is a simple soul
    called Simplicity.
    Enter Love and Conscience.

FRAUD. But here come two of the ladies; therefore make ready.
    But which of us all shall first break the matter?

DISSIMULATION. Marry, let Simony do it, for he finely can flatter.

USURY. Nay, sirs, because none of us shall have pre-eminence above
    other,
    We will sing in fellowship together like brother and brother.

SIMONY. Of troth agreed my masters, let it be so.

SIMPLICITY. Nay and they sing, I'll sing too.

              The Song.

    Good Ladies take pity and grant our desire.

CONSCIENCE REPLY. Speak boldly and tell me what is't you require.

---

[6]If.

[7]A fancy way to say "simply." (The Latin philosophical expression *I per se I* means "the letter I simply as itself, the letter I.")

[8]Coin worth about half a pound.

[9]Income from a priest's parish.

[10]Rent it out.

THEIR REPLY. Your service, good Ladies, is that we do crave.
HER REPLY. We like not, nor list not, such servants to have.
THEIR REPLY. If you entertain us, we trusty will be:
But if you refrain us, then most unhappy.
We will come, we will run, we will bend at your beck,
We will ply, we will hie, for fear of your check.[11]
HER REPLY. You do feign, you do flatter, you do lie, you do prate,
You will steal, you will rob, you will kill in your hate.
I deny you, I defy you, then cease of your talking:
I refrain you, I disdain you, therefore get you walking.
CONSCIENCE. What, Fraud, Dissimulation, Usery, and Simony,
How dare you for shame presume so boldly
As once to shew yourselves before Love and Conscience,
Not yielding your lewd lives first to repentance.
Think you not that God will plague you for your wicked practices,
If you intend not to amend your vile lives so amiss?
Think you not God knows your thoughts, words, and works,
And what secret mischiefs in the hearts of you lurks?
Then how dare you to offend his heavenly majesty
With your dissembling deceit, your flattery and your usury?
FRAUD. Tut sirs, seeing Lady Conscience is so scripolous,[12]
Let us not speak to her, for I see it is frivolous:
But what say you, Lady Love, will you grant us favor?
LOVE. I'll no such servants, so ill of behavior:
Servants more fitter for Lucre then Love;
And happy are they which refrain for to prove[13]
Shameless, pitiless, graceless, and quite past honesty.
Then who of good conscience but will hate your company?
USURY. Here is scripolous Conscience, and nice[14] Love indeed.
Tush, if they will not, other will;[15] I know we shall speed.
[Conscience chooses Simplicity to be her servant;
Love and Conscience exit] [. . .]

---

[11]Discipline.
[12]Scrupulous (possibly intended as a comic mistake).
[13]Refuse to show themselves.
[14]Refined.
[15]Will take us on as servants.

DISSIMULATION. Tush there be a thousand places where we our
    selves may provide.
    But look sirs, here commeth a lusty Lady towards us in haste,
    But speak to her if you will, that we may be all placed.
    Enter Lady Lucre.
USURY. I pray thee do, for thou art the likeliest to speed.[16]
DISSIMULATION. Why then I'll to't with a stomach[17] in hope of
    good speed.
    Fair Lady, all the gods of good fellowship kiss ye (I would say
    bliss ye).
LUCRE. Thou art very pleasant and full of thy roperipe[18] (I would
    say rhetoric).
DISSIMULATION. Lady you took me at the worst I beseech you,
    therefore,
    To pardon my boldness, offending no more.
LUCRE. We do: the matter is not great. But what wouldest thou
    have?
    How shall I call thee, and what is't thou do'st crave?
DISSIMULATION. I am called Dissimulation, and my earnest request
    Is to crave entertainment for me and the rest,
    Whose names are Fraud, Usury, and Simony:
    Great carers for your health, wealth, and prosperity.
LUCRE. Fraud, Dissimulation, Simony, and Usury,
    Now truly I thank you for proffering your service to me.
    You are all heartly welcome, and I will appoint straight way,
    Where each one in his office in great honor shall stay.
    But Usury, didst thou never know my Grandmother, the old
    Lady Lucre of Venice?
USURY. Yes Madam, I was servant unto her and lived there in bliss.
LUCRE. But why camest thou into England, seeing Venice is a city
    Where Usury by Lucre may live in great glory?
USURY. I have often heard your good grandmother tell,
    That she had in England a daughter which her far did excel,
    And that England was such a place for Lucre to bide,
    As was not in Europe and the whole world beside.

[16]Be successful.

[17]Enthusiasm.

[18]Ripe for the gallows.

Then lusting greatly to see you, the country, and she being
dead,
I made haste to come over to serve you in her stead.
LUCRE. Gramercy, Usury, and I doubt not but that you shall live
here as pleasantly,
Ay and pleasanter too, if it may be . [. . .]
Well Usury, I thank thee, but as for Fraud and Dissimulation,
I know their long continuance and after what fashion.
Therefore Dissimulation, you shall be my steward,
An office that every man's case by you must be preferred.
And you Fraud shall be my rent-gatherer, my leetor[19] of leases
and my purchaser of land,
So that many old bribes will come to thy hand.
And Usury because I know you be trusty, you shall be my secre-
tary
To deal amongst merchants, to bargain and exchange money.
And Simony because you are a sly fellow, and have your tongue
liberal,
I will place you over such matters as are ecclesiastical.
And though I appoint sundry offices where now you are in,
Yet jointly I mean to use you together oft times in one thing:
ALL. Lady, we rest at your command in ought we can or may. [. . .]
Exeunt, Dissimulation and Lucre, [Simony and Usury]
[. . .]
Enter Usury and Conscience.
USURY. Lady Conscience, is there anybody within your house, can
you tell?
CONSCIENCE. There is nobody at all be ye sure, I know certainly
well.
USURY. You know when one comes to take possession of any piece
of land,
There must not be one within, for against the order of law it
doth stand.
Therefore I thought good to ask you, but I pray you think not
amiss,
For both you, and almost all others knows, that an old custom
it is.

[19]Designated official (?).

CONSCIENCE. You say truth. Take possession when you please,
    good leave I render ye;
    Doubt you not, there is neither man, woman nor child, that
    will or shall hinder you.
USURY. Why then I will be bold to enter.   *Exit.*
CONSCIENCE. Who is more bold then Usury to venture?
    He maketh the matter dangerous[20] where is no need at all,
    But he thinks it not perilous to seek every man's fall.
    Both he and Lucre hath so pinched us, we know not what to do,
    Were it not for Hospitality, we knew not whither to go.
    Great is the misery that we poor Ladies abide,
    And much more is the cruelty of Lucre and Usury beside.
    O Conscience thou art not accounted of, O Love thou art little
    set by,
    For almost everyone, true Love and pure Conscience doth deny;
    So hath Lucre crept into the bosom of man, woman, and child,
    That everyone doth practice his dear friend to beguile.
    But God grant Hospitality be not by them over-pressed,
    In whom all our stay and chiefest comfort doth rest.
    But Usury hates Hospitality, and cannot him abide,
    Because he for the poor and comfortless doth provide.
    Here he comes, that hath undone many an honest man,
    And daily seeks to destroy, deface, and bring to ruin if he can.
    Now sir, have you taken possession as your dear Lady willed
    you?
    Enter Usury.
USURY. I have done it, and I think you have received your money,
    But this to you: my Lady willed me to bid you provide some
    other house out of hand.
    For she would not, by her will, have Love and Conscience to
    dwell in her land.
    Therefore I would wish you to provide ye,
    So ye should save charges, for a less house may serve.[21]
CONSCIENCE. I pray you heartily let us stay there, and we will be
    content
    To give you ten pound a year, which is the old rent.

---

[20]Pretends the action is fraught with danger.
[21]Save expenses since a smaller house will be sufficient.

USURY. Ten pound a year! that were a stale jest,
   If I should take the old rent to follow your request;
   Nay after forty pound a year, you shall have it for a quarter:[22]
   And you may think too, I greatly befriend ye in this matter.
   But no longer then for a quarter to you I'll set it,
   For perhaps my Lady shall sell it, or else to some other will let it.
CONSCIENCE. Well, sith we are driven to this hard and bitter drift,
   We accept, it and are contented to make bare and hard shift.
USURY. Then get you gone, and see at a day your rent be ready.
CONSCIENCE. We must have patience perforce, seeing there is no
   remedy.
   Exit Conscience.
USURY. What a fool was I, it repents me I have let it so reasonable,
   I might so well have had after threescore, as such a trifle:
   For seeing they were distressed, they would have given largely.
   I was a right sot, but I'll be overseen[23] no more, believe me.
   *Enter Mercador [an Italian merchant with a heavy
   accent, meeting Usury].*
MERCADOR. Ah my good a friend a Master Usury, be my trot you
   be very well met:
   Me be much beholding unto you for your good will, me be in
   your debt.
   But a me take a your part so much against a scald[24] old churl
   called Hospitality,
   Did speak against you, and says you bring good honest men to
   beggary.
USURY. I thank you, sir. Did he speak such evil of me as you now
   say?
   I doubt not but to reward him for his treachery one day.
MERCADOR. But I pray tell a me how fare a my Lady all dis while?
USURY. Marry, very well, sir, and here she comes if myself I do not
   beguile.
   Enter Lucre
LUCRE. [. . .] Usury, tell me, how have you sped in that you went
   about?

---

[22]Quarter of a year (a short lease that gives the tenant little security).

[23]Outsmarted.

[24]Scurvy, miserable.

USURY. Indifferently, Lady, you need not to doubt,
    I have taken possession; and because they were destitute,
    I have let it for a quarter, my tale to conclude.
    Marry, I have a little raised the rent, but it is but after forty
        pound by the year;
    But if it were to let now, I would let it more dear.
LUCRE. Indeed 'tis but a trifle, it makes no matter,
    I force it not greatly, being but for a quarter.
MERCADOR. Madonna, me tell ye vat you shall do, let dem to
        stranger[25] dat are content
    To dwell in a little room, and to pay much rent;
    For you know da French mans and Flemings in dis country be
        many,
    So dat they make shift to dwell ten houses in one very gladly,
    And be content a for pay fifty or three score pound a year
    For dat which da English mans say twenty mark is to deare.
LUCRE. Why Signior Mercador, think you not that I
    Have infinite numbers in London that my want doth supply?
    Beside in Bristol, Northhampton, Norwich, Westchester, Can-
       terbury,
    Dover, Sandwich, Rye, Portsmouth, Plymouth, and many moe,
    That great rents upon little room do bestow.
    Yes, I warrant you, and truly I may thank the strangers for this,
    That they have made houses so dear, whereby I live in bliss.
    Exeunt.
                 [. . .]
    Enter Hospitality.
HOSPITALITY.
    Oh what shall I say? Usury hath undone me, and now he hates
        me to the death,
    And seeks by all means possible for to bereave me of breath.
    I cannot rest in any place, but he hunts and follows me every-
        where,
    That I know no place to abide, I live so much in fear.
    But out, alas, here comes he that will shorten my days.
    Enter Usury

---

[25]Foreigner. (Mercador refers to immigrants who were forced to live in crowded
quarters at high rents, which then drove up rents for native workers.)

USURY.
   O have I caught your old gray beard? You be the man whom
      the people so praise:
   You are a frank gentleman, and full of liberality.
   Why, who had all the praise in London or England, but Master
      Hospitality?
   But I'll master you now, I'll hold you a groat.
HOSPITALITY. What, will you kill me?
USURY. No, I'll do nothing but cut thy throat.
HOSPITALITY. O help, help, help, for God's sake.
   Enter Conscience running apace.
CONSCIENCE. What lamentable cry was that I heard one make?
HOSPITALITY. O Lady Conscience, now or never help me.
CONSCIENCE. Why, what wilt thou do with him, Usury?
USURY. What will I do with him? Marry, cut his throat, and then no
   more.
CONSCIENCE. O dost thou not consider that thou shalt dearly
   answer for Hospitality that good member? Refrain it therefore.
USURY. Refrain me no refraining, nor answer me no answering,
   The matter is answered well enough in this thing.
CONSCIENCE. For God's sake spare him, for country sake spare him,
   for pity sake spare him, for Love sake spare him, for Conscience
   sake forbear him.
USURY. Let country, pity, Love, Conscience, and all go in respect of
   my self;
   He shall die: come ye feeble wretch, I'll dress ye like an elf.
CONSCIENCE. But yet Usury, consider the lamentable cry of the
   poor,
   For lack of Hospitality, fatherless children are turned out of
   door.
   Consider again the complaint of the sick, blind and lame,
   That will cry unto the Lord for vengeance on thy head in his
   name.
   Is the fear of God so far from thee that thou hast no feeling at
   all?
   O repent Usury! leave Hospitality, and for mercy at the Lord's
   hand call.
USURY. Leave prating, Conscience, thou canst not mollify my heart,
   He shall in spight of thee and all other feel his deadly smart.

Yet I'll not commit the murder openly,
But haul the villain into a corner, and so kill him secretly.
Come ye miserable drudge, and receive thy death. *Haul him in.*
HOSPITALITY. Help good Lady, help, he will stop my breath.
CONSCIENCE. Alas I would help thee, but I have not the power.
HOSPITALITY. Farewell Lady Conscience, you shall have Hospitality
in London nor England no more.

Thomas Wilson (1528–1581)

Thomas Wilson, a Protestant and a humanist, was tutor to King
Edward VI and, after exile under the Catholic Queen Mary, became a
parliamentarian and councilor to Queen Elizabeth. He is best known
for two important firsts: he wrote The Rule of Reason *(1551), the first*
comprehensive book about logic in English, and The Art of Rhetoric
(1553), the first comprehensive how-to book about English language
usage. The selection here is from a later work, A Discourse upon Usury
(1572). Written as a debate in dialogue form, the Discourse *leaves no*
question where Wilson's sentiments lie: his dedication of the book to
the Earl of Leicester recommends executing all money-lenders. At the
end the Lawyer, who defends lending at interest, concedes defeat to the
Preacher, who takes a thoroughly conservative line. But Cambridge
scholars such as Wilson were trained to argue on both sides of an issue,
and Wilson lets the Lawyer, despite his cynical tone and occasional
sophistries, make a reasonable case in favor of money-lending.

from *A Discourse upon Usury*[1]

The Preacher:

I know a gentleman born to five hundred pound land, and entering
into usury upon pawn of his land did never receive above a thousand pound of neat money, and within certain years running still
upon usury, and double usury, and usury upon usury (the merchants terming it usance and double usance by a more cleanly
name), he did owe to Master Usurer five thousand pound at the
last, borrowing but one thousand pound at first; so that his land

[1]Thomas Wilson, *A Discourse upon Usury*. London, 1572.

was clean gone, being five hundred pounds inheritance, for one thousand pound in money and the usury of the same money for so few years, and the man now beggeth. I will not say but this gentleman was an unthrift diverse ways in good cheer, nay in evil cheer I may call it, in wearing gay and costly apparel, in roistering with many servants more than needed, and with mustering in monstrous great hose, in haunting evil company, and lashing out fondly and wastefully at cards and dice, as time served. And yet I do say, he lost more by the usurer than he did by all those unthrifty means, for his vain expenses was not much more than a thousand pound because he had no more; whereas the usurer had not only his thousand pound again but four times more, which is five thousand pound in the whole, and for want of this payment the five hundred pound land was wholly his. And this gain only he had for time. They say time is precious. He may well say, time was precious to him that paid so dearly for it; or rather the usurer may say that time was very precious to him that took so much unto him.

Now Lord God, what a strange thing is this, that God suffering the sun to shine upon us freely and the air to be common to all, as well poor as rich, without any gain taking, that we not considering so liberal a goodness of God, should so far be from charity that we will sell time and air so dearly, having it of God so freely. [. . .]

To lend freely is a kind of liberality and bountifulness, when a man departeth from his own to help his neighbor's want, without any hope of lucre or gain at all, for he is benefitted that borroweth and feeleth great comfort in his great need. Whereas lending for gain is a chief branch of covetousness, and makes him, that before might have been counted bountiful, to be now reckoned a greedy gainer for himself, seeking his own welfare upon good assurance, without any care at all what becometh of his neighbor, gnawing him unmercifully to satisfy his own wretched and most greedy hunger, directly turning a most beautiful virtue into a most filthy abominable vice. Yea, usury is a manifest and voluntary known theft, which men do use knowingly and wittingly, for either they think they do evil, and forbear it never a wit, or (that which is worst of all) they think they do well, and so, by oft using of this filthiness, do lull themselves in sin without any sense or feeling of their most wretched wickedness and horrible dealing. Christ for his bitter passion be merciful unto us and give us his fear, that we may live after his law, and follow his holy will, for surely, as we live now, either the Bible is not God's word, or else we are not of God, such contrariety is between our lives and our lessons.

The scripture commandeth, Thou shalt not steal, thou shalt not kill, thou shalt not commit adultery, thou shalt not bear false witness, thou shalt not lend out thy money for gain, to take any thing for the loan of it, and yet we do all these things, as though there were neither scripture that forbad us, nor heaven for us to desire, nor hell to eschew nor God to honor nor devil to dread. And this last horrible offence, which I count greater, or as great, as any of the rest is so common amongst us that we have no sense to take it for sin, but count it lawful bargaining, and judge them goodly wise men that having great masses of money by them will never adventure any jot thereof in lawful occupying, either to carry out our plenty or to bring in our want, as good merchants use and ought to do, but living idle at home will set out their money for profit and so enrich themselves with the labor and travail of others, being themselves none other than drones that suck the honey which other painful bees gather with their continual travail of diverse flowers in every field. And whether these men be profitable or tolerable to a commonweal, or no, I report me[2] to you. Besides that, God doth utterly forbid them, whose commandment ought to be obeyed if we be Christians and of God, as we profess to be.

And therefore for my part, I will wish some penal law of death to be made against those usurers, as well as against thieves or murderers, for that they deserve death much more than such men do, for these usurers destroy and devour up, not only whole families, but also whole countries and bring all folk to beggary that have to do with them, and therefore are much worse than thieves or murderers, because their offence hurteth more universally and toucheth a greater number, the one offending for need, and th'other upon wilfulness. And that which is worst, under the color of friendship, men's throats are cut, and the doers counted for honest and wise men amongst others that have so ungodly gathered goods together. What is the matter that Jews are so universally hated wheresoever they come? Forsooth, usury is one of the chief causes, for they rob all men that deal with them and undo them in the end. And for this

[2]Appeal [to your judgment].

cause they were hated in England and so banished worthily, with whom I would wish all these Englishmen were sent that lend their money or their goods whatsoever for gain, for I take them to be no better then Jews. Nay, shall I say they are worse then Jews. For go whither you will throughout Christendom, and deal with them, and you shall have under ten in the hundred,[3] yea sometimes for six at their hands, whereas English usurers exceed all God's mercy, and will take they care not how much, without respect had to the party that borroweth what loss, danger, hindrance soever the borrower sustaineth. And how can these men be of God that are so far from charity, that care not how they get goods so they may have them? O Lord, have mercy upon us, and deal not with us according to our manifold wickedness, neither reward us according to our iniquities! Great are our sins that we have committed and more in number then are the sands upon the sea shores. Lord, if thou narrowly mark our naughtiness and wicked doings, who shall be able to stand before thee in judgement? But thou Lord art merciful, and wilt forgive them that call upon thee in faith with a repentant mind, which God grant unto us all for his dear son's sake Jesus Christ, to whom with the father and the holy ghost be all honor and glory for ever and ever. Amen.

The Lawyer:

Every man in his faculty, I see well, ought first to be heard. You have said much, and very godly; but whether politically and altogether aptly I cannot constantly affirm, for that I see all commonweals in the Christian world are governed otherwise than you preach. And therefore I must think you take the scriptures amiss and do not expound them according to the very meaning of the Holy Ghost. And I tell you plain, it is not in you preachers to judge precisely what usury is. For as divines cannot tell what herb is best for every disease but the physicians that are best practiced and acquainted therewith, so it is not in simple divines to say what contract is lawful and what is not, but in skillful lawyers to show and in wise magistrates to determine the truth and right hereof. And such contracts as the laws do allow for lawful a good man may use the same with a safe conscience. And public laws made according to

---

[3] A loan at less than ten percent.

good reason and justice are the ordinances of God, and the magistrate is the minister of God to a good man for good. I grant you may preach generally against it, as you do, but to say particularly and precisely what it is, is not within the compass of your profession. [. . .]

[W]hereas you say no man should lend for any gain and that all men should lend freely to them that have need without any respect of profit, I do think you do deal over precisely and go about to bring men to that straightness as they never were in at any time. For, as I hear some say, usury is never hurtful but when it biteth; otherwise it may be allowed and suffered. [. . .] For whatever you say of love towards our neighbor, me thinketh no man should love his neighbor better than himself, which they seem to do that lend to other freely and want themselves. And I have heard say that *Caritas incipit a se*: charity beginneth first at itself. And use we not in common phrase to say Near is my coat to my skin, but my shirt is nearer? As who should say, I will be a friend unto my neighbor and help him so much as I am able, but I will not so help him, by St. Mary, as I will harm myself, which is not God's will that I should do. You have heaped a number of scriptures together, alleged doctors, and brought forth reasons for the detestation of usury, wherein you have done well; but better you should have done, in my mind, if you had weighed usury more straightly by the rule of charity and not directly to call all those usurers that take anything more than they have lent, for so the case may fall out that he sinneth who hath borrowed if he will not make recompense. Therefore in such cases circumstances ought to be considered, and so judgment given upon the matter.

Neither ought I to deal with all men in one sort. For as there be three sorts of dealings among men, that is, gift, bargaining, and lending, so there are three sorts of men, the stark beggar, the poor householder, and the rich merchant or gentleman. To the first I ought to give freely, not only to lend freely; to the second I ought to lend either freely or mercifully; with the third I may deal straightly, and ask mine own with gain, as I take it, without offence to God or man. For when I deal with him that maketh gain of my money with his trade and occupying, and is well able to pay me again, being enriched by my means chiefly, why should not I in reason have part of his advantage, when by my goods he is grown rich? For be it that two, three or four be in consort, whereof two puts forth their money, and the other two use their labor and industry for increasing the same money by lawful trade, is not reason that these, although they be idle at home, who have disbursed large sums of money to adventure freely with others, should have reasonable gain with them? God forbid else. [. . .]

Some there be that say all usury is against nature. Whereas I think clean contrary. For if usury were against nature, it should be universally evil, but God hath said that to a stranger a man may put out his money for usury,[4] but if it had been against nature, God would not have granted that liberty. So that I take it to agree both with law and nature that I should do good unto him that doth good unto me or else I should be unthankful, than which there cannot be a greater or more horrible fault upon earth; and rewards given for good turns done or pleasure received for benefits bestowed are so common, that whoso offendeth herein is pointed at and counted a churl, and shall have want when he would have.[5] Moreover, who may not give his own freely, or what is he that will not or may not take anything that is given? What is more free than gift? Or what is he that will shew such discourtesy not to receive a gift, when it is freely offered? And what other thing do they that seek to borrow money but entreat marvelously and offer frankly for the time and use of money? [. . .] Even in God's law, if I be not deceived, usury is not forbidden. For is it not in St. Luke's gospel that God said He would come and ask the money lent with the usury, blaming him that did not put it forth for gain?[6] And in Deuteronomy it is plain: Thou shalt not lend to thy brother for gain, but to a stranger. [. . .]

And yet to lend money simply is counted usury, whereas there is no man that lendeth but sustaineth loss for the want of it, because he might better benefit himself by employing it in diverse ways than to suffer it to be in another man's hands, besides the danger that

[4]Deuteronomy 23.20: "Unto a stranger thou mayest lend upon usury, but thou shalt not lend upon usury unto thy brother" (Geneva Bible). Compare Antonio: "If thou wilt lend this money, lend it not / As to thy friends . . . But lend it rather to thine enemy" (1.3.127–130).

[5]And will not get what he needs when he needs it.

[6]In Christ's parable (Luke 19.12–27), the servants who return their master's money with interest are rewarded, but the "wicked servant" who returns exactly what was entrusted to him is chided: "Wherefore . . . gavest not thou my money into the bank, that at my coming I might have required mine own with usury?" (King James version).

may happen when a man's money is out of his own hands; for surer it cannot be than in a man's own possession. Then away with this preciseness, on God's name, to make every lending for gain to be plain usury, and that one penny over is sin before God, which neither I nor yet Master Merchant here can well believe fully, for I would have all things weighed by reason in matters of contracts and bargains, and not so to mince things as though there were no mean.[7] For I do not take usury to be as whoredom or theft is. In these sins there is no mean to make any virtue, for he that offendeth but once in whoredom is an offender, and he that stealeth never so little is a thief, and neither of their doings in any respect or by any circumstance is or can be good, whereas the lending of money or other goods for gain may be very beneficial unto him that borroweth. As for example: a man is bound to pay 300 pounds at a certain day or else he loseth perhaps 40 pounds good land: were it not charity and a good deed to help this man, that his land should not be lost for ever? And none offence neither, as I take it, to do a good turn and to receive another.

---

[7]Chop the issue so finely that there is no middle ground or moderate solution.

Shylock on Stage

The Merchant of Venice is one of the most frequently performed of Shakespeare's plays. In the past century, and especially since the Holocaust, it is also the play whose performance is most likely to cause pain and even to arouse calls for censorship. Much hinges on the actors' and directors' choices in embodying Shylock, and those choices in part reflect changing cultural preconceptions. We have little direct evidence for how Shylock was performed by Shakespeare's own company, but we know that in 1741 Charles Macklin famously acted Shylock as a scary villain rather than a figure of comedy; earlier Shylocks were, presumably, played for laughs.

The most famous performances in the nineteenth century, with the compelling initiative of Edmund Kean, complicated the character, often bringing out sympathetic elements to the point where, as William Hazlitt says in a selection in this section, "he becomes a half-favourite with the philosophical part of the audience, who are disposed to think that Jewish revenge is at least as good as Christian injuries." As actors stressed the sympathetic elements of Shylock's character (Sir Henry Irving's performance, described in the selection by William Winter, is a seminal instance) so by contrast they sometimes stressed the less lovely aspects of Portia and Bassanio—their self-righteousness as insiders in comparison to Shylock's perpetual outsider. Reviews of such performances tend to praise the way in which Shylock is supposedly depicted as somehow typically Jewish, even as the representative of a so-called "race": stereotyping that had once been a source of laughter or contempt was now sometimes enlisted in the cause of a sentimentalized Shylock.

In the notable 1970 National Theatre production (TV film version, 1973) starring Laurence Olivier, Shylock was dressed as an assimilated businessman and the carving knife he bore in many earlier productions was reduced to a decorous penknife for cleaning his fingernails. The production was at a great distance from productions that made Shylock an exotic figure swathed in Oriental robes; but Olivier made his final exit to the accompaniment of the great Hebrew prayer, the Kaddish, suggesting that Shylock's story was an episode in the long history of anti-Semitism.

This section concludes with several reviews of actors from the American Yiddish theater playing the part of Shylock. The idea of a Jew as Shylock was at the time a newsworthy oddity. The final selection, by the critic Desmond MacCarthy, takes the opportunity of one such performance to survey the tradition of theatrical Shylocks.

Laurence Olivier as Shylock. By permission of Cleveland State University Library, Special Collections.

In the production of *The Merchant of Venice*, directed by Jonathan Miller at the National Theatre (London) in 1970, and televised in the United States in 1973, Laurence Olivier's Shylock was costumed as a dignified businessman of the late nineteenth century. Gone were the beard and exotic costume that had become commonplace among stage Shylocks since at least the eighteenth century. Compare Olivier's top-hatted Shylock with the more bizarre costume adopted by Arthur Bourchier in the illustration on the next page.

Signed postcard of Arthur Bourchier (1864–1927) as Shylock. Hulton Archive, copyright 2001 Getty Images, Inc.

The English actor Arthur Bourchier played Shylock in the season 1905–1906, when he was manager of the Garrick Theatre in London. His beard, turban, and robes make this Shylock an exotic figure from some unspecified eastern region, and as much of an outsider to Venetian society as can be imagined. Bourchier began his career as an undergraduate at Oxford and went on to many successes both in classical roles (including, notably, Shakespeare's *Henry VIII*) and more popular roles: each Christmas for many years he produced a stage version of *Treasure Island*, casting himself as the rascally pirate Long John Silver.

William Hazlitt (1778–1830)

William Hazlitt's criticism, whether of painting, drama, poetry, sports, politics, or politicians, is fervid, racy, usually right, and never uninteresting. Hazlitt was influenced as a young man by his association with Samuel Taylor Coleridge, a poet and critic in what we now think of as the first generation of Romantic poets; later he was allied with the younger Romantics, especially his friends Charles Lamb and Leigh Hunt. He was passionately attached to the idea of liberty, which he believed was manifested in the French Revolution. Hazlitt wrote incessantly to eke out a living for himself through journalism and lecturing. The following selection comes from his collection of essays on Characters of Shakespeare's Plays *(1817). In it he writes about* The Merchant of Venice *with a sharp eye for stagecraft, despite his own claim that "The stage is not in general the best place to study" Shakespeare's characters, because the theater "is too often filled with traditional commonplace conceptions." But Hazlitt, using the powerful lens of Edmund Kean's performance as Shylock, as well as his own habit of contrarian thought, pierces through many commonplaces about the play. In his view, Shylock is indeed "malignant," but with ample cause. The Christian's appeal for mercy from Shylock is, according to Hazlitt, "the rankest hypocrisy or the blindest prejudice" in light of their treatment of him. Hazlitt's focus on the* characters *of Shakespeare's plays tends to blur certain historical considerations about the culture of Shakespeare's age but sharpens his sympathy and his indignation.*

from Characters of Shakespeare's Plays[1]

The Merchant of Venice

This is a play that in spite of the change of manners and of prejudices still holds undisputed possession of the stage. Shakespeare's malignant has outlived Mr Cumberland's benevolent Jew.[2] In proportion as Shylock has ceased to be a popular bugbear, "baited with the rabbles' curse,"[3] he becomes a half-favourite

---

[1]William Hazlitt, *Characters of Shakespeare's Plays*, 3rd ed., London: John Templeman, 1838, pp. 248–256.

[2]Richard Cumberland's (1732–1811) very bad play *The Jew* (1779) featured a benevolent character named Sheva who, in gratitude for being saved from mobs in Spain and London, gives £10,000 to his English benefactor.

[3]Quoting Macbeth's defiant line: "I will not yield / To kiss the ground before young Malcolm's feet / And to be baited with the rabble's curse" (5.8.27–29).

with the philosophical part of the audience, who are disposed to think that Jewish revenge is at least as good as Christian injuries. Shylock is *a good hater*; "a man no less sinned against than sinning."[4] If he carries his revenge too far, yet he has strong grounds for "the lodged hate he bears Antonio," which he explains with equal force of eloquence and reason. He seems the depositary of the vengeance of his race; and though the long habit of brooding over daily insults and injuries has crusted over his temper with inveterate misanthropy, and hardened him against the contempt of mankind, this adds but little to the triumphant pretensions of his enemies. There is a strong, quick, and deep sense of justice mixed up with the gall and bitterness of his resentment. The constant apprehension of being burnt alive, plundered, banished, reviled, and trampled on, might be supposed to sour the most forebearing nature, and to take something from that "milk of human kindness,"[5] with which his persecutors contemplated his indignities. The desire of revenge is almot inseparable from the sense of wrong; and we can hardly help sympathising with the proud spirit, hid beneath his "Jewish gaberdine," stung to madness by repeated undeserved provocations, and labouring to throw off the load of obloquy and oppression heaped upon him and all his tribe by one desperate act of "lawful" revenge, till the ferociousness of the means by which he is to execute his purpose, and the pertinacity with which he adheres to it, turn us against him, but even at last, when disappointed of the sanguinary revenge with which he had glutted his hopes, and exposed to beggary and contempt by the letter of the law on which he had insisted with so little remorse, we pity him and think him hardly dealt with by his judges. In all his answers and retorts upon his adversaries, he has the best not only of the argument but of the question, reasoning on their own principles and practice. They are so far from allowing of any measure of equal dealing, of common justice or humanity between themselves and the Jew, that even when they come to ask a favour of him, and Shylock reminds them that "on such a day they spit upon him, another

---

[4]Paraphrasing King Lear: "I am a man / More sinned against than sinning" (3.2.59–60).

[5]Lady Macbeth fears that Macbeth's nature "is too full o' the milk of human kindness" to assasinate King Duncan (1.5.17).

spurn'd him, another called him dog, and for these courtesies request he'll lend them so much monies"—Antonio, his old enemy, instead of any acknowledgment of the shrewdness and justice of his remonstrance, which would have been preposterous in a respectable Catholic merchant in those times, threatens him with a repetition of the same treatment—

"I am as like to call thee so again,
To spit on thee again, to spurn thee too."

After this, the appeal to the Jew's mercy, as if there were any common principle of right and wrong between them, is the rankest hypocrisy, or the blindest prejudice; and the Jew's answer to one of Antonio's friends, who asks him what his pound of forfeit flesh is good for, is irresistible. [Hazlitt quotes 3.1.44–61, beginning "To bait fish withal" to "it shall go hard but I will better the instruction."]

The whole of the trial-scene, both before and after the entrance of Portia, is a master-piece of dramatic skill. The legal acuteness, the passionate declamations, the sound maxims of jurisprudence, the wit and irony interspersed in it, the fluctuations of hope and fear in the different persons, and the completeness and suddenness of the catastrophe, cannot be surpassed. Shylock, who is his own counsel, defends himself well, and is triumphant on all the general topics that are urged against him, and only fails through a legal flaw. Take the following as an instance:—

"SHYLOCK. What judgment shall I dread, doing no wrong?
You have among you many a purchas'd slave,
Which, like our asses, and your dogs, and mules,
You use in abject and in slavish part,
Because you bought them:—shall I say to you,
Let them be free, marry them to your heirs?
Why sweat they under burdens? let their beds
Be made as soft as yours, and let their palates
Be season'd with such viands? you will answer,
The slaves are ours:—so do I answer you:
The pound of flesh, which I demand of him,
Is dearly bought, is mine, and I will have it:

If you deny me, fie upon your law!
There is no force in the decrees of Venice:
I stand for judgment: answer; shall I have it?"

[4.l.89–103]

The keenness of his revenge awakes all his faculties; and he beats back all opposition to his purpose, whether grave or gay, whether of wit or argument, with an equal degree of earnestness and self-possession. His character is displayed as distinctly in other less prominent parts of the play, and we may collect from a few sentences the history of his life—his descent and origin, his thrift and domestic economy, his affection for his daughter, whom he loves next to his wealth, his courtship and his first present to Leah, his wife! "I would not have parted with it" (the ring which he first gave her) "for a wilderness of monkies!" What a fine Hebraism is implied in this expression![6]

Portia is not a very great favourite with us; neither are we in love with her maid, Nerissa. Portia has a certain degree of affectation and pedantry about her, which is very unusual in Shakespeare's women, but which perhaps was a proper qualification for the office of a "civil doctor," which she underakes and executes so successfully. The speech about Mercy is very well; but there are a thousand finer ones in Shakespeare. We do not admire the scene of the caskets; and object entirely to the Black Prince Morocchius. We should like Jessica better if she had not deceived and robbed her father, and Lorenzo, if he had not married a Jewess, though he thinks he has a right to wrong a Jew. The dialogue between this newly-married couple by moonlight, beginning "On such a night," &c. is a collection of classical elegancies. Launcelot, the Jew's man, is an honest fellow. The dilemma in which he describes himself placed between his "conscience and the fiend," the one of which advises him to run away from his master's service and the other to stay in it, is exquisitely humorous. [. . .]

The graceful winding up of this play in the fifth act, after the tragic business is despatched, is one of the happiest instances of Shakespeare's knowledge of the principles of the drama. We do not

---

[6]Hebraism or not, Hazlitt, who wrote quickly and quoted from memory, gets Shylock's line slightly wrong: "I would not have *given it* for a wilderness of monkeys" (3.1.101–102). Also, he forgets that Leah gave the ring to Shylock, not vice-versa.

mean the pretended quarrel between Portia and Nerissa and their husbands about the rings, which is amusing enough, but the conversation just before and after the return of Portia to her own house, beginning "How sweet the moonlight sleeps upon this bank," and ending "Peace! how the moon sleeps with Endymion, and would not be awaked." There is a number of beautiful thoughts crowded into that short space, and linked together by the most natural transitions.

When we first went to see Mr. Kean in Shylock,[7] we expected to see, what we had been used to see, a decrepid old man, bent with age and ugly with mental deformity, grinning with deadly malice, with the venom of his heart congealed in the expression of his countenance, sullen, morose, gloomy, inflexible, brooding over one idea, that of his hatred, and fixed on one unalterable purpose, that of his revenge. We were disappointed, because we had taken our idea from other actors, not from the play. There is no proof there that Shylock is old, but a single line, "Bassanio and *old* Shylock, both stand forth,"—which does not imply that he is infirm with age—and the circumstance that he has a daughter marriageable, which does not imply that he is old at all. It would be too much to say that his body should be made crooked and deformed to answer to his mind, which is bowed down and warped with prejudices and passion. That he has but one idea, is not true; he has more ideas than any other person in the piece: and if he is intense and inveterate in the pursuit of his purpose, he shows the utmost elasticity, vigour, and presence of mind, in the means of attaining it. But so rooted was our habitual impression of the part from seeing it caricatured in the representation, that it was only from a careful perusal of the play itself that we saw our error. The stage is not in general the best place to study our author's characters in. It is too often filled with traditional common-place conceptions of the part, handed down from sire to son, and suited to the taste of *the great vulgar and the small*.[8]—"'Tis an unweeded garden: things rank and gross do

---

[7]Edmund Kean (1787/90–1833), English tragic actor known especially for his Shakespearean villains, had his first hit playing Shylock at Drury Lane in 1814. Instead of the red beard and wig that had become traditional in playing Jewish characters, his Shylock was a dark, knife-wielding menace but also sympathetic as an abused object of prejudice.

[8]A paraphrase by Abraham Cowley (1618–1677) of a line by the Latin poet Horace.

merely gender in it!"[9] If a man of genius comes once in an age to clear away the rubbish, to make it fruitful and wholesome, they cry, "'Tis a bad school: it may be like nature, it may be like Shakespeare, but it is not like us." Admirable critics!—

Heinrich Heine (1797–1856)

Heinrich Heine was the greatest German lyric poet of his time. Although he converted to Christianity, he retained (as this excerpt shows) his strong feelings for Judaism, and partly from this his constant concern about oppressors and oppressed. The passage presented here, about a performance of The Merchant of Venice *and his reaction to Shylock, is typical of the Romantic strain in nineteenth-century Shakespeare criticism in its assumption of a continuity between stage life and real life, its grasping after universality instead of historical specificity ("The spirit of Shakespeare rises above the little squabble of two religious sects"), and in what may seem to us its over-the-top sentimentality, as Heine imagines himself searching for Shylock in the Venetian ghetto.*

from *Shakespeare's Maidens and Women*[1]

When I saw this play at Drury Lane,[2] there stood behind me in the box a pale, fair Briton, who at the end of the Fourth Act fell to weeping passionately, several times exclaiming, "The poor man is wronged!" It was a face of the noblest Grecian style, and the eyes were very large and black. I have never been able to forget those large and black eyes that wept for Shylock![3]

---

[9]Hazlitt slightly misremembers *Hamlet*, "Fie on't, ah fie! 'tis an unweeded garden / That grows to seed. Things rank and gross in nature / Possess it merely" (1.2.135–137).

---

[1]Heinrich Heine, *Shakespeares Mädchen und Frauen (Shakespeare's Maidens and Women)*, excerpted in an anonymous translation in The Variorum Edition of *The Merchant of Venice*, ed. H. H. Furness. Philadelphia: J. P. Lippincott, 1888.

[2]One of the two main "legitimate" theaters in London, a vast amphitheater.

[3]The production was by William Charles Macready in 1840; the identity of the pale, fair Briton with the large black eyes has not been established.

When I think of those tears I have to rank *The Merchant of Venice* with the tragedies, although the frame of the piece is decorated with the merriest figures of masks, of satyrs, and of Cupids, and the poet meant the play for a comedy. [. . .] But the genius of the poet, the genius of Humanity that reigned in him, stood ever above his private will; and so it happened that in Shylock, in spite of all his uncouth grimacings, the poet vindicates an unfortunate sect, which, for mysterious purposes, has been burdened by Providence with the hate of the rabble both high and low, and has reciprocated this hate—not always with love.

But what do I say? The spirit of Shakespeare rises above the little squabble of two religious sects, and the drama shows us neither Jew nor Christian exclusively, but oppressor and oppressed, and the mad, bitter exultation of the latter when they can pay back to their haughty tormentors with interest the shames they have suffered. There is not the slightest trace in this play of a religious difference. [. . .]

In truth, with the exception of Portia, Shylock is the most respectable person in the play. He loves money, he does not hide this love—he cries it out aloud in the marketplace, but there is something he prizes above money; satisfaction for a tortured heart—righteous retribution for unutterable shames; and although they offer him the borrowed sum tenfold, he rejects it, and the three thousand, ay and ten times three thousand, ducats he would not regret if he can but buy a pound of his enemy's flesh therewith.

Ay, Shylock does indeed love money, but there are things he loves still more, among them his daughter, "Jessica, my girl." Although he curses her in his rage, and would see her dead at his feet with the jewels in her ears and the ducats in the coffin, he loves her more than ducats and jewels. Debarred from public intercourse, outcast from Christian society, and thrust back upon a narrow domestic life, to the poor Jew there remains only devotion to his home, and this is manifested in him with the most touching intensity. [. . .]

Portia represents that after-bloom of Greek art which, in the sixteenth century, impregnated the world, from Italy out, with its delightful fragrance, and which we at the present day love and treasure under the name of "the Renaissance." Portia is at the same time the representative of the serene good fortune which is the opposite of the gloomy lot that Shylock represents. What a rosy bloom, what a ring of purity, is there in all her thoughts and speeches! How warm with joy her words, how beautiful all her images, mostly borrowed from mythology! How sad, on the contrary, how incisive and repulsive, are the thoughts and speeches of Shylock, who uses only Old Testament similitudes! [. . .]

[As a visitor in Venice:] At last I, wandering hunter after dreams that I am, I looked around everywhere on the Rialto to see if I could not find Shylock. I could have told him something that would have pleased him—namely, that his cousin, Herr von Shylock in Paris, had become the mightiest baron in Christendom, invested by her Catholic Majesty with that Order of Isabella which was founded to celebrate the expulsion of the Jews and Moors from Spain. But I found him nowhere on the Rialto, and I determined to seek my old acquaintance in the Synagogue. The Jews were just then celebrating their Day of Atonement, and they stood enveloped in their white talars,[4] with uncanny motions of the head, looking almost like an assemblage of ghosts. There the poor Jews had stood, fasting and praying, from earliest morning;—since the evening before they had taken neither food nor drink, and had previously begged pardon of all their acquaintance for any wrong they might have done them in the course of the year, that God might thereby also forgive them their wrongs—a beautiful custom, which, curiously, is found among this people, strangers though they be to the teaching of Christ.

Although I looked all round the Synagogue, I nowhere discovered the face of Shylock. And yet I felt he must be hidden under one of those white talars, praying more fervently than his fellow-believers, looking up with stormy, nay frantic wildness, to the throne of Jehovah, the hard God-King! I saw him not. But towards evening, when, according to the Jewish faith, the gates of Heaven are shut, and no prayer can then obtain admittance, I heard a voice, with a ripple of tears that were never wept by eyes. It was a sob that could come only from a breast that held in it all the martyrdom which, for eighteen centuries, had been borne by a whole tortured people. It was the death-rattle of a soul sinking

[4]Shawls worn by men during religious services.

down dead tired at heaven's gates. And I seemed to know the voice, and I felt that I had heard it long ago, when, in utter despair it moaned out, then as now, "Jessica, my girl!"

William Winter (1836–1917)

William Winter served as drama critic for the New York Tribune *from 1865 to 1909. His reviews, biographies, and other writing provide an extraordinarily full record of the Anglo-American theater in that period. With admirable recall for the minute specifics of costume, gesture, and intonation, Winter in the selection presented here describes a landmark performance in 1879 by Sir Henry Irving (1838–1905). Irving was the most famous actor-manager of his period. He had sole control over the acting company in which he was both star and director. His leading lady and equal in artistic achievement and fame was Ellen Terry, who played Portia in this production. Irving famously interpolated a pathetic silent scene, which Winter evokes, of Shylock's knocking at the door of the dark home from which Jessica has just fled.*

from *Shakespeare on the Stage*[1]

Irving's Shylock entered, for the first time, preceding Bassanio, who, obviously, had found him in the mart and spoken to him abut a loan of money. He was seen to be a man stricken in years—his shoulders a little bowed, his knees a little bent, his face lined and wrinkled, his hair going gray—*old* Shylock in every detail—but hardy, resolute, formidable, possessing the steel-sinewy, nervous vitality of the Hebrew race, and animated by indomitable will. His aspect was distinctively Jewish, and it was Orientally pictorial. His demeanor revealed a mind intensely interested, veiling that interest by a crafty assumption of indifference. His detested enemy had applied to him to borrow money: that fact was singular, was astonishing; there might be no consequence in it, or there might proceed from it the opportunity, for which he had long hungered and thirsted, to strike that enemy dead. Bassanio must be made to

[1]William Winter, *Shakespeare on the Stage.* New York: Moffatt, Yard and Co., 1911, pp. 179–197.

Ellen Terry as Portia. The Hulton Archive, copyright 2001 Getty Images, Inc.

This photograph, probably taken in 1890, shows the English actress Ellen Terry (1848–1927) costumed as Portia (disguised as the young lawyer) in the courtroom scene. Terry teamed with the actor-manager Henry Irving in the production described in the selection by William Winter. In her left hand she holds the legal document that will defeat Shylock's plea to take a pound of Antonio's flesh. Terry's Portia is a serious and dignified figure in the photograph, less playful or glamorous than other actresses have sometimes made her.

repeat his request, and the matter must be carefully considered. One skirt of the Jew's gabardine—a garment of rich material but of sober hue and well-worn—was caught up at the side and held in the right hand, which also held a black crutch-stick, grasping it near the middle and more as though it were a weapon than a prop. Throughout the opening scene the mention by Shylock of the ducats desired by Antonio was made in a lingering, caressing tone, involuntarily expressive of his love of money, and the thumb and first two fingers of whichever hand happened to be free—for he shifted his staff occasionally from one hand to the other—were, from time to time, moved slowly, as though in the act of counting coins. The first speech, "Three thousand ducats—Well?" only noted the sum, with an accent of inquiry; the second speech, "For three months: Well?" indicated watchful expectation of something to follow; but the third speech, "Antonio shall become bound," was uttered with a strong emphasis on the merchant's name and on the word "bound," accompanied by a momentary flash of lurid fire in the dark, piercing, baleful eyes, a quick contraction of the muscles of the arm and hands, instantly succeeded by a perfect resumption of self-control, as the calm, cold voice, reiterated the recurring question, "Well?" The utterance of the declaration, "I *will* be *assured* I may" was sharp, incisive, almost fierce, but the tone quickly softened in delivery of the words that immediately follow. The rebuff beginning "Yes, to smell pork," was ejaculated in a bitter tone of protest, till the closes, when the words "nor *pray* with you" were spoken in accents of deep solemnity. Then Shylock saw and recognized the approaching figure of Antonio—a fact signified in the expression of his face, before he asked, with an entire change of manner, in a nonchalant, indifferent way, "What news on the Rialto?" He then raised his left hand, as though to shade his eyes, and gazed intently into the distance, saying "Who is he comes here?" There was in the action of Irving's Shylock, at that and at some other points, a viperous impartment of the Jew's inherent treachery and deep-seated malice—the duplicity which is characteristically false in circumstances in which it would be much easier to be true. [. . .]

In Irving's arrangement of the comedy the Second Act contained three scenes, the second being devoted to Lorenzo's love affairs, and the third, exceptionally picturesque and illuminative, devoted to

Shylock, in his relation to the incident of Jessica's elopement. In this latter scene the place represented was a street in front of Shylock's house. At the back a finely painted drop afforded a spacious view of romantic Venice, in the dim starlight.[2] A high bridge, spanning a canal, extended across the stage, from the upper left-hand corner to a point forward on the right. The bridge was accessible by steps. At the right of and below it was a building, fashioned from a projecting hood above the door—the "pent house" mentioned by Lorenzo. At the left of the stage, in the foreground, bordering the canal, was placed the house of Shylock, on the front of which was a prominent balcony. Launcelot and Shylock entered from that dwelling, the former in haste and perturbation, as if retreating from his harsh employer. Shylock's speech of dismissal to him—"Well, thou shalt see"—was spoken by Irving in a strain of censorious sarcasm, and the Jew's parting from his daughter, immediately before her flight, was effected in a mood of querulous anxiety, Shylock showing himself oppressed by the presentiment of impending disaster: "There is some ill a-brewing towards my rest." At mention of Bassanio, when Launcelot said, "My young master doth expect your reproach," there was a quick accession of severity in Shylock's fact and demeanor, and the tone in which, to the menial's blundering speech, he replied, "So I do—*his*," was grim with expectancy of revenge. When he ended his authoritative delivery of the mandate, to Jessica, "Lock up my doors," he entered the house, was absent for a moment, and then returned, wearing a cloak and an orange-tawny, turban-like head-dress, and carrying a lantern and a staff. Hearing the voice of Launcelot, who was speaking in a hurried undertone to Jessica, but not hearing the words, he swiftly advanced to his daughter, as Launcelot sped away, seized her by the wrist, looked suspiciously upon her face and harshly put the question to her— pointing with his stick after the departing servant—"*What says* that fool of Hagar's offspring—ha?" Reassured by Jessica's ready lie, he turned from her, murmuring, "The patch is kind enough," and then, with the old proverb about the wisdom of precaution on his lips, ascended to the bridge and passed across it, out of sight. The

---

[2]Like other spectacular Victorian productions, Irving's provided richly detailed stage pictures, using backdrops and elaborate props. The stage pictures were the product of historical research into sixteenth-century Venice, but the result was romantic and fanciful.

elopement of Jessica with Lorenzo was then effected, in a gondola, which moved smoothly away in the canal, and the scene became tumultuous with a revel of riotous maskers, who sang, danced, frolicked, and tumbled in front of Shylock's house, as though obtaining mischievous pleasure in disturbing the neighborhood of the Jew's decorous dwelling. Soon that clamorous rabble streamed away; there was a lull in the music, and the grim figure of Shylock, his staff in one hand, his lantern in the other, appeared on the bridge, where for an instant he paused, his seamed, cruel face, visible in a gleam of ruddy light, contorted by a sneer, as he listened to the sound of revelry dying away in the distance. Then he descended the steps, crossed to his dwelling, raised his right hand, struck twice upon the door with the iron knocker, and stood like a statue, waiting—while a slow-descending curtain closed in one of the most expressive pictures that any stage has ever presented. [. . .]

Throughout the Trial Scene [Irving's] acting was perfect in symmetry, particularly of expressive detail, cumulative power, and tragic effect. All indication of passion had disappeared from his visage and person. He seemed the authentic personification of the Mosaic Law, the righteous minister of Justice; the ordained avenger. In the presence of that majestic Hebrew the observer became, for a moment, completely oblivious that Shylock is not only a villain but a trickster; that his nature, like his quest, is abhorrent; that the "bond" to which he appeals, and by virtue of which he so ostentatiously craves "the law," was obtained by the hypocritical pretense of friendship and magnanimity; and that he is now proceeding in his actual character, that of a dissembling scoundrel, to do a murder under the compulsory sanction of a Court of Justice. The illusion, however, was only momentary. Every evil passion poisons the mind that harbors it, till, if the inevitable degradation be not stayed, the character is vitiated, the body is ravaged, the soul is polluted. That truth was legibly written in the countenance of Irving's Shylock, as the Jew stood there, in the Courtroom, no thoughtful observer could fail to read it. [. . .] On entering the Court, Shylock advanced a little way, paused, and slowly gazed around until his eyes found Antonio, upon whom his look then settled, with evident gloating satisfaction—a cruel, deadly look of sanguinary hatred—and then he stepped a little forward and gravely bowed toward the Duke's throne. The address of that magistrate was heard by him with patient but wholly unmoved attention, and his reply was spoken with dignity and decisive force. [. . .]

There was bland simplicity in his question "On *what* 'compulsion' *must* I?" and he listened with weariness and growing impatience to the speech about "The quality of mercy," feeling it be to irrelevant, futile, and tedious: his answer to it was abrupt and decisive. When Portia, in pitiful entreaty, said, "Bid me *tear* the bond," he laid his left hand heavily on both of their hands, to stay the action, and answered, without even a tremor, "When it is *paid*, according to the tenor." At "So says the bond—doth it not, noble judge?" he laid the point of his knife on the words in that document, held open by Portia, and when she enquired, "Are there balances here, to weigh the flesh?" he caused an hysterical laugh, by the grisly promptitude with which he brought fort the "balance" from his bosom—an action which seemed to imply that he had carried the implement there, to comfort him by its touch, with assurance of his certain revenge. The relentless statement "'Tis not *in* the bond" was horrible in its icy implacable resolve, and he uttered with infernal exultation the summons to the Merchant, "A sentence! *Come!* PREPARE!" In the subsequent resolute, persistent effort to extricate himself with at least financial profit from the ruins of his defeated scheme of murder the stalwart force of the Jew's character was splendidly maintained, and at the final catastrophe, the collapse, both physical and mental, was denoted with consummate skill. In making his exit from the Court Shylock moved slowly and with difficulty, as if he had been stricken by a fatal weakness and were opposing it by inveterate will. At the door he nearly fell, but at once recovered himself, and with a long, heavy sigh he disappeared. The spectacle was intensely pathetic, awakening that pity which naturally attends upon despoiled greatness of character and broken, ruined power, whether that character and that power be malignant or benign. [. . .]

[Irving] restored the Fifth Act, which, after the time of Edmund Kean, had frequently been omitted.[3]

---

[3]The tradition of dropping Act 5, so that the play ends after the trial scene, places the emphasis on Shylock, deemphasizes the music and romance of Act 5, and contributes to the sense of a "tragic" *Merchant*.

Reviews of Yiddish-Speaking Actors in the Role of Shylock

The first three newspaper reviews printed here refer to the Jewish actor Jacob P. Adler's performance as Shylock in 1903. Adler was a leading figure in a briefly thriving theatrical scene that served Yiddish-speaking Jewish immigrants from Russia and Eastern Europe. Yiddish companies frequently performed Shakespeare's plays in translation, sometimes adapted to the tastes of their audience. In a departure from tradition, Adler played his Shylock in Yiddish while the rest of the cast spoke English. The first selection (about a pre–New York performance) is from a Jewish publication; the others are from leading New York newspapers. These reviews are followed by one of a later Yiddish-speaking actor, Maurice Schwartz.

from *The American Hebrew*, May 15, 1903

The True Shakespeare's Jew

It is the pleasure of the literary man who happens to be a "modern" Jew, to settle Shylock's fate by taking him as an example of the prejudice of Shakespeare's time. But Shakespeare's Jew left the stage when the audience left his playhouse. Shylock, as Shakespeare must have conceived him, died with the performers instructed by him. Since then, the players of Shylock have put into the character the prejudices of their own time, varying from ridicule when Shylock was a comic character, to dislike when he became a money-lender.

The Shylock presented by Jacob P. Adler (for the first time with an English-speaking company, last Saturday night, in Philadelphia) was "the Jew that Shakespeare drew,"[1] at least in outlines, which Mr. Adler filled in with great intelligence; it was the Jew which Shakespeare would have constructed had he known more of the details of Jewish life.

[1] The line "This is the Jew that Shakespeare drew" was supposed to have been said by the poet Alexander Pope on seeing Charles Mackin's performance in 1771.

I pride myself on a little bit of racial pride, and to be loyal have often strained the limits of truth to see something pardonable in Shylock's desire to make carrion of Antonio; but I must confess that I could never see anything praiseworthy in his unbusinesslike insistence on the pound of flesh. The audiences were in the right: Shylock was a villain. The vindictive, persistent, and implacable Shylock deserved the spurning of the contemptible Gratiano, whatever Portia's subsequent decision might have been.

Mr Adler's Jew rests on a desire to present a consistent man, whose affection for his daughter, whose kindness to his brethren, whose general sense of justice could not have been perverted by a senseless desire for revenge which would have resulted in the death of his enemy.

Mr. Adler's Shylock was the portrait of a man of strong feelings, who earns his wealth in the midst of foes who hold him in the greatest contempt. To him comes one who has frequently expressed his contempt, and as a jest, and perhaps to have the haughty merchant under deep personal obligation to him, he proposes his "merry" bond. With the connivance of intimate friends of this same honest merchant, young Lorenzo elopes with Shylock's daughter and as a token of his affection takes with him a valuable box of jewels. Shylock loves his daughter with staid paternal affection, and her unfaithfulness intensifies his hatred of Antonio. In the course of time the "merry" bond is forfeited, and Antonio must pay his creditor.

It is the condition of the bond; the pound of flesh is his; and legally, so Shylock seems to argue, he may take it. But when a life is to be forfeited his intention is not to pursue the merchant to the very end, but demanding justice according to that law which Venice had established, rest with the granting of life to the merchant who had reviled him. The Jew is an alien. He has had no voice in the making of the law; let then the penalty fall on Venice if it contravene the law of its own creation. When he sharpened the knife to cut the pound of flesh from the bankrupt, when he produced the contract insisting on its validity to the letter, Shylock slyly noted whether the proud merchant quailed, and when Portia declared that the law award the penalty, he rushed toward the merchant and allowed himself to be restrained. The judgment of the court follows. It legalizes the elopement of his daughter and the robbery; it takes from him his property and compels him to become a Christian if he would remain alive. The great injustice of such justice evokes the exclamation, "Is *this* your law?" With a shrug of the shoulders and an expression of exalted contempt, he turns away and leaves the hall of justice with unspoken reproach for such law and justice.

Shylock is not exceptional in any respect. Capable of anger as well as of affection. Capable of strength and humility. Capable of joy and weeping; not unlike others in virtues and vices. A good hater and a good lover; he is strong in his control of himself, but he is stronger in his indifference to that outside world which taunts him with that degradation which they themselves have produced. In brief, Mr. Adler has revived the Jewish Shylock. He takes a place in the synagogue, not among the nobility but among those who are typical. The impersonation was distinguished for its consistency, and the introduction of numerous illuminating touches. The gestures, the voice, the walk, the appearance and dress were complete in every detail. The elopement of Jessica almost overwhelms him; he tears his clothes as a sign of mourning; but he goes to Bassanio's house, not to enjoy himself, but to be among the merchants and also to assist the prodigal in scattering the money he had borrowed on his friend's life; nothing grand in that, but thoroughly human; true to himself, at least.

Much might be said of certain passages in the production: the fine affection for his daughter; the entrance with the mob of revilers; the negotiations with Antonio; the trial scene and when he discovers the loss of his daughter and his money; but finest of all was his departure from the court. Gratiano had been making a number of passes at him, which he had beaten off after the manner of a bird, with weak clutchings of the hands; then he brushes the impress of Gratiano's hand from his sleeve, arranges his hair and coat, his beard, and with calm contempt for the court and all those interested in the wrongful miscarriage of justice, passes out, leaving a stern sense of disapproval of the whole proceeding.

It was a new Shylock. It deserves attention. Mr Adler will present his interpretation in New York in the month of June, when his company will be better drilled, and he himself will feel at home in the midst of a company speaking English in the theaters where his art must be all the more true because so few will understand his words.

from *New York Times*, May 26, 1903

THE YIDDISH SHYLOCK
Jacob Adler and the Augustin Daly Production
An Interesting Performance at the American
Before a Large and Enthusiastic House

Jacob Adler, who has for many years been known as the great
Yiddish tragedian of the Bowery,[2] appeared as Shylock last night
at the American Theatre, speaking his part in Yiddish, with an
English-speaking support, and the magnificent production used
four years ago by the late Augustin Daly.[3] The spacious audito-
rium was so crowded with his friends, and others who were
attracted by his fame, that the reference on the program to the
ordinance against standees seemed a hollow mockery. He received
an enthusiastic welcome, and was followed breathlessly to the
end. If he failed to command a place among the greatest inter-
preters of the part, this was largely, no doubt, due to the fact that
to make Shylock fully sympathetic to a Jewish audience is virtually impossible.

There are, roughly speaking, two views of the character. To
those who have studied the esthetic of the Elizabethan theatre and
the traditional treatment of the Jew on the Shakespearean stage,
there is little doubt that Shylock was acted essentially as a comic
grotesque—a man hated and baited after the manner of Marlowe's
Jew of Malta (who, indeed, seems to have served as a prototype)
and in the end brought to a cruel defeat—enlivened by such exultation, even laughter, as was natural to a Jew-hating people whose
national amusement was bear baiting.

This medieval conception of the Jew was Shakespeare's point
of departure in creating Shylock; but it was only that. He overlaid
the rough ground plan with a character so truly and sympatheti-
cally rendered that one sees Shylock, as it were, in the full round

[2]The Bowery, a main street on the lower East Side of New York, where Jewish immigrants from Eastern Europe settled around the turn of the twentieth century. The
Yiddish theater was a thriving enterprise there, and Jacob Adler (1855–1926) was
one of its stars.

[3]Daly (1838–1899) was a leading American actor, producer, and playwright.

of life. To those inclined to sympathize with the downtrodden, it thus became possible to conceive of him in a radically different light—to make of him a sort of hero of his race, a demigod whose very sins were to be pitied, not hated, and whose fate was to be viewed as the tragedy of a great race. Such are the revenges brought about by the whirligig of time[4] in this matter of Shakespearean interpretations!

To Adler, as to all other modern actors, the Elizabethan Shylock is of course out of the question; and to him more than to another it is needful to represent the Jew in his most sympathetic and most exalted light. But in order to do this it is necessary to ennoble in the acting such passages as tend to buffoon his character, and, if they cannot be ennobled, to cut them.

Adler failed, in so far as he did fail, because his artistic good sense impelled him to give, on the whole, a simple, unaffected, and naturalistic rendering of the part, to eschew the Hebrew prophet of the modern sentimentality, and to stick to the Shylock of Shakespeare—and of the Ghetto.[5] He thus fell, as it were, between two stools.

The audience laughed heartily at national traits and applauded Shylock's outbursts of indignation against the Christians; but it failed to be swayed with full dramatic force for the simple reason that it was both repelled and mystified.

In attitude and demeanor he was the Jewish money lender—dignified, but in a manner that was matter-of-fact and unimaginative. The grim austerity of Irving[6] and the malignancy of Mansfield[7] were alike absent. It was probably because of this lack of spiritual exaltation in the character, rather than because of any studied design, that so many of his lines raised a laugh. The laughs are in the lines right enough, and no doubt were welcomed by Shakespeare's company; but they are well nigh fatal to any interpretation of the part which can sway the deeper emotions of Mr. Adler's audience.

---

[4]A paraphrase of Feste's line about the outwitted Malvolio in *Twelfth Night*: "And thus the whirligig of times brings in his revenges" (5.1.376).

[5]The first recorded English use of the Italian word—meaning the place in a city where Jews were forced to live—is in Coryate, *Crudities*.

[6]On Irving, see the selection by William Winter in this section of Contexts materials.

[7]The American actor Richard Mansfield (1854?–1907) starred as Shylock in 1893.

It was for a similar reason that the lines went for so little in which Shylock is reminded alternately of his own losses and Antonio's disasters. It bears every evidence of being a bravura passage, and it is usually played as such. Mansfield reveled in the quick transitions from the heights of exultation to the abyss of chagrin; and if Irving did not do so, it was seemingly because he lacked the physical and the temperamental force.

Mr. Adler has the requisite abilities, as those who have been familiar with his work at the Windsor and the People's Theatres are abundantly aware; but he failed of full effect in the passage, as it seemed, because he feared to overstep the bounds of what is realistically possible. Whatever dignity he achieved by his sober reading came at the cost of a strong theatric effect.

*[The following story appeared on page 2 of
the same day's edition of the* New York Times*]*

JEWS, PANIC-STRIKEN, LEAVING ST. PETERSBURG

**Fear Similar Outrages to Those at Kishineff at the
Celebration to be Held on Friday**

A dispatch from St. Petersburg [. . .] confirms the report that the Jews in that city are in fear that similar outrages to those in Kishineff[8] may occur in the Russian capital during the celebration of the two hundredth anniversary of the founding of St. Petersburg, which will be held on May 29.

All the Jews who are possessed of the means are preparing to go to Finland, while the poor Jews are panic stricken.

The authorities hope to avoid rioting through diverting the attention of the masses by giving free shows at the theaters and other entertainments.

---

[8]In April 1903, a pogrom (originally a Russian word for a riot against Jews) occurred with official approval in Kishinev in Russian-ruled Moldavia. Mobs killed and looted for two days before police intervened. Forty-five Jews died, 600 were wounded, and 1,500 Jewish homes were pillaged.

from *New York Herald*, May 26, 1903

JACOB P. ADLER'S SHYLOCK SCORES

Gave Effective Performance of the Role in Yiddish at American Theatre

OTHERS PLAYED IN ENGLISH
Miss Meta Maynard a Graceful Portia,
but Rest of Cast Not Very Strong

Shylock in Yiddish, with the rest of the company speaking English—that was the novelty presented in last night's rendition of *The Merchant of Venice* at the American Theatre.

In Yiddish Shylock, represented by Jacob P. Adler, was more intelligible than the English company. His make-up, his gestures, his manner, his elocution carried conviction with them, even to that portion of his audience which could not understand the words. Yet his methods were of the simplest. He used no undue emphasis.

He was the hounded and persecuted Hebrew of the Middle Ages—servile, fawning, submissive in manner, save for an occasional snarl when his enemies had driven him to bay. Only when he felt himself backed up by the power of the law did he allow a gleam or a gesture of triumph to escape him. Even then his suppliant whine to the Duke and to Daniel, come to judgment in the person of Portia, showed that he felt the necessity of protection. His final breakdown when Duke and Daniel arrayed themselves against him was pathetic in its helplessness and overwhelming but noiseless agony.

There was less assumption of dignity in this Shylock than in the Shylocks with which an English-speaking audience is familiar. His hatreds were the malevolent hatreds of a man who feels that hate is impotent unless he can summon cunning to his aid. With infinite art Mr. Adler suggested the impression that this Shylock belonged to a race so buffeted by fortune, so accustomed to defeat that his temporary triumph left him too dazed for the full expression of his gratification, and as the full measure of his disasters dawned slowly upon his brain they crushed him into a condition of abject and pitiable despair. Only at the last did he gather himself together with a consciousness of having been wronged and stalked off the stage with an air of pride and disdain. [. . .]

Of the company which supported Mr. Adler not much can be said in commendation. The Portia of Miss Meta Maynard had its graceful moments, but it lacked sparkle and vivacity in the lighter scenes and impressiveness in the weightier ones. The Antonio of Mr. Balfour and the Bassanio of Mr. Ryan presented a goodly exterior, and they spoke their lines in a rotund and distinct voice. The Launcelot Gobbo of Robert C. Turner was played without any unctuousness of humor. The Old Gobbo of Beverly W. Turner showed more originality and was an entirely creditable performance.

The audience, which crowded every seat in the large theatre, was generous in its tribute to Mr. Adler, but showed little favor for any of the company except Miss Maynard, who received a few faint rounds of applause here and there.

Mr. Adler was called on repeatedly before the curtain at the end of every act in which he had made an appearance, was overwhelmed with floral tributes and was at the close compelled to make a little speech of thanks.

Maurice Schwartz (1890–1960), star and founding producer of the Jewish Arts Theater, had one of his most successful performances in a play called (in Yiddish) Shaylock und Zayn Tokhter *(Shylock and His Daughter), in 1947. His earlier Shylock, reported in this newspaper account, was an act on a vaudeville program—a variety show with songs, dances, comedians, dumb animal acts, and occasionally, as here, a serious theatrical turn.*

from *New York Times*, April 21, 1930 (Copyright © by the New York Times Co. Reprinted by permission.)

MAURICE SCHWARTZ A FERVID SHYLOCK

Yiddish Actor in Scenes From 'Merchant of Venice' at Palace

To make his début on the English-speaking stage, Maurice Schwartz has come north to the Palace this week from his Yiddish Art Theatre at Broadway and Twenty-eighth Street, and in what must seem the paradoxical surroundings of the variety stage he takes his bows as Shylock. Before audiences which have just listened to the mad Jim McWilliams and will next observe the equally irresponsible Ben Blue, he makes a striking and indicative appearance in a short anthology of scenes from *The Merchant of Venice.*

They do not include the court room scene, but in those that he has chosen Mr. Schwartz has been careful to include what will round out his altogether emotional interpretation. He begins quietly with the dread bargaining between Shylock, Antonio and Bassanio, moves into the parting scene with Jessica and later with the two scornful young men of Venice, and concludes with the apostrophe to Tubal. It is a passionate, furious portrait that he creates, precise and controlled in diction and held closely to the rhythm of the verse. It leaves no doubt on the part of Mr. Schwartz as to the tragic implications of the character. The "Hath not a Jew eyes?" speech is delivered in a sort of frenzy, full of despair and near madness, and the quieter scene with Tubal is likewise replete with revenge and dark foreboding. Perhaps as a concession to this vaudeville setting Mr. Schwartz has chosen to stress the background of a Venetian carnival where it occurs in the play, and the emphasis has not resulted fortunately. The music, while successful in setting a mood, is at present too loud and continuous to serve as an effective incidental accompaniment. But over and above these details this Shylock has an undeniable stature, the more remarkable for its swift and sure creation in the heart of a vaudeville bill.

Desmond MacCarthy (1877–1952)

Under the pseudonym "Affable Hawk," the English critic Desmond MacCarthy wrote regularly for the New Statesman *(where the following review appeared); he was later senior literary critic for the (London)* Sunday Times. *From his days as an undergraduate at Cambridge, MacCarthy was associated with the loosely affiliated group of friends that has become known as "Bloomsbury," among its members Virginia Woolf, Vanessa Bell, John Maynard Keynes, and Lytton Strachey. In this review, of a 1919 production of* Merchant *in London, starring Maurice Moscovitch (1871–1949), a Russian-born star of the American Yiddish Theater who went on to a career in Hollywood, MacCarthy helpfully contrasts Moscovitch's approach to that of some precursors.*

from "Shylocks Past and Present"[1]

On returning to England I inquired whose acting was being most admired in London, and I was told that Maurice Moscovitch's acting in the part of Shylock at the Court Theatre had roused the critics into saying enthusiastic things about him. Having missed my colleague's comments I do not know how far my praise falls short of theirs. Perhaps after their comments mine will seem cold; I do not feel coldly about his performance—far from it.

Mr. Maurice Moscovitch is, I am informed, a Russian subject and by birth a Jew.[2] He has surmounted triumphantly the drawback of acting in a foreign tongue; proving himself the best elocutionist in the cast, only keeping a slight accent such as an actor might even assume to stress the difference between Shylock and the Venetians. His birth has given Mr. Moscovitch one huge advantage. His Shylock is a realistic Shylock, and being himself a Jew, instinct prompts him to all those gestures and movements which an actor of another race can only acquire by painstaking mimicry. For deprecating movements of the hands, shrugs, dubious slantings of the head, agitated shakings of the wrists, for a certain pervasive subserviency of manner, for effusiveness in cajolery, for homely expansiveness in joy, for childish abandonment to weeping (poor miserable, puckered face!), for gusto in *schadenfreude*,[3] his Shylock is perfect. Wherever in the list of famous Shylocks you finally decide to place Mr. Moscovitch, this is certain—he is "damned good to steal from." But I have got much more praise to give than that (see lower down). What I have said would be consistent with his having played Shylock as a little Yiddish pawnbroker, who at painful moments might squirm his way into our sympathies and at triumphant ones wake in us a desire to stamp on him. Shylock has been played like that; the text will stand it. And if then in the trial scene Portia is given a false beard and paunch, and Jessica is played as more of a sly hussy (the text will support this interpretation, too) than even

[1]Desmond MacCarthy, "Shylocks Past and Present" [1920] in *Drama*. New York: Putnam, 1940, pp. 15–20.

[2]Moscovitch made his English-language debut in this production in 1919 and went on to play many other English parts on both stage and screen.

[3]German word (literally, "shame-joy") for the pleasure we take in someone else's misfortune.

Miss Nesbitt[4] makes her, the play can be a great deal better pulled together than the Court Theatre company succeeds in doing. Their performance, however, aims at something better, but it is dreadfully out of gear. Very little imagination has been spent on the production. Mr. Fagan[5] does not seem to have made up his mind what the total effect of the play is to be; what dominant mood should be sustained in us by it. He has merely trusted Shakespeare to muddle through to some kind of emotional result: "We'll say all the words and go on and off when Shakespeare tells us and accompany the words with more or less expected gestures, and then the glory of his creative imagination will shine upon you." Ah, if it were only as simple as that!

In conducting an orchestral symphony, it is not sufficient to see that the flutes come in at the right places, and the fiddles and trombones at theirs, and that the performers play the notes written down for them; the parts have to be blended. The composition must be interpreted. The conductor must carry the whole of it in his head, and according to his interpretation he will modify the prominence of this passage, or bring out the quality of that instrument at such and such a moment, knowing in each case it will effect the emotional value of what is past and to come. He may not be able to define what he wants to convey, or know why this or that stress is important, but he feels that it is so. He has an emotional conception of the whole and in proportion to the fineness, sureness, and richness of that conception so (setting aside their varying skill) will the playing of the individual musicians be good.

The parallel between a symphony and a piece like *The Merchant of Venice* is close. The producer has to decide how much realism in the acting is needed in this scene, how subordinate realism must be in that; when the audience is glad to forget that all this is happening in Venice or anywhere on earth, when they must be sharply reminded again of time and place; how rampant the fun should be, not only judging it as though it were an independent comic turn, but from the point of view of its being also a transition to something else. Does it matter if Gobbo kills the casket scene

---

[4]English actress Cathleen Nesbitt (1888–1982) played a wide range of roles during her long career, including, on Broadway, Mrs. Higgins in *My Fair Lady*.

[5]James Bernard Fagan (1873–1933), director, playwright, and actor-manager; later Hollywood screenwriter. Fagan led the Court (now Royal Court) Theatre at the time of this production.

when he enters? Shall we be reminded by Jessica's voice, when she speaks from the window, that she is a wily, caressing little runaway, capable of stealing her dead mother's ring from her father and exchanging it for a monkey, or is that side of her character better kept out of sight until it is wanted to bring out the pathos of Shylock? Or shall we hear first and last only the voice of a beautiful girl in love? How sympathetic is Shylock himself to be? How unreal are the Venetian gallants to appear? How simple and young or how unfeeling? How like fairyland is Portia's palace to be? How like a real court of justice the Trial Scene?

I can imagine many people, and I am tempted to include Mr. Fagan among them, saying: "But Shakespeare himself has decided all these questions; he was the greatest of dramatists; we need only read the play and go straight along." The answers may be in the written book, but it is not easy to find them. Every speech which advances a plot, or creates atmosphere or expresses character is a many-faceted thing. Take by itself a passage or dialogue—its largest facet may be obvious; but when you come to put it in its setting, it by no means follows that the strongest beam of light should flash at that moment from that facet. I have been drawn into making these remarks because great as the pleasure is which the company at the Court Theatre have lately given to an unexacting public, they would give a great deal more if attention were directed to this side of their art.

By an irony of fate, the element in their performance (namely, the acting of Mr. Maurice Moscovitch) which makes it worth seeing, explodes the whole play as they act it. His Shylock is a piece of dignified realism introduced among the tame, histrionic conventions of the stock Shakespearean touring company. No one will blame Mr. Fagan for allowing an actor of Mr. Moscovitch's talent a free hand, but no array of terms can express the reprobation he deserves as a producer for not bringing the acting of the others into some sort of harmony with him. One adjective will suggest the quality of Mr. Moscovitch's Shylock; it is Rembrandtesque. Imagine, then, the aesthetic effect of a figure by Rembrandt introduced into a Maclise illustration of Shakespare.[6] His Shylock reminds one of those old Jews Rembrandt was fond of painting, of the dramatic realism of

---

[6]Daniel Maclise (1806–1870) won fame but not much critical praise for his lithograph portraits of contemporary celebrities and his vast fresco paintings of historical subjects.

their poses, their picturesqueness, their dignity, and of the passion which smoulders in their dark, impersonal eyes. I do not myself believe that a Rembrandtesque Shylock is consistent with the finest production of *The Merchant of Venice* conceivable. To continue to use painting as an indication of a possible presentment of character, the quality which a Tintoretto[7] figure possesses would blend better the stormy, tragic human elements of the play with the unreality, suavity, gaiety, and tenderness of the rest.

Until the ugly loud-voiced Irishman, Macklin,[8] persuaded "Lun" Rich to try him in the part at Covent Garden in 1725, Shylock was never played realistically. The immediate effect was tremendous. Macklin's performance kept George II awake all night and moved Pope to compose a couplet which on internal evidence no one would attribute to him. If he could see Mr. Moscovitch perhaps he would exclaim again:

> This is the Jew
> That Shakespeare drew.

Macready made Shylock (according to George Lewis) into "an abject, sordid, irritable, argumentative Jew";[9] he did not show him as a vindictive man whose vengeance is a retribution of wrongs to his sacred nation and himself, nor did his acting bring out that passionate passage (so necessary to the pathos) in which Shylock refers to his dead Leah. In both these respects M. Moscovitch was certainly admirable. Irving's Shylock, as some readers will remember, was extremely dignified and full of that vivid unreality which Irving infused into all his successful parts. His Shylock turned the Venetians into "a wilderness of monkeys."[10] Baited, betrayed, forlorn,

---

[7]Tintoretto (1518–1594), one of the greatest Venetian painters of his time.

[8]Charles Macklin (1690/99–1797), the first actor known to have played Shylock as a melodramatic villain rather than as a figure of broad comedy. John "Lun" Rich built and was the first manager of the Covent Garden Theater, one of the two major London theaters, along with Drury Lane.

[9]William Charles Macready (1793–1873), actor and manager, at different times, of both Covent Garden and Drury Lane. G. H. Lewes (1817–1878) wrote influentially on a wide variety of subjects, including theater, and was the husband, in all but official name, of the novelist George Eliot.

[10]MacCarthy sardonically reapplies Shylock's statement that he would not have sold his wife Leah's ring "for a wilderness of monkeys" (3.2.102).

implacable, Irving's Shylock was so dignified and pathetic that it made nonsense of the play; yet in itself it was a beautiful performance.[11] Mr. Moscovitch does not attain to that imaginative dignity; yet dignified he is—except in his exit in a sort of convulsion from the Trial Scene, half supported by Tubal. During the trial itself he has moments of true dignity; but the physical and moral collapse should come before, not after his last words:

> I pray you, give me leave to go from hence;
> I am not well: send the deed after me,
> And I will sign.

This is important not only from the point of view of Shylock's character (for life has taught him resignation as well as cruelty), but as a means of modulating the scene into another key. It is a hopeless task to attempt to make the whole Trial Scene realistic. The only performance I have seen in which it seemed credible that a pound of flesh was actually going to be cut from a man's breast before our eyes was a Japanese version of the play, which Sada Yacco and Kawakami brought over here nearly twenty years ago. After the Portia speeches, Kawakami, as the Shylock of the piece, made faces like a man who has swallowed bitter medicine. In their acting the emphasis on the physical was extraordinary.

Where Mr. Moscovitch excelled and other Shylocks have fallen short of him, was in exhibiting in the Jew a lurking doubt that Justice will be done him; a doubt which makes him all the more resolutely implacable. Shylock's contempt for Antonio as a sentimentalist, a plunger, a bad merchant and a Christian was splendidly brought out. And a still subtler point he marked with extraordinary skill. Shylock's hatred is not a wild passion, it is a tamed passion; it is caged within another—a passion for legality. When the law will not allow him to be revenged, we feel he will not attempt to satisfy his revenge by violence—as Antonio might do. In the manner in which Mr. Moscovitch made the word bond, "my bond, my bond," echo through the whole play, was expressed the longing for security of an oppressed people to whom the law is the only, but by no

---

[11]On Sir Henry Irving's performance, see the selection by William Winter in this section of Contexts materials.

means certain, refuge. The sound of his voice at those moments will linger in my memory. His Shylock had the first quality it should possess; he was passionate in hate, in business, in family and race-feeling, in revenge and in despair.

Maurice Moscovitch as Shylock (1930), drawn by Dan Solowey. Courtesy of The Studio of Dan Solowey, www.solowey.com.

The Jewish actor Maurice Moscovitch played Shylock in the production used by the critic Desmond MacCarthy as the occasion for his article, "Shylocks Past and Present." The drawing is later than the original production.

Friendʃhip and Marriage

"Say How I Loveд You" (4.1.272)

People in the Renaissance had considerable latitude to express same-sex affection. An exalted ideal of male friendship, especially, had deep roots both in classical precedent and in more recent ideas of chivalry and noble behavior. Conversely, the idea of a special homosexual identity, in the modern sense, had not yet emerged (the word itself first appears in the language at the end of the nineteenth century); sexual contact between people of the same sex was generally considered a sinful action that any fallen human might be capable of. When Ben Jonson wrote a eulogy in the First Folio of Shakespeare's work, "To the Memory of My Beloved," the poem was extraordinary but the title was not. On the other hand, when Shakespeare wrote a series of adoring sonnets to a young man, he created an apparent mystery that for several centuries has left readers fruitlessly guessing about the exact nature of the author's emotions.

The friendship in *The Merchant of Venice* between the older Antonio and his dear friend Bassanio has attracted special attention from modern critics and has informed the characterization of Antonio in some modern productions. Their affection has parallels in many comedies of the period, including Shakespeare's *Two Gentlemen of Verona*, *Much Ado About Nothing*, and *Twelfth Night*. So does the potential for conflict between male friendship and male-female sexual love which plays itself out in Act 5 of *Merchant*: again, that conflict is a staple of Shakespeare's comedies (and also appears in the tragic *Othello* and the tragicomic *The Winter's Tale*).

The following selections include two essays about male friendship. The first, by the French essayist Michel de Montaigne, while it draws on classical ideas, movingly recalls the author's actual relationship with his now-dead friend, Étienne de la Boétie. An excerpt from Francis Bacon's essay "Of Friendship" follows; it takes a more pragmatic view of the value of friendship. This section also contains two of Shakespeare's Sonnets addressed to his "fair friend."

Michel de Montaigne (1533–1592)

Michel de Montaigne used the French word essais—*attempts, trials, probings—to name the kind of writing he did, and with which he created a new genre and a new way of representing the world. That way begins with Montaigne's most intimate experience of his own thinking and feeling: his subject, he insisted, whether he was writing about idleness or constancy or sleeping or lying, the force of imagination, ancient authors, recent history, or the vanity of words, was always the changeable, fallible, brilliant human being Michel de Montaigne. The style of the* Essays *embodies the unconstrainable liveliness of the mind in action.*

In his essay "Of Friendship," Montaigne treats a subject that had engaged ancient writers (such as Cicero) as well as more recent Renaissance writers who idealized male friendship, but Montaigne's essay movingly arises out of personal experience. He was twenty-four when he met the slightly older Étienne de la Boétie; although La Boétie died only six years later, their mutual affection—more important to Montaigne than marriage, more satisfying than his active political life—was the author's greatest joy and its loss his greatest grief. The Essays *were translated into English in 1603 by John Florio and were read in that version by Shakespeare (a long passage in* The Tempest, *for instance, very closely echoes Montaigne's essay "Of Cannibals"). In the following selection from Florio's translation, I have omitted Montaigne's quotations from classical authors.*

from "Of Friendship"[1]

There is nothing to which Nature hath more addressed us than to society. And Aristotle saith, that perfect law-givers have had more

---

[1]Michel de Montaigne, "Of Friendship," in *Essays*, trans. John Florio. London, 1603.

regardful care of friendship than of justice. And the utmost drift of its perfection is this. For generally, all those amities which are forged and nourished by voluptuousness or profit, public or private need, are thereby so much the less fair and generous, and so much the less true amities, in that they intermeddle other causes, scope, and fruit with friendship, than it self alone. Nor do those four ancient kinds of friendships—natural, social, hospitable, and venerian[2]—either particularly or conjointly beseem[3] the same.

That from children to parents may rather be termed respect. Friendship is nourished by communication, which by reason of the over-great disparity cannot be found in them, and would haply[4] offend the duties of nature: for neither all the secret thoughts of parents can be communicated unto children, lest it might engender an unbeseeming familiarity between them, nor the admonitions and corrections (which are the chiefest offices of friendship) could be exercised from children to parents. [. . .]

To compare the affection toward women unto it, although it proceed from our own free choice, a man cannot, nor may it be placed in this rank: Her fire, I confess it [. . .] to be more active, more fervent, and more sharp. But it is a rash and wavering fire, waving and diverse: the fire of an ague subject to fits and stints, and that hath but slender hold-fast of us. In true friendship, it is a general and universal heat, and equally tempered, a constant and settled heat, all pleasure and smoothness, that hath no pricking or stinging in it, which the more it is in lustful love, the more is it but a ranging and mad desire in following that which flies us. [. . .] Friendship is enjoyed according as it is desired, it is neither bred, nor nourished, nor increaseth but in jouissance,[5] as being spiritual, and the mind being refined by use and custom. Under this chief amity, these fading affections have sometimes found place in me [. . .] so are these two passions entered into me in knowledge one of another, but in comparison never: the first flying a high, and keeping a proud pitch, disdainfully beholding the other to pass her points far under it.

[2]Erotic.
[3]Accord with.
[4]Perhaps.
[5]Both joy and enjoyment (French).

Concerning marriage, besides that it is a covenant which hath nothing free but the entrance, the continuance being forced and constrained, depending elsewhere than from our will, and a match ordinarily concluded to other ends: A thousand strange knots are therein commonly to be unknit, able to break the web, and trouble the whole course of a lively affection; whereas in friendship, there is no commerce or business depending on the same, but itself. Seeing (to speak truly) that the ordinary sufficiency of women cannot answer[6] this conference and communication, the nurse of this sacred bond: nor seem their minds strong enough to endure the pulling of a knot so hard, so fast, and durable. And truly, if without that, such a genuine and voluntary acquaintance might be contracted, where not only minds had this entire jouissance, but also bodies, a share of the alliance, and where a man might wholly be engaged, it is certain that friendship would thereby be more complete and full.[7] But this sex could never yet by any example attain unto it, and is by ancient schools rejected thence.

And this other Greek licence[8] is justly abhorred by our customs, which notwithstanding, because according to use it had so necessary a disparity of ages, and difference of offices between lovers, did no more sufficiently answer the perfect union and agreement, which here we require. [. . .] For even the picture the Academy makes of it, will not (as I suppose) disavow me, to say thus in her[9] behalf: That the first fury, inspired by the son of Venus in the lover's heart, upon the object of tender youths-flower, to which they allow all insolent and passionate violences, an immoderate heat may produce, was simply grounded upon an external beauty; a false image of corporal generation: for in the spirit it had no power, the sight whereof was yet concealed, which was but in his infancy, and before the age of budding.[10] For, if this fury did seize upon a base minded courage,[11] the means of its pursuit, [were] riches, gifts, favor to the advance-

---

[6]Cannot match.

[7]If a voluntary relationship with a woman could be achieved that equally engaged body and soul, the resulting friendship would be all the stronger for its physicality.

[8]Greek homosexual relations between an older man and a younger man.

[9]On the subject of Greek homosexuality.

[10]The love was only physical because the beloved boy was too young for his spiritual side to have developed.

[11]A person of base mind or spirit.

ment of dignities, and such like vile merchandise, which they reprove. If it fell into a most generous mind, the interpositions were likewise generous: Philosophical instructions, documents to reverence religion, to obey the laws, to die for the good of his country: examples of valor, wisdom and justice. [. . .]

As for the rest, those we ordinarily call friends and amities are but acquaintances and familiarities, tied together by some occasion or commodities[12] by means whereof our minds are entertained. In the amity I speak of they intermix and confound themselves one in the other, with so universal a commixture that they wear out and can no more find the seam that hath conjoined them together. If a man urge me to tell wherefore I loved him, I feel it cannot be expressed but by answering, Because it was he, because it was my self. [. . .] We sought one another before we had seen one another, and by the reports we heard one of another, which wrought a greater violence in us than the reason of reports may well bear: I think by some secret ordinance of the heavens, we embraced one another by our names. And at our first meeting, which was by chance at a great feast, and solemn meeting of a whole township, we found ourselves so surprised, so known, so acquainted, and so combinedly bound together, that from thence forward nothing was so near unto us, as one unto another. [. . .] This [friendship] hath no other idea than of itself, and can have no reference but to itself. It is not one especial consideration, nor two, nor three, nor four, nor a thousand: It is I wot[13] not what kind of quintessence of all this commixture, which having seized all my will, induced the same to plunge and lose itself in his, which likewise having seized all his will, brought it to lose and plunge itself in mine, with a mutual greediness, and with a semblable[14] concurrence. I may truly say "lose," reserving nothing unto us that might properly be called our own, nor that was either his or mine. [. . .]

If in the friendship whereof I speak, one might give unto another, the receiver of the benefit should bind his fellow. For each seeking more than any other thing to do each other good, he who yields both matter and occasion is the man sheweth himself liberal,

[12]By chance or convenience.
[13]Know.
[14]Similar.

giving his friend that contentment to effect towards him what he desireth most.[15] [. . .]

This perfect amity I speak of is indivisible; each man doth so wholly give himself unto his friend that he hath nothing left him to divide elsewhere: moreover he is grieved that he is not double, triple, or quadruple, and hath not many souls, or sundry wills, that he might confer them all upon this subject. Common friendship may be divided; a man may love beauty in one, facility of behavior in another, liberality in one, and wisdom in another, paternity in this, fraternity in that man, and so forth: but this amity which possesseth the soul, and sways it in all sovereignty, it is impossible it should be double. If two at one instant should require help, to which would you run? Should they crave contrary offices of you, what order would you follow? Should one commit a matter to your silence, which if the other knew would greatly profit him, what course would you take? Or how would you discharge your self? A singular and principal friendship dissolveth all other duties, and freeth all other obligations. The secret I have sworn not to reveal to another, I may without perjury impart it unto him who is no other but my self. It is a great and strange wonder for a man to double himself; and those that talk of tripling know not, nor cannot reach unto the height of it. Nothing is extreme, that hath his like. And he who shall presuppose that of two I love the one as well as the other, and that they inter-love one another, and love me as much as I love them: he multiplieth in brotherhood a thing most singular, and a lonely one, and than which one alone is also the rarest to be found in the world. [. . .]

Since the time I lost him [. . .] I do but languish, I do but sorrow: and even those pleasures all things present me with, instead of yielding me comfort, do but redouble the grief of his loss. We were co-partners in all things. All things were with us at half; methinks I have stolen his part from him. [. . .] I was so accustomed to be ever two, and so inured to be never single, that methinks I am but half my self.

---

[15]Compare this idea with Seneca's "On Benefits" (see p. 164).

Francis Bacon (1561–1626)

Bacon's essay about male friendship, like his essay about usury, casts (to use a phrase from the essay) a "dry light" on its subject. (For an introduction to Bacon and his Essays, see p. 171.) Bacon considers the advantages of friendship, without which solitary man inhabits a lonely wilderness. Friendship allows a man to express his joys and griefs, doubling the one and halving the other. It provides a man with a source of good counsel. And it provides man with "another himself," who can extend the man's abilities beyond his singular time and place. Bacon's style, as always, is incisive, but the friendship he describes seems a more utilitarian thing than the emotion that Antonio feels for his friend Bassanio.

from "Of Friendship"[1]

It had been hard for him that spake it to have put more truth and untruth together in few words, than in that speech, "Whosoever is delighted in solitude, is either a wild beast or a god." For it is most true, that a natural and secret hatred and aversation[2] towards society, in any man, hath somewhat of the savage beast; but it is most untrue, that it should have any character at all of the divine nature, except it proceed, not out of a pleasure in solitude, but out of a love and desire to sequester a man's self for a higher conversation: such as is found to have been falsely and feignedly in some of the heathen [. . .] and truly and really in diverse of the ancient hermits and holy fathers of the church. But little do men perceive what solitude is and how far it extendeth. For a crowd is not company; and faces are but a gallery of pictures; and talk but a tinkling cymbal, where there is no love.[3] The Latin adage meeteth with[4] it a little: *Magna civitas, magna solitudo;*[5] because in a great town friends are scattered; so that there is not that fellowship, for the most part, which is in less neighborhoods. But we may go further, and affirm most truly, that

[1]Francis Bacon, The Essays or Counsels, Civil and Moral of Francis, Lord Verulam, Viscount St. Alban, London, 1629, pp. 149–163.
[2]Aversion.
[3]See 1 Corinthians 13.1, "Though I speak with the tongues of men and angels, and have not love, I am as sounding brass or a tinkling cymbal" (Geneva Bible).
[4]Approximates.
[5]"Great city, great solitude."

it is a mere and miserable solitude to want true friends; without which the world is but a wilderness; and even in this sense also of solitude, whosoever in the frame of his nature and affections is unfit for friendship, he taketh it of the beast, and not from humanity.

A principal fruit of friendship is the ease and discharge of the fulness and swellings of the heart, which passions of all kinds do cause and induce. We know diseases of stoppings, and suffocations, are the most dangerous in the body; and it is not much otherwise in the mind; you may take sarza[6] to open the liver, steel to open the spleen, flowers of sulphur for the lungs, castoreum[7] for the brain; but no receipt openeth the heart, but a true friend; to whom you may impart griefs, joys, fears, hopes, suspicions, counsels, and whatsoever lieth upon the heart to oppress it, in a kind of civil shrift or confession. [. . .] But one thing is most admirable (wherewith I will conclude this first fruit of friendship), which is, that this communicating of a man's self to his friend works to contrary effects, for it redoubleth joys and cutteth griefs in halves. For there is no man that imparteth his joys to his friend, but he joyeth the more; and no man that imparteth his griefs to his friend, but he grieveth the less. So that it is in truth, of operation[8] upon a man's mind, of like virtue as the alchemists use to attribute to their stone for man's body:[9] that it worketh all contrary effects, but still to the good and benefit of nature. But yet without praying in aid of[10] alchemists, there is a manifest image of this in the ordinary course of nature. For in bodies, union strengtheneth and cherisheth any natural action; and on the other side, weakeneth and dulleth any violent impression: and even so it is of minds.

The second fruit of friendship is healthful and sovereign for the understanding, as the first is for the affections. For friendship maketh indeed a fair day in the affections, from storm and tempests; but it maketh daylight in the understanding, out of darkness and confusion of thoughts. Neither is this to be understood only of faithful counsel, which a man receiveth from his friend;

---

[6]Sarsparilla.

[7]Castor oil.

[8]In its way of operating.

[9]The mysterious "alchemist's stone" supposedly had the power to cure all ills.

[10]Making claims in behalf of.

but before you come to that, certain it is that whosoever hath his mind fraught with many thoughts, his wits and understanding do clarify and break up in the communicating and discoursing with another; he tosseth his thoughts more easily; he marshalleth them more orderly, he seeth how they look when they are turned into words: finally, he waxeth wiser than himself, and that more by an hour's discourse than by a day's meditation. [. . .] Neither is this second fruit of friendship, in opening the understanding, restrained only to such friends as are able to give a man counsel (they indeed are best); but even without that, a man learneth of himself and bringeth his own thoughts to light and whetteth his wits as against a stone, which itself cuts not. In a word, a man were better relate himself to a statue or picture than to suffer his thoughts to pass in smother.[11]

Add now, to make this second fruit of friendship complete, that other point, which lieth more open and falleth within vulgar observation—which is faithful counsel from a friend. Heraclitus[12] saith well in one of his enigmas, "Dry light is ever the best"; and certain it is that the light that a man receiveth by counsel from another is drier and purer than that which cometh from his own understanding and judgment, which is ever infused and drenched in his affections and customs. So as there is as much difference between the counsel that a friend giveth and that a man giveth himself, as there is between the counsel of a friend and of a flatterer. For there is no such flatterer as is a man's self; and there is no such remedy against flattery of a man's self, as the liberty of a friend. [. . .]

After these two noble fruits of friendship (peace in the affections and support of the judgment), followeth the last fruit, which is like the pomegranate, full of many kernels; I mean aid, and bearing a part, in all actions and occasions. Here the best way to represent to life the manifold use of friendship is to cast and see how many things there are, which a man cannot do himself; and then it will appear that it was a sparing[13] speech of the ancients, to say that a friend is another himself; for that a friend

---

[11]To be smothered.

[12]According to the Greek philosopher Heraclitus (540–480 BCE), the universe is made of opposites reconciled by fire.

[13]Unexaggerated.

is far more than himself. Men have their time, and die many times, in desire of some things which they principally take to heart: the bestowing of a child, the finishing of a work, or the like. If a man have a true friend, he may rest almost secure that the care of those things will continue after him. So that a man hath, as it were, two lives in his desires. A man hath a body, and that body is confined to a place; but where friendship is, all offices of life are as it were granted to him and his deputy, for he may exercise them by his friend. How many things are there which a man cannot, with any face or comeliness, say or do himself? A man can scarce allege his own merits with modesty, much less extol them; a man cannot sometimes brook to supplicate or beg; and a number of the like. But all these things are graceful in a friend's mouth, which are blushing in a man's own. So again, a man's person hath many proper relations, which he cannot put off: a man cannot speak to his son but as a father, to his wife but as a husband, to his enemy but upon terms; whereas a friend may speak as the case requires and not as it sorteth with the person. But to enumerate these things were endless. I have given the rule: where a man cannot fitly play his own part, if he have not a friend, he may quit the stage.

William Shakespeare (1564–1616)

The majority of Shakespeare's 154 sonnets are addressed to a young man, handsome, rich, and headstrong, possibly an aristocrat and the poet's patron. The Sonnets were written in the mid-1590s, close in time to the writing of The Merchant of Venice. *The sonnet—a difficult form of fourteen lines—migrated to England from Italy, where, nearly 200 years earlier, the poet Petrarch had written a sequence of sonnets to an idealized woman he called Laura. In its English revival, by poets such as Spenser, Sidney, and Daniel, the object of the poet's adoration became more sexualized.*

There was nothing unexpected about Shakespeare's joining the fashion for sonneteering. But of all the English sonnet sequences, his is the only one that features a male object of affection. The sonnets tell a complex, shadowy story involving this "fair" young man, a "dark lady" with whom first the poet and then both the poet and the young man are sexually involved, and a "rival poet" who vies for the young man's favor. No contemporary, as far as we know, registered embarrassment or surprise at Shakespeare's choice of subject matter. It was only in the nineteenth century that an influential critic, Henry Hallam, in his Introduction to the Literature of Europe *(1837), could "wish that Shakespeare had never written them," because, he said, "There is a weakness and folly in all excessive and misplaced affection." But the nature and placing of the poet's "affection" is a matter for debate. We can distinguish between the overtly sexual content of the "dark lady" sonnets and the sometimes strongly erotic tone of the sonnets to the young man.*

In the nineteenth century the poet Matthew Arnold said that with these poems Shakespeare unlocked his heart. We might reply that the heart has more mysteries than any key can open, partly because the heart, like other organs, is involved in a history of changing perceptions and expressions.

Sonnet 20

A woman's face with Nature's own hand painted[1]
Hast thou, the master-mistress[2] of my passion;
A woman's gentle heart, but not acquainted
With shifting change, as is false women's fashion;
An eye more bright than theirs, less false in rolling,[3]
Gilding the object whereupon it gazeth;
A man in hue all hues in his controlling,[4]
Which steals men's eyes and women's souls amazeth.
And for a woman wert thou first created,
Till Nature, as she wrought thee, fell a-doting,[5]

---

[1]The face is adorned like a woman's but by nature rather than cosmetic art.

[2]Having both male and female properties.

[3]Wandering.

[4]A man whose appearance ("hue") makes him able to dominate others; a man who can control his own appearance.

[5]Nature fell in love with her own creation.

And by addition me of thee defeated,[6]
By adding one thing to my purpose nothing.[7]
    But since she pricked thee out[8] for women's pleasure,
    Mine be thy love and thy love's use their treasure.[9]

Sonnet 29

When in disgrace with fortune and men's eyes
I all alone beweep my outcast state,
And trouble deaf heaven with my bootless[1] cries,
And look upon myself, and curse my fate,
Wishing me like to one more rich in hope,
Featured like him, like him with friends possessed,
Desiring this man's art, and that man's scope,[2]
With what I most enjoy contented least;[3]
Yet in these thoughts myself almost despising,[4]
Haply I think on thee,—and then my state,
Like to the lark at break of day arising
From sullen earth, sings hymns at heaven's gate;
    For thy sweet love remembered such wealth brings
    That then I scorn to change my state[5] with kings.

[6]Deprived.

[7]The penis added by Nature is of no use to the speaker.

[8]Designated you, as with a checkmark; gave you a penis.

[9]I get your love and women get the sexual excess added by Nature ("use" means "utility" and also "usury").

---

[1]Useless.

[2]Range of power or social possibilities.

[3]Envying others, I am discontented with the things that (usually) give me pleasure.

[4]Hating myself because of the things I think I lack, and hating myself for having such (unworthy) thoughts.

[5]Of mind; also a pun on "state" meaning "throne."

Women and Marriage

Shakespeare grew up in a society of male social privilege ruled over by one of the most powerful women who has ever lived. At Queen Elizabeth's instruction, preachers throughout England read to their congregations the "Homily of the State of Matrimony," which affirmed the hierarchical law of gender laid down by St. Paul, that wives should submit to their husbands because the husband is the head of the wife. (The Queen lived and died single.) Women attended the theater as audience but were represented on stage by men. However affectionate the relations of women to one another, conditions did not encourage them to write about the value of female friendships in a way comparable to the extensive literature of male friendship. Shakespeare's romantic comedies, with their bright, active young women who lead the plays toward their endings in marriage, are in part a response to the anxieties that attend the project of male dominance. In pairings like Portia and Nerissa, Rosalind and Celia (*As You Like It*), Beatrice and Hero (*Much Ado About Nothing*), Shakespeare imagined female friendships as loving as that of Antonio and Bassanio, even as the plots move with comic inexorability toward heterosexual marriage.

The two selections presented here do not come from the dispiritingly large literature of outright, flagrant misogyny. In their different ways, both the Elizabethan homily and Richard Mulcaster's tract on education suggest that women, like men, deserve respect and nurture; but the fact that these things had to be argued suggests the great difference between sixteenth-century and twenty-first-century western ideas about gender. They are signs of a growing tendency in Protestant England to what has been called "companionate marriage," in which an older idea of wives as property was giving way to the idea of the family as a cooperative enterprise. Shakespeare's comedy, which can imagine Portia, Nerrisa, and Jessica, is also a sign of that cultural shift.

"An Homily of the State of Matrimony" (1563)

In 1547 the Church of England published a book of Certain Sermons or Homilies. *As the fuller title makes plain, these were "appointed [or ordered] to be read" during the year from pulpits throughout the king-dom. The intention was to supply a set of readings for the use of clergy incapable of writing their own sermons and to enforce uniformity of doctrine. A second volume of homilies (the word indicates a slightly informal sermon) followed under Queen Elizabeth in 1563. Some of those homilies (like the one on matrimony) deal with social issues and tell us how a society governed according to the dictates of the official Church ought to function. The fact that the entire country was made to hear the homilies once a year tells us that society did not in fact always function in that ideal way. The homily on matrimony tells us, follow-ing scripture, that women should be obedient to their husbands and that husbands should be the heads of their wives. It also deals exten-sively with wife-beating—the sort of thing that wouldn't be a problem if men acted as wise governors of compliant wives.*

from *Certain Sermons or Homilies*

The word of almighty God doth testify and declare whence the original beginning of matrimony cometh, and why it is ordained. It is instituted of God to the intent that man and woman should live lawfully in a perpetual friendship, to bring forth fruit, and to avoid fornication. [. . .] The devil will assay[1] to attempt all things to inter-rupt and hinder your hearts and godly purpose, if ye will give him entry. For he will either labor to break this godly knot once begun betwixt you, or else at the least he will labor to encumber it with divers griefs and displeasures.

And this is the principal craft, to work dissension of heart of the one from the other, that whereas now there is pleasant and sweet love betwixt you, he will in the stead thereof bring in most bitter and unpleasant discord. And surely that same adversary of ours doth, as it were from above, assault man's nature and condition. For this folly is ever from our tender age grown up with us, to have a desire to rule, to think highly of our self, so that none thinketh it meet to give place to another. That wicked voice of stubborn will and self-love is more meet to break and dissever the love of the heart than to preserve concord. Wherefore married persons must apply their minds in most earnest wise to concord, and must crave continually of God the help of his holy spirit so to rule their hearts,

[1]Try.

and to knit their minds together, that they be not dissevered by any division or discord. [. . .]

But to this prayer must be joined a singular diligence, whereof St. Peter giveth this precept, saying, "You husbands, deal with your wives according to knowledge, giving honor to the wife, as unto the weaker vessel, and as unto them that are heirs also of the grace of life, that your prayers be not hindered."[2] This precept doth particularly pertain to the husband, for he ought to be the leader and author of love, in cherishing and increasing concord, which then shall take place if he will use moderation and not tyranny, and if he yield something to the woman. For the woman is a weak creature, not endued[3] with the like strength and constancy of mind; therefore they be the sooner disquieted, and they be the more prone to all weak affections and dispositions of mind, more than men be, and lighter they be, and more vain in their fantasies and opinions. These things must be considered of the man, that he be not too stiff, so that he ought to wink at some things and must gently expound all things, and to forebear. Howbeit,[4] the common sort of men do judge that such moderation should not become a man, for they say it is a token of womanish cowardness, and therefore they think it is a man's part to fume in anger, to fight with fist and staff. [. . .] But he which will do all things with extremity and severity, and doth use always rigor in words and stripes, what will that avail in the conclusion? Verily nothing but that he thereby setteth forward the Devil's work, he banisheth away concord, charity, and sweet amity, and bringeth in dissension, hatred, and irksomeness, the greatest griefs that can be in the mutual love and fellowship of man's life. [. . .]

Now as concerning the wife's duty: what shall become her? Shall she abuse the gentleness and humanity of her husband, and at her pleasure turn all things upside down? No, surely, for that is far repugnant against God's commandment. For thus doth St. Peter preach to them "Ye wives, be ye in subjection to obey your own husband."[5] To obey is another thing than to control or command,

[2]1 Peter 3.7.
[3]Endowed.
[4]However.
[5]1 Peter 3.1.

which yet they may do to their children and to their family;[6] but as for their husbands, them must they obey, and cease from commanding, and perform subjection. For this surely doth nourish concord very much, when a wife is ready at hand at her husband's commandment, when she will apply herself to his will, when she endeavoreth herself to seek his contentment, and to do him pleasure, when she will eschew all things that might offend him. [. . .]

If we be bound to hold out our left cheek to strangers which will smite us on the right cheek,[7] how much more ought we to suffer[8] an extreme and unkind husband? But yet I mean not that a man should beat his wife, God forbid that, for that is the greatest shame that can be, not so much to her that is beaten as to him that doth the deed. But if by fortune thou chancest upon such an husband, take it not too heavily, but suppose thou that thereby is laid up no small reward hereafter, and in this lifetime no small commendation to thee, if thou can'st be quiet. But yet to men, thus I speak, let there be none so grievous fault as to compel you to beat your wives. [. . .] And this thing may be well understood by the laws the Paynims[9] have made, which do discharge her any longer to dwell with such an husband, as unworthy to have any further company with him that doth smite her. For it is an extreme point, thus so vilely to entreat[10] her like a slave, that is to follow thee of[11] thy life, and so joined unto thee beforetime in the necessary matters of living. And therefore a man may well liken such a man (if he may be called a man rather than a wild beast) to a killer of his father or his mother. And whereas we be commanded to forsake our father and mother for our wives' sake, and yet thereby do work them none injury, but do fulfill the law of God; how can it not appear then to be a point of extreme madness to entreat her despitefully for whose sake God hath commanded thee to leave parents? Yea, who can suffer such despite? Who can worthily express the inconvenience, that is, to see

---

[6]The "family" the wife commands includes servants as well as her own children.

[7]In Matthew 5.39, Jesus says, "resist not evil, but whosoever will smite thee on thy right cheek, turn to him the other too" (King James version). Also in Luke 6.29.

[8]Endure.

[9]Pagans, specifically Muslims.

[10]Treat.

[11]All of.

what weepings and wailings made in the open streets, when neighbors run to'gether to the house of so unruly a husband, as to a Bedlam-man,[12] who goeth about to overturn all that he hath at home? Who would not think it were better for such a man to wish the ground to open and swallow him, than once ever after to be seen in the market? But peradventure thou wilt object that the woman provoketh thee to this point. But consider thou again, that the woman is a frail vessel, and thou art therefore made the ruler and head over her, to bear the weakness of her in this subjection.

Richard Mulcaster (1530–1611)

As headmaster of the distinguished Merchant Tailors' School in London, Richard Mulcaster had among his pupils such future literary figures as Edmund Spenser and Thomas Kyd. His book Positions *(1581) is a proposal for children's education, based not on rote learning and even including such extracurricular activities as music and sports. In Chapter 38, excerpted here, he turns to the education of girls—itself an unusual move, since not everyone agreed with the idea that girls should be educated. But Mulcaster was writing under the exceptionally learned Queen Elizabeth, to whom the book was dedicated. While most of his proposals for a girl's education have the goal of making her a good wife, Mulcaster also appreciates the abilities and attainments of women as valuable in their own right and even as potentially valuable for the commonwealth in which he envisages them playing an active role. Mulcaster's attitudes reflect those of other humanist scholars, like Erasmus and Sir Thomas More. And they suggest that the learned and witty Portia, in* The Merchant of Venice, *is a figure not inconceivable in the imagination of at least one Elizabethan educator.*

from *Positions . . . Necessary for the Training Up of Children*[1]

When I did appoint the persons which were to receive the benefit of education I did not exclude young maidens, and therefore seeing I

---

[12]Madman (from the hospital for the insane called Bethlehem, pronounced Bedlam).

---

[1]Richard Mulcaster, *Positions . . . Necessary for the Training Up of Children.* London, 1581, Chapter 38.

made them one branch of my division, I must of force say somewhat more of them. [. . .]

And to prove that they are to be trained, I find four special reasons, whereof any one, much more all may persuade any their most adversary,[2] much more me, which am for them with tooth and nail. The first is the manner and custom of my country, which allowing them to learn, will be loth to be contraried[3] by any of her countrymen. The second is the duty which we owe unto them, whereby we are charged in conscience not to leave them lame in that which is for them. The third is their own towardness,[4] which God by nature would never have given them to remain idle or to small purpose. The fourth is the excellent effects in that sex when they have had the help of good bringing up, which commendeth the cause of such excellency, and wisheth us to cherish that tree whose fruit is both so pleasant in taste and so profitable in trial. What can be said more? Our country doth allow it, our duty doth enforce it, their aptness calls for it, their excellency commands it. [. . .]

In all good and generally authorised histories, and in many particular discourses, it is most evident, that not only private and particular women, being very well trained, but also great princesses and gallant troups of the same sex have shewed forth in themselves marvelous effects of virtue and valor. And good reason why. For where naturally they have to shew, if education procure shew, is it a thing to be wondered at?[5] Or is their singularity less in nature, because women be less accustomed to shew it, and not so commonly employed, as we men be? Yet whensoever they be,[6] by their dealings they shew us that they have no dead flesh nor any base mettle. Well, I will knit up this conclusion and burn daylight no longer, to prove that carefully which all men may see clearly, and their adversaries grieve at because it confutes their folly, which upon some private error of their own, to seem faultless in words,

---

[2]Even their harshest opponents.
[3]Contradicted.
[4]Aptitude.
[5]Is it surprising that education should bring out their natural virtues?
[6]Whenever they are employed or given a chance.

where they be faithless in deeds,[7] blame silly[8] women as being the only cause why they went awry. [. . .]

But now having granted [women] the benefit and society of our education, we must assign the end,[9] wherefor their train[10] shall serve, whereby we may apply it the better. Our own train is without restraint for either matter or manner, because our employment is so general in all things: theirs is within limit, and so must their train be. If a young maiden be to be trained in respect of marriage, obedience to her head and the qualities which looks that way must needs be her best way; if in regard of necessity to learn how to live,[11] artificial train must furnish out her trade; if in respect of ornament to beautify her birth, and to honor her place, rarities in that kind and seemly for that kind do best beseem such; if for government, not denied them by God, and devised them by men, the greatness of their calling doth call for great gifts, and general excellencies for general occurrences. Wherefore having these different ends always in eye, we may point them their train in different degrees. But some Timon[12] will say, what should women do with learning? Such a churlish carper will never pick out the best, but be always ready to blame the worst. If all men used all points of learning well, we had some reason to allege against women, but seeing misuse is common to both the kinds,[13] why blame we their infirmities whence we free not ourselves? Some women abuse writing to that end, some reading to this, some all that they learn any way, to some other ill some way. And I pray you what do we? I do not excuse ill, but bar them from accusing, which be as bad themselves, unless they will first condemn themselves and so proceed in their plea with more discretion after a repentant discovery. [. . .]

For though the girls seem commonly to have a quicker ripening in wit than boys have, for all that seeming yet it is not so. Their nat-

[7]Women's critics, who have committed errors (presumably sexual) out of their own foolishness, blame women so that through their self-righteous words they can seem blameless of their bad deeds.

[8]Innocent.

[9]Purpose.

[10]Training.

[11]Make her own living (as opposed to marrying).

[12]A famous hater of humanity, not only of women.

[13]Genders.

ural weakness, which cannot hold[14] long, delivers very soon, and yet there be as prating boys as there be prattling[15] wenches. Besides, their brains be not so much charged, neither with weight nor with multitude of matters, as boys' heads be, and therefore like empty casks they make the greater noise. [. . .]

For the matter what they shall learn, thus I think. [. . .] Reading if for nothing else it were, as for many things else it is, is very needful for religion, to read that which they must know and ought to perform, if they have not whom to hear in that matter which they read;[16] or if their memory be not steadfast, by reading to revive it. If they hear first and after read of the selfsame argument, reading confirms their memory. Here I may not omit many and great contentments, many and sound comforts, many and manifold delights, which those women that have skill and time to read, without hindering their houswifery, do continually receive by reading of some comfortable and wise discourses, penned either in form of history or for direction to live by.

As for writing [. . .] many good occasions are oftentimes offered where it were better for them to have the use of their pen, for the good that comes by it, than to wish they had it, when the default[17] is felt; and for fear of evil, which cannot be avoided in some, to avert that good, which may be commodious[18] to many.

Music is much used, where it is to be had, to the parents' delight, while the daughters be young, more than to their own, which commonly proveth true when the young wenches become young wives. For then lightly forgetting music when they learn to be mothers, they give it in manifest evidence that in their learning of it they did more seek to please their parents than to pleasure themselves. [. . .

[14]Retain.
[15]"Prating" and "prattling" both mean "idle chatter."
[16]They have to read it themelves if they don't have someone to tell it to them.
[17]Lack.
[18]Advantageous.

"Mark the Music"
(5.1.88)

The Merchant of Venice is full of the sounds of music, from the pompous trumpets that herald the entrance of Portia's suitors to the didactic song that accompanies Bassanio's choosing; from the raucous music of the revellers who steal away Jessica in the night to the "touches of sweet harmony" that play for Jessica and Lorenzo as they await the musical announcement of Portia's return to Belmont in Act 5. There is nothing unusual about this. In their original staging, Shakespeare's comedies were full of songs and dancing, and even the most tragic Elizabethan play had instrumental accompaniment. In *The Merchant of Venice* music serves not only as background or punctuation but also as a suggestion of characters' ethical attitudes. Shylock despises the music of revelry—"the drum / And the vile squealing of the wry-necked fife"—and bids Jessica shut the windows ("stop my house's ears") to exclude the "sound of shallow fopp'ry" from his "sober house" (2.5.28–35). For Shylock, the celebratory music is a sign of wasteful frivolity. In Lorenzo's very different scale of values, responsiveness to music indicates a person's fullness of humanity. By Lorenzo's measure, "The man that hath no music in himself," who is deaf to "the concord of sweet sounds" proves that "The motions of his spirits are dull as night / And his affections dark as Erebus. / Let no such man be trusted" (5.1.83–88). Lorenzo tells Jessica that the music we hear is a wordly counterpart of the sound of the heavenly spheres. The smallest orb in the starry sky "in his motion like an angel sings"; an immortal soul can hear that angelic harmony, but "whilst this muddy vesture of decay"—our mortal bodies—"Doth grossly close it in, we cannot hear it" (5.1.61–65).

The ideas that underlie Lorenzo's little discourse on music were centuries old, and in 1595 their days were numbered. Galileo, whose telescope and mathematical deductions would overthrow the entire astronomical scheme of starry spheres, was born in 1564, the same year as Shakespeare. But old ideas often live on alongside new ones; *The Merchant of Venice* echoes some of the principal texts of that older system. Among the selections that follow are influential passages from the medieval writings of Boethius and Macrobius. In one of the selections below, from Burton's *The Anatomy of Melancholy,* music is recommended as an antidote to the kind of pervasive sadness that afflicts the strangely melancholy merchant Antonio. Burton also elaborates delightfully on Lorenzo's claim that music can tame wild animals. But Shylock was not alone in doubting the social and moral value of music. In the selection from Castiglione's *The Courtier,* a speaker defends musical training against a previous speaker's charge that musical appreciation is a sign of effeminate weakness. And in the Puritan Philip Stubbes (*The Anatomy of Abuses*), Shylock could find an odd ally.

Boethius (c. 475–525)

The Roman philosopher Boethius wrote The Consolation of Philosophy, *one of the most influential books in the history of Christianity, while he was in prison, awaiting execution. It was translated from Latin into English repeatedly, in the medieval period by Chaucer, among others, and in Shakespeare's lifetime by Queen Elizabeth herself. "Dame Philosophy" appears to the condemned author and reconciles him to his lot by inculcating a Christianized version of the Platonic idea of a supreme Good, and the providential rightness of all things, including death.*

Boethius translated and wrote many other influential works, among them De Institutione Musica, *or* On Music *(c. 503), from which the following brief selection is translated. Its tripartite division of music influenced ideas we hear expressed in* The Merchant of Venice, *especially in Lorenzo's speeches to Jessica in Act 5. (See also the selection from Macrobius's* Commentary on Cicero's The Dream of Scipio, *that follows this selection).*

from *On Music*

The Three Kinds of Music, and the Power of Music

There are three kinds of music: first, the music of the universe; second, human music; third, instrumental music. [. . .]

The first kind, the music of the universe, is observable in the combination of elements in the heavens and the changing of the seasons. For how could the swiftly moving mechanism of the heaven be silent in its course? Although this sound does not reach our ears (for which there are many reasons) it is impossible that the rapid motions of such vast bodies could move without sound, especially since the courses of the stars are so harmoniously joined and adapted to one another that nothing more perfectly well fitted could be imagined. For some orbit in a higher sphere and others in a lower, and all revolve with such exact impulses that from their diversity of movement a fixed order can be discovered. Therefore a fixed order of modulation cannot be lacking in the heavenly revolution. [. . .]

What human music is, anyone may understand by examining his own nature. For what else unites the incorporeal activity of the reason with the body but a certain harmony and, as it were, a tuning of low and high sounds into a single consonance? What else joins together the parts of the soul itself, which in the opinion of Aristotle is a joining together of the rational and the irrational? What causes the blending of the body's elements or holds its parts together in established adaptation? The third kind of music is that which is said to reside in certain instruments. Instrumental music is produced by tension, as in strings, or by blowing [. . .] or by some kind of percussion, as in concave brasses which produce a variety of sounds.

Macrobius (fl. 400)

In the sixth book of his De re publica, *Cicero (105–43 BCE), the great Roman statesman and philosopher, narrates the dream of Scipio (c. 185–129 BCE), the Roman general who destroyed Carthage. In his dream, Scipio's father and grandfather reveal his destiny and, in the process of showing him the workings of the universe, explain how its concentric spheres produce a vast music, inaudible to mortal ears. Hundreds of years after Cicero's death, the Latin author Macrobius (fl. 400) wrote an extensive* Commentary *(c. 430) on* The Dream of Scipio, *elaborating it and in subtle ways making it acceptable to Christian readers. Cicero's text with Macrobius's commentary influenced Chaucer and other medieval writers. The ideas in these linked documents continued to have currency in Shakespeare's time, even as the entire earth-centered universe was being displaced by the heliocentric view.*

Cicero, from *The Dream of Scipio*[1]

As I looked out from this spot,[2] everything appeared splendid and wonderful. Some stars were visible which we never see from this region, and all were of a magnitude far greater than we had imagined. Of these the smallest was the one farthest from the sky and nearest the earth, which shone forth with borrowed light. And, indeed, the starry spheres easily surpassed the earth in size. From here the earth appeared so small that I was ashamed of our empire which is, so to speak, but a point on its surface. As I gazed rather intently at the earth my grandfather said, "How long will your thoughts continue to dwell upon the earth? Do you not behold the regions to which you have come? The whole universe is comprised of nine circles, or rather spheres. The outermost of these is the celestial sphere, embracing all the rest, itself the supreme god, confining and containing all the other spheres. In it are fixed the eternally revolving movements of the stars. Beneath it are the seven underlying spheres, which revolve in an opposite direction to that of the celestial sphere. One of these spheres belongs to that planet which on earth is called Saturn. Below it is that brilliant orb, propitious and helpful to the human race, called Jupiter. Next comes the ruddy one, which you call Mars, dreaded on earth. Next, and occupying almost the middle region, comes the sun, leader, chief, and regulator of the other lights, mind and moderator of the universe, of such magnitude that it fills all with its radiance. The sun's companions, so to speak, each in its own sphere, follow—the one

[1]Macrobius, *Commentary on the Dream of Scipio*, ed. William Harris Stahl. New York: Columbia University Press, 1952, pp. 71–74, 185–187.

[2]Scipio, the narrator of his dream, has been granted a privileged view downward upon the earth (at the center of the spheres that form the universe) and outward to the other starry spheres.

Venus, the other Mercury—and in the lowest sphere the moon, kindled by the rays of the sun, revolves. Below the moon all is mortal and transitory, with the exception of the souls bestowed upon the human race by the benevolence of the gods. Above the moon all things are eternal. Now in the center, the ninth of the spheres, is the earth, never moving and at the bottom. Towards it all bodies gravitate by their own inclination."

I stood dumbfounded at these sights, and when I recovered my senses I inquired: "What is this great and pleasing sound that fills my ears?" "That," replied my grandfather, "is a concord of tones separated by unequal but nevertheless carefully proportioned intervals, caused by the rapid motion of the spheres themselves. The high and low tones blended together produce different harmonies. Of course such swift motions could not be accomplished in silence and, as nature requires, the spheres at one extreme produce the low tones and at the other extreme the high tones. Consequently the outermost sphere, the star-bearer, with its swifter motion gives forth a higher pitched tone, whereas the lunar sphere, the lowest, has the deepest tone. Of course the earth, the ninth and stationary sphere, always clings to the same position in the middle of the universe. The other eight spheres, two of which move at the same speed, produce seven different tones, this number being, one might almost say, the key to the universe. Gifted men, imitating this harmony on stringed instruments and in singing, have gained for themselves a return to this region, as have those who have devoted their exceptional abilities to a search for divine truths. The ears of mortals are filled with this sound, but they are unable to hear it.[3] Indeed, hearing is the dullest of the senses: consider the people who dwell in the region about the Great Cataract, where the Nile comes rushing down from lofty mountains; they have lost their sense of hearing because of the loud roar. But the sound coming from the heavenly spheres revolving at very swift speeds is of course so great that human ears cannot catch it; you might as well try to stare directly at the sun, whose rays are much too strong for your eyes."

I was amazed at these wonders, but nevertheless I kept turning my eyes back to earth.

---

[3]Compare: "But whilst this muddy vesture of decay / Doth grossly close [the soul] in, we cannot hear it" (5.1.64–65).

Macrobius, from *Commentary on The Dream of Scipio*

In the first book of our commentary, Eustachius, my son dearer to me than life itself, our discussion progressed as far as the motions of the starry sphere and the seven underlying spheres. At this point let us take up their musical harmonies.

"What is this great and pleasing sound that fills my cars?" I asked.

"That," replied my grandfather, "is a concord of tones separated by unequal but nevertheless carefully proportioned intervals, caused by the rapid motion of the spheres themselves. The high and low tones blended together produce different harmonies. Of course such swift motions could not be accomplished in silence, and, as nature requires, the spheres at one extreme produce the low tones and at the other extreme the high tones. Consequently the outermost sphere, the star-bearer, with its swifter motion gives forth a higher-pitched tone, whereas the lunar sphere, the lowest, has the deepest tone. Of course the earth, the ninth and stationary sphere, always keeps the same position in the middle of the universe. The other eight spheres, two of which move at the same speed, produce seven different tones, this number being, one might almost say, the key to the universe. Gifted men, imitating this harmony on stringed instruments and in singing, have gained for themselves a return to this region."

Since we have explained the order of the spheres and have pointed out how the seven underlying spheres rotate in the opposite direction to the celestial sphere's motion, it is fitting for us next to investigate the sounds produced by the onrush of such vast bodies. [. . .] Now it is well known that in the heavens nothing happens by chance or at random, and that all things above proceed in orderly fashion according to divine law. Therefore it is unquestionably right to assume that harmonious sounds come forth from the rotation of the heavenly spheres, for sound has to come from motion, and Reason, which is present in the divine, is responsible for the sounds being melodious.

Pythagoras[4] was the first of all Greeks to lay hold of this truth. He realized that the sounds coming forth from the spheres were regulated by divine Reason, which is always present in the sky, but he had difficulty in determining the underlying cause and in finding ways by which

[4]Greek philosopher and mathematician (c. 580–c. 500). None of his writings are extant, but the tradition of his work influenced Plato and later philosophers. The story told here of Pythagoras and the musical hammers belongs to that tradition.

he might discover it. When he was weary of his long investigation of a problem so fundamental and yet so recondite, a chance occurrence presented him with what his deep thinking had overlooked.

He happened to pass the open shop of some blacksmiths who were beating a hot iron with hammers. The sound of the hammers striking in alternate and regular succession fell upon his ears with the higher note so attuned to the lower that each time the same musical interval returned, and always striking a concord. Here Pythagoras, seeing that his opportunity had been presented to him, ascertained with his eyes and hands what lie had been searching for in his mind. He approached the smiths and stood over their work, carefully heeding the sounds that came forth from the blows of each. Thinking that the difference might be ascribed to the strength of the smiths he requested them to change hammers. Hereupon the difference in tones did not stay with the men but followed the hammers. Then he turned his whole attention to the study of their weights, and when he had recorded the difference in the weight of each, he had other hammers heavier or lighter than these made. Blows from these produced sounds that were not at all like those of the original hammers, and besides they did not harmonize. He then concluded that harmony of tones was produced according to a proportion of the weights, and made a record of all the numerical relations of the various weights producing harmony.

Next he directed his investigation from hammers to stringed instruments, and stretched intestines of sheep or sinews of oxen by attaching to them weights of the same proportions as those determined by the hammers. Again the concord came forth which had been assured by his earlier well-conceived experiment, but with a sweeter tone, as we might expect from the nature of the instruments.

Baldassare Castiglione (1478–1529)

Baldassare Castiglione was an eminent courtier (he served as ambassador for various Italian princes, including the Pope) as well as the author of Il libro del cortegiano *(1528), the definitive guide to the Italian Renaissance ideal of aristocratic behavior. It records the (fictitious) dialogues supposedly held in the palace of the Duke of Urbino over the course of four evenings in 1507. Among the subjects is the role of music in the social life of an eminent man. In the selection below, the Count defends musical education against another courtier's charge that indulgence in music makes a man too much like a woman. Castiglione's work was translated into English by Sir Thomas Hoby in 1561, and this very influential version of* The Book of the Courtier—*four separate printings during Queen Elizabeth's reign—is used here.*

from *The Courtier,* translated by Sir Thomas Hoby

[T]he Count, beginning afresh: "My lords (quoth he), you must think I am not pleased with the Courtier if he be not also a musician, and besides his understanding and cunning upon the book, have skill in like manner on sundry instruments. For if we weigh it well, there is no ease of the labors and medicines of feeble minds to be found more honest and more praiseworthy in time of leisure than it. And principally in courts, where (beside the refreshing of vexations that music bringeth unto each man) many things are taken in hand to please women withal, whose tender and soft breasts are soon pierced with melody and filled with sweetness. Therefore no marvel that in the old days and nowadays they have always been inclined to musicians, and counted this a most acceptable food of the mind."

Then the Lord Gaspar: "I believe music (quoth he) together with many other vanities is meet for women, and peradventure for some also that have the likeness of men, but not for them that be men indeed; who ought not with such delicacies to womanish their minds and bring themselves in that sort to dread death."

"Speak it not," answered the Count. "For I shall enter into a large sea of the praise of music and call to rehearsal how much it hath always been renowned among them of old time and counted a holy matter; and how it hath been the opinion of most wise philosophers that the world is made of music, and the heavens in their moving make a melody, and our soul framed after the very same sort, and therefore lifteth up itself and (as it were) reviveth the virtues and force of it with music. Wherefore it is written that Alexander was sometime so fervently stirred with it that (in a manner) against his will he was forced to arise from banquets and run to weapon, afterward the musician changing the stroke and his manner of tune, pacified himself again and returned from weapon to banqueting. And I shall tell you that grave Socrates when he was well stricken in years learned to play upon the harp. And I remember I have understood that Plato and Aristotle will have a man that is well brought up, to be also a musician; and declare with infinite reasons the force of music to be to very great purpose in us, and for many causes (that should be too long to rehearse) ought necessarily to be learned from a man's childhood, not only for the superficial melody that is heard, but to be sufficient to bring into us a new habit that is good and a custom inclining to virtue, which maketh the mind more apt to the conceiving of felicity, even as bodily exercise maketh the body more lusty, and not only hurteth not civil matters and warlike affairs, but is a great stay to them. [. . .] Do ye not then deprive our Courtier of music, which doth not only make sweet the minds of men, but also many times wild beasts tame; and whoso savoreth it not, a man may assuredly think him not to be well in his wits.

Robert Burton (1577–1640)

Robert Burton is famous for one great book, The Anatomy of Melancholy, *which appeared in 1621 and was expanded in various editions until 1651. Burton never quite defines melancholy—it includes but is certainly not confined to what we might call depression—but he uses it as a coverall term for all sorts of ailments, minor and great, that stand in the way of human happiness. Expansively purusing his subject, Burton draws on anecdotes, ancient myths, folk wisdom, and medical lore. At times his book seems to satirize the very learning it so amply draws upon. It is, not least of all, a work of great good humor and in itself an antidote to melancholy. In the selection presented here, Burton explains the joyful benefits of music. (Recall, by contrast, Jessica's puzzled statement that she is never merry when she hears sweet music (5.1.69).) In this selection, some Latin phrases have been translated into English, and Burton's citations of his scholarly authorities have been deleted.*

from *The Anatomy of Melancholy*[1]

Music a Remedy

Many and sundry are the means which philosophers and physicians have prescribed to exhilarate a sorrowful heart, to divert those fixed and intent cares and meditations, which in this malady so much offend; but in my judgment none so present, none so powerful, none

---

[1]Robert Burton, *The Anatomy of Melancholy*, ed. Floyd Dell. New York: Tudor Publishing Co., 1927, pp. 478–479.

so apposite, as a cup of strong drink, mirth, music, and merry company. [. . .] Music is a tonic to the saddened soul, a Roaring Meg[2] against melancholy, to rear and revive the languishing soul, affecting not only the ears, but the very arteries, the vital and animal spirits; it erects the mind, and makes it nimble. This it will effect in the most dull, severe, and sorrowful souls, expel grief with mirth, and if there be any clouds, dust, or dregs of cares yet lurking in our thoughts, most powerfully it wipes them all away, and that which is more, it will perform all this in an instant: cheer up the countenance, expel austerity, bring in hilarity, inform our manners, mitigate anger. [. . .] It doth extenuate fears and furies, appeaseth cruelty, abateth heaviness and to such as are watchful it causeth quiet rest; it takes away spleen and hatred, be it instrumental, vocal, with strings, wind; it leadeth us by the spirit, it cures all irksomeness and heaviness of the soul. Laboring men, that sing to their work, can tell as much, and so can soldiers when they go to fight, whom terror of death cannot so much affright, as the sound of trumpet, drum, fife, and such like music, animates; the fear of death [. . .] music driveth away. It makes a child quiet, the nurse's song; and many times the sound of a trumpet on a sudden, bells ringing, a carman's whistle, a boy singing some ballad tune early in the street, alters, revives, recreates, a resless patient that cannot sleep in the night, etc. In a word, it is so powerful a thing that it ravisheth the soul, the queen of the senses, by sweet pleasure (which is an happy cure) and corporal tunes, pacifies our incorporeal soul, and rules it without words, and carries it beyond itself, helps, elevates, extends it. Scaliger[3] gives a reason for these effects, because the spirits about the heart take in that trembling and dancing air into the body, are moved together, and stirred up with it, or else the mind, as some suppose, harmonically composed, is roused up at the tunes of music. And 'tis not only men that are so affected, but almost all other creatures. You know the tales of Hercules, Gallus, Orpheus, and Amphion, happy spirits, Ovid calls them, that could make stocks and stones, as well as beasts, and other animals, dance after their pipes: the dog and hare, wolf and lamb; the noisy jackdaw, the croaking crow, and Jupiter's eagle, as Philostratus[4] describes it in his *Images*, stood all

[2]Possibly referring to a famously large and noisy cannon.

[3]Julius Caesar Scaliger (1484-1558), French-born scholar of language and poetics.

[4]Philostratus of Lemnos, second-century Greek writer, whose *Images* describe sixty-five paintings on mythological themes.

gaping upon Orpheus; and trees, pulled up by the roots, came to hear him, and the pine brought her friend the oak. [. . .] Arion made fishes follow him, which, as common experience evinceth, are much affected with music. All singing birds are much pleased with it, especially nightingales [. . .] and bees amongst the rest, though they be flying away, when they hear any tingling sound, will tarry behind. Harts, hinds, horses, dogs, bears, are exceedingly delighted with it. Elephants, Agrippa[5] adds, and in Lydia in the midst of a lake there be certain floating Islands (if ye will believe it) that after music will dance.[6]

Philip Stubbes (fl. 1583–1591)

Puritan Philip Stubbes, as we have seen (p. 169), denounced usury in the place he calls Ailgna, and he also managed to find the social and religious downside of music. In The Anatomy of Abuses, *this section of dialogue follows a longer one subtitled "The Horrible Vice of Pestiferous Dancing Used in Ailgna," replete with biblical and modern examples of how "Dancing stirreth up lust." In this selection, Stubbes is especially anxious about what he considers the effeminizing (or "womanishing") effect of music on men.*

from *The Anatomy of Abuses*[1]

Of Music in Ailgna[2] and How It Allureth to Vanity

PHILOPONUS. I say of music, as Plato, Aristotle, Galen,[3] and many others have said of it, that it is very ill for young heads, for a certain kind of smooth sweetness in it, alluring the auditory to effeminacy, pussilanimity, and loathsomeness of life, much like unto honey; for as honey and such like other sweet conserves received into the stomach doth delight at the first, but afterwards maketh the stom-

---

[5]Second-century Greek skeptical philosopher.
[6]"Mr. Carew of Anthony, in *Descrip[tion] of Cornwall*, saith of whales, that they will come and show themselves dancing at the sound of a trumpet" [Burton's note].

---

[1]Philip Stubbes, *The Anatomy of Abuses*. London, 2nd ed., 1585, pp. 109–112.
[2]"Anglia" spelled backward.
[3]Greek philospher and physician (129–c. 216) whose ideas about medicine were influential well into the seventeenth century.

ach queasy, and unable to receive meat of hard digesture, so sweet
music at the first delighteth the ears, but afterward corrupteth and
depraveth the mind, making it queasy, and inclined to all licentiousness of life whatsoever. And right, as good edges are not sharpened
(but obtused) by being whetted upon soft stones, so good wits, by
hearing of soft music, are rather dulled than sharpened, and made
apt to all wantonness and sin. And therefore writers affirm Sappho[4]
to have been expert in music, and therefore whorish. [. . .]

SPUDEUS. I have heard it said (and I thought it very true) that
music doth delight both man and beast, reviveth the spirits, com-
forteth the heart, and maketh it apter to the service of God.

PHILOPONUS. I grant music is a good gift of God, and that it
delighteth both man and beast, reviveth the spirits, delighteth the
heart, and maketh it readier to serve God; and therefore did David
both use music himself, and also commend the use of it to his posterity (and being used to that end, for man's private recreation,
music is very laudable). But being used in public assemblies and private conventicles,[5] as a directory to filthy dancing, through the
sweet harmony and smooth melody thereof, it estrangeth the mind,
stirreth up filthy lust, womanisheth the mind, ravisheth the heart,
enflameth concupiscence, and bringeth in uncleanness. [. . .]

SPUDEUS. What say you then of musicians and minstrels, who
live only upon the same art?

PHILOPONUS. I think that all good minstrels, sober and chaste
musicians (speaking of such drunken sockettes[6] and bawdy parasites
as range the [country], rhyming and singing of unclean, corrupt, and
filthy songs, in taverns, ale-houses, inns, and other public assemblies),
may dance the wild Morris[7] through a needle's eye.[8] For how should
they bear chaste minds, seeing that their exercise is the pathway to all
uncleanness? There is no ship so balanced with massy matter as their
heads are fraught with all kinds of bawdy songs, filthy ballads, and
scurvy rhymes, serving every purpose and for every company.

[4]Greek lyric poet (c. 610–c. 580 BCE) who lived much of her life on the island of Lesbos.
[5]Meetings.
[6]Sugary, preserved fruits, a rich dessert.
[7]A traditional English dance in which the participants wear bells, step high, and make a lot of noise.
[8]Alluding to Jesus's saying that it is easier for a camel to pass through a needle's eye than for a rich man—or, in Stubbes's version, a musician—to enter the kingdom of heaven.

Further Reading

Adelman, Janet. "Her Father's Blood: Race, Conversion, and Nation in *The Merchant of Venice*. *Representations* 81 (2003): 4–30.

Auden, W. H. "Brothers and Others." In *The Dyer's Hand and Other Essays*. New York: Random House, 1962.

Barber, C. L. *Shakespeare's Festive Comedy*. Princeton: Princeton University Press, 1959.

Boose, Linda. "The Comic Contract and Portia's Golden Ring." *Shakespeare Studies* 20 (1987): 241–254.

Brown, John Russell, ed. *The Merchant of Venice*. London: Methuen, 1985.

Cohen, Walter. "*The Merchant of Venice* and the Possibilities of Historical Criticism." *ELH* 49 (1982): 765–782.

Cook, Ann Jennalie. *Making a Match: Courtship in Shakespeare and His Society*. Princeton: Princeton University Press, 1991.

Danson, Lawrence. *The Harmonies of "The Merchant of Venice."* New Haven: Yale University Press, 1978.

Edelman, Charles, ed. *The Merchant of Venice (Shakespeare in Performance)*. Cambridge: Cambridge University Press, 2002.

Gross, John. *Shylock: Four Hundred Years in the Life of a Legend*. London: Chatto and Windus, 1992.

Halio, Jay L. ed. *The Merchant of Venice*. Oxford: Oxford University Press, 1993.

Holland, Peter. "*The Merchant of Venice* and the Value of Money." *Cahiers Elisabéthains: Late Medieval and Renaissance Studies* 60 (2001): 13–30.

Holmer, Joan Ozark. "*The Merchant of Venice:*" *Choice, Hazard, and Consequence*. New York: St. Martin's, 1995.

Hutson, Lorna. *The Usurer's Daughter: Male Friendship and Fictions of Women in Sixteenth-Century England*. London: Routledge, 1994.

Kahn, Coppélia. "The Cuckoo's Nest: Male Friendship and Cuckoldry in *The Merchant of Venice*." In *Shakespeare's Rough Magic*, ed. Peter Erickson and Coppélia Kahn. Newark, DE: University of Delaware Press, 1985.

Kaplan, M. Lindsay, ed. *William Shakespeare: "The Merchant of Venice": Texts and Contexts*. New York: Palgrave, 2002.

Kermode, Frank. "The Mature Comedies." In *Early Shakespeare*, Stratford-upon-Avon Studies, 3. London: Edward Arnold, 1961.

Lewalski, Barbara. "Biblical Allusion and Allegory in *The Merchant of Venice*." *Shakespeare Quarterly* 13 (1962): 317–343.

Mahood, M. M., ed. *The Merchant of Venice*. Cambridge: Cambridge University Press, 1987.

McPherson, David C. *Shakespeare, Jonson, and the Myth of Venice*. Newark, DE: University of Delaware Press, 1990.

Newman, Karen. "Portia's Ring: Unruly Women and Structures of Exchange in *The Merchant of Venice*." *Shakespeare Quarterly* 38 (1987): 19–33.

Rabkin, Norman. "Meaning and *The Merchant of Venice*." In Rabkin, *Shakespeare and the Problem of Meaning*. Chicago: University of Chicago Press, 1981.

Rackin, Phyllis. "Androgyny, Mimesis, and the Marriage of the Boy Heroine on the English Renaissance Stage." *PMLA* 102 (1987): 29–41.

———. "The Impact of Foreign Trade on *The Merchant of Venice*." *Shakespeare-Jahrbuch* 138 (2002): 73–88.

Roth, Cecil. *A History of the Jews in England*. Oxford: Oxford University Press, 1941; 3rd ed. rev. 1964.

Shapiro, James. *Shakespeare and the Jews*. New York: Columbia University Press, 1996.

Tawney, R. H. *Religion and the Rise of Capitalism*. New York: Harcourt Brace, 1926; Penguin Books, 1947.